I was

Thursday's Child

- a memoir

From the 1930's and wartime England,
to colonial Nigeria and Australia

Jillian Jelliffe

NENGE BOOKS, Australia

I was Thursday's Child.

Published by NENGE BOOKS, Australia
ABN 26809396184
Email: nengebooks1@gmail.com

Author - Jillian Jelliffe

This book or parts thereof may not be reproduced in any form, stored in a retrieval system, or transmitted in any form by any means – electronic, mechanical, photocopy, recording or otherwise – without prior written permission of the publisher.

Text and photographs - Copyright © Jillian Jelliffe 2017.

Cover design - Michael Jelliffe

All rights reserved.

ISBN-13: 978-0-6480675-1-1

The original manuscript for this book received First Prize and Certificate of Merit in a 'Writing Women's Stories' workshop by the Zonta Club of Coffs Harbour, May 2001.

This is dedicated to my beloved family,

whether they be past, present or future.

Thursday's Child

Monday's child is fair of face
 Tuesday's child is full of grace
Wednesday's child is full of woe
 Thursday's child has far to go
Friday's child is loving and giving
 Saturday's child works hard for a living
But the child that is born on the Sabbath day
 Is loving and bright and good and gay.

Anon

Jillian, 1945

Contents

Glossary	....	6
Prologue	....	9
The Journey Commences	....	15
School Days Begin	....	26
Life in Our Street 1935	....	36
Lee-on-Solent.	....	41
A Happy Period	....	45
The End of an Era	....	57
First Family Breakdown	....	64
World War II and RNS	....	76
German Measles and Cornwall 1940	....	81
The War Hots Up	....	87
Mother Returns, Treyarnon Bay School	....	96
Somerset, RNS Haslemere	....	102
Confirmation, Doodle Bugs, School Cert.	....	110
Student Days	....	120
Training Hospitals	....	126
Ear Surgery and a Real Job	....	134
Marriage 1951	....	149
To Nigeria, January 1952	....	158
Azare	....	175
Michael Alistair, Jos	....	191
Peter Andrew, Kano	....	201
Hepatitis A and Kaduna	....	212
Ibadan University.	....	219
John Anthony, England	....	223
We Emigrate to Australia	....	231
Richard Alan, Goondiwindi	....	238
Coffs Harbour and Journey's End	....	242
My Other Pilgrimage	....	252
Epilogue	....	256

Glossary

Acidosis	Condition caused by cyclical vomiting, fat intolerance, starvation
Ack-ack	Anti-aircraft (guns)
A.D.O.	Assistant District Officer
All Clear	Long steady blast on siren indicating current air raid is over
Arthrodesis	Insertion of a titanium or other metal cup in hip joint
Arthroplasty	Plastic surgery applied to joint eg hip
Auroscope	Instrument for looking into ear
Bacon (Roger)	Philosopher and scientist born 1214
Balkan Beam	Strong wooden bean erected over bed, from which orthopaedic equipment can be slung
Bayan gida	(Hausa) literally back of the house (toilet)
B.C.G.	Vaccination against TB
Billingsgate	London fish market
Bitter aloes	Bitter non-poisonous juice of aloes to discourage chewing nails
Burberry	Popular make of raincoat in UK
Cockade	Rosette or half moon of pleated stiff cotton used as decoration on hat
Comox	Town on east coast of Vancouver Island, BC Canada
C.R.H.	Catering Rest House
Delabole	Place in Cornwall famous for its slate tiles
Doodle Bugs	Flying Bombs, V1's Buzz Bombs used by Germany in 1944
D.O.	District Officer
E.C.T.	Electro-convulsive therapy
Elevenses	mid-morning snack, morning tea, smoko (Australian)
Elsan	Chemical toilet
Emirs	Moslem rulers
Errand boy	Delivery boy on a bicycle
Flander's fields	Battleground in Belgium, WW1
Fort Blockhouse	Portsmouth Submarine Base
Gasthof	(Austrian) guesthouse
Genuflection	Bending the knee
Gibbet	Gallows
Gloaming	Evening twilight
G.P.	General practitioner, doctor
Ground nuts	Peanuts
Hausa	People group inhabiting Northern Nigeria, of Bantu/Hamitic origin. Also Hamitic language used in commerce over much of

	West Africa
Harmattan	Hot parching Sahara desert wind
Heath W Robinson	Known for his entertaining drawing of weird inventions
House Physician	Junior hospital resident medical officer in medical ward
House Surgeon	Junior hospital resident medical officer in surgical ward
In loco parentis	In place of a parent ie. guardian
Jerry	Chamber pot
Kit car	Small truck, utility
Land girl	Member of the women's land army, UK
Langa langa	Thin strip of metal used to cut grass
Lisle	Fine cotton used for stockings
Louis XIVth	King of France pictured with heavy jowls
Maisonette	Two storey flat
Mantoux	Skin test for sensitivity to Tuberculosis
Mastoidectomy	Removal of infected bone from mastoid process located behind the ear
Medical registrar	Senior resident doctor in medical wards
Metrology	Science, system of weights and measures
Merchant Taylors	Boys public school founded in London by Worshipful Company of Merchant Taylors around 1500AD, relocated to Moore Park
M.O.	Medical officer
Moral Re-Armament.	Ideological campaign launched in 1938 b Frank Buckman, UK
Monsieur du Bain.Fr.	Gentleman of the Bath
M.T.B.	Motor Torpedo Boats
O.B.E.	Officer of the Order of the British Empire
Objets d'art	Artistic objects
O.H.	Miss H M Oakley Hill (headmistress of RNS)
O.T.	Occupational Therapy or therapist
Old Uncle Tom Cobley.	Cornish character in a song
Orangery	Hot house for protection of orange trees, particularly in 17th century mansions in UK
Osteopath	Manipulator of the spine
Paludrine	Anti malarial medication
Pickford's	Furniture removals and storage firm
Pentathol	Anaesthetic administered by injection. (Sodium Pentathol)
Pie or Pye dog	Nondescript type of dog found largely in Africa and Asia
Piece de resistance.	Main creation of the occasion
Press ganged	Pressed into service against one's will
Privy	Private place for toilet purposes
P.W.D.	Public Works Department

Proselytizing	Attempting to convert one to another faith
Pyrexia	Fever
Racing Demon	A card game, a form of patience for more that one player
Resident	Senior District Officer
R.N.S.	Royal Naval School
R.N.V.R.	Royal Naval Volunteer Reserve
Rounders	Softball
Rubella	German measles
Salle de chambre	(French) Bedroom
Scull	Way to propel a row boat using one oar supported in a notch in the transom (stern)
Solent, The	Stretch of water between Portsmouth and the Isle of Wight
Stooks	Sheaves of corn, wheat, oats, barley etc stacked upright in the field to dry out
Sisal	Strong, durable grass used for rope
St Trinians	Caricature of English girls school with black stocking and gym tunics
String heddles	Used in weaving to separate and control warp threads
Tan-Sad	A popular British collapsible perambulator
Tilley lamp	Kerosene pressure lamp
Tow-path	Wide path beside the river used by horses towing barges
W.R.N.S.	Women's Royal Naval Service i.e. Wrens
Yoruba	Predominant tribe in the western region of Nigeria
Zebo Cattle	Humped African cattle

Prologue

I was an English child, born on a Thursday in 1928, and my life took me in a circle almost around the world until eventually I landed with my family in a small town on the east coast of Australia. Here I dug in and put down deep roots but en route I experienced a world that seems to be no more.

The twentieth century was a very fast changing and interesting period of history and life in the first half is worth recording. Otherwise our descendants will have little concept of how their still-living grandparents coped before the availability of electricity, plastics, computers and credit cards. When there were no antibiotics, incubators for babies, safe anaesthetics, common vaccines, contraceptives, tranquillisers, disposable nappies, or insecticides. And worst of all, no Television… not anywhere!

How did we get on when very few people owned cars, there were no passenger planes and certainly no jets? When travelers had to take five or six weeks sailing from Europe to Australia by ocean liner. When few homes possessed a phone, and that only used for local calls (our first one, in 1937, was like a black daffodil on a stem with separate ear piece attached by a chord) and urgent messages went by telegram or overseas cable, delivered in a small yellow envelope by a boy on a bicycle. When a family was lucky to have a radio this had valves which had to warm up and was bedeviled with static.

There were no refrigerators, washing machines, dishwashers, freezers, electric stoves, kettles, toasters or other electrical gadgets in the kitchen, nor air conditioning, electric fires, fans or vacuum cleaners. No supermarkets, washing detergents, water in the tap or solar heating. Bath water had to be carried upstairs in cans or heated by a gas geyser or chip heater, and flushing toilets and sewerage were not universal, even into the 1960s. There were no inner-spring mattresses, electric blankets, wall-to-wall carpets or en-suites. People got by with a chamber pot under the bed and a privy down the garden path.

When there was no air mail. All mail went by sea so Australia seemed (and was) a very long way from England. A wrist watch was a luxury and, like clocks, was wound up daily. There were no C.D's, cassette tapes, Hi Fi's, electric guitars or keyboards or battery operated toys or clocks. There was no public 'musack' in lifts or waiting rooms or through telephones. Music in public places was always live, with town bands, palm court orchestras, dance bands and Salvation Army meetings on street corners. Collieries and factories, police, and the armed services formed brass bands which regularly entertained the public from park bandstands and on the sea fronts. Most middle class homes aspired to piano or pianola and most people enjoyed singing.

There were no motor mowers, chain saws or whipper snippers in the back yard (or even Hill's hoists), and of course mobile phones, walkmen, calculators, computers and the Internet had not even been imagined. Altogether it was a much quieter world with little road or air traffic and very many fewer people to populate it. Large families would seldom see all their children reach adulthood and many women died in childbirth. Life expectation was more than twenty years less than now, and children in particular spent quite a lot of time in bed, sick. On the streets it was very common to see people on crutches and children in calipers, crippled with polio. Tuberculosis was rife and there was a lot of spitting, with notices prohibiting it in public places and busses. Nearly everyone smoked, frequently a pipe. Nearly everyone wore hats for fashion. People were concerned about good manners and men always stood aside for the ladies (oh well ... nearly always).

The employment scene was quite different. There were scores of tellers in the banks, clerks and typists in the office, domestic servants in houses, shop assistants behind counters road gangs on the highways and labourers in the fields, milking shed, factories and at the coal face, which all ran on people power, without automation. These competent workers are no longer needed in any number, so the dignity of work is denied them. Their descendants, replaced by computers, heavy machinery and new technological inventions, must subsist on a non-career of casual work wherever they can find it, or the dole. Technology has made even the housewife self-sufficient, with the washing machine taking over from the local laundry or washer woman, the supermarket from local family tradesmen, and electrical gadgets and better house design taking over from domestic help.

It is hard for young people to understand why we 'oldies' often think of those apparently bleak and hard-working times with some nostalgia. Could it be because the pace was so much slower? Before TV we spent much more time talking with each other and making our own entertainment. It was normal for a couple to wander up the road on a warm summer evening and visit friends, without fear of interrupting their television viewing. Children were expected to make themselves useful. Shoes must be polished daily, the fowls fed, errands run, tables laid and belongings kept tidy, but they also spent more time curled up with a book, doing a jig-saw puzzle or fixing up their stamp collections.

We girls sewed, knitted, mended and learnt dress-making and how to recite, sing and play the piano. Boys learnt carpentry and bicycle maintenance, chopped wood, shot rabbits and pigeons, fished and got into mischief. Children had adventures. When forced indoors they would know how to play chess, draughts, snakes and ladders, Monopoly or cards, paint a water colour or build a model, hang around dad in his workshop or their mother baking in the kitchen.

There was time for charades at Christmas, which all the generations joined in as a matter of course; time for singing carols and Gilbert and Sulivan round the piano or gathering the family round to play parlour games on Sunday. There was nothing else to do after church as everything closed down... cinemas, shops, sporting fixtures. Not having cars we donned raincoats, sou'westers and gum boots and walked long distances in the rain, cheeks rosy as apples, water trickling down inside our necks, coming home to an open fire and toast made in front of it on a toasting fork.

The housewife's week ran roughly to a programme. Monday wash day, Tuesday ironing, Wednesday flues and floors, Thursday baking, Friday to town shopping, Saturday dusting and polishing, or such like. Menus, before the second world war, also ran to a pattern, with the Sunday roast joint of mutton or sirloin re-appearing as cold meat and salad on Monday and shepherd's pie or a concoction optimistically called curry (perhaps helped out by hard boiled eggs) on Tuesday. On other days our fare was liable to be a traditional dish such as Lancashire Hot-Pot, steak and kidney pie or pudding, Irish stew, liver and onions with bacon, braised beef or mutton and caper sauce or a fish dish, all accompanied by potatoes and a couple of vegetables. We never dreamed that one day our kitchens would produce Italian pasta one day and Thai food the next and that rice, couscous and pasta would edge out potatoes in popularity. The only spaghetti we knew about was in tins supplied by Heinz.

Nowadays, the expectation of middle class newly-weds to own their own home, to fill it straight away with quality furniture, with a car in the garage and golf clubs in the boot, has resulted in the need for two incomes, much anxiety when unemployment or bad health threatens, and twenty five years slavery to the bank, doubling the price of the house to which they are chained. Child-bearing tends to be delayed and the rearing shared. A mother's role has altered and small children spend much time in the care of outsiders who may not be family members. In adolescence peer pressure holds more sway than parental guidance. Meals are snatched on the run or eaten in front of T.V. stealing precious opportunity for communication and family togetherness. Life is lived by the clock, and always in a hurry. Children now are more sexually informed at six than I was at sixteen. Are we, our society, any better for all this change? Do parents feel happier and children more secure than in the past?

Although I fully appreciate the modern gadgets that I use constantly, and which make my life easy and interesting now, I am nevertheless so glad that I spent my early years in a quieter and slower era before the age of technology overwhelmed us. It wasn't so bad. We worked harder physically, walked or cycled a lot, which was probably good for our health, and were more creative as we had to make do. We probably formed deeper and more faithful relationships and spent more time doing things together as a family, which kept us in touch. On the whole, if we didn't like it we had to lump it and this is possibly not a bad way to develop character.

I hope my story will keep alive for future generations a little of how it was then, both the good and the bad of it.

Jillian Jelliffe, 2000

Places in England mentioned in my story.

Chapter One

The Journey Commences

Judging mainly from remarks made or overheard during my early years, I built up a picture of myself as a rather unattractive child, somehow managing to combine knock knees and bandy legs and bunions; dead straight hair (when little girls wanted to look like Princess Elizabeth, if not Shirley Temple); deep-set blue eyes (with possibly a hint of a squint) and definitely an inquisitive nose; also I could not keep still in spite of constant exhortations. Making these natural endowments even less appealing, I felt personally to blame for having yellow teeth (because un-brushed), black fingernails (ditto), a dirty nose (insufficiently blown), and a loud voice like a Billingsgate fishwife (which I was constantly bid to keep down). I was often affectionately called "Funny Face", "Wriggle-bottom" and "Chatterbox". Also I couldn't pronounce my "R's" and had a look on my face that prompted grown-ups frequently to tell me to take off.

As I approached puberty I sprouted hair in alarming places and in prodigious quantity, and by my early teens I had lost any hope of ever winning the battle against masculinity, which threatened to give me a black moustache, thick black eyebrows meeting in the middle, and whiskers on my chin like a great-aunt, who I met only once but was strongly impressed by. As if all that was not bad enough, when confronted with small swellings appearing on my chest, at age 11, I became convinced that I was destined to develop an enormous bosom, and spent two whole days in deep despair until a different mirror angle failed to show them up at all.

On the more positive side, I had boundless energy, inquisitiveness (which was often my downfall), enormous enthusiasm for life and a trusting and friendly disposition. My imaginative life was very real to me and resulted in my being alternatively very timid and very courageous, often taking on different characters according to the story that I was currently enjoying, and seeing myself in the light of these role models.

I compensated for the poor physical deal by participating in the forefront of anything that was going on, and grabbing the limelight as best I could, which is probably why people frequently felt the need to squash me. On the whole I found the world an exciting place, full of mostly kindly people, and I usually jumped in feet first to sample whatever life had to offer next. This prompted one of my teachers to advise me, (no doubt in response to my habit of putting my hand up with the wrong answer before she had finished putting the question), "Jill, your motto should be 'Look before you leap'!"

E. N. R. Fletcher

It's hard to say where I come from in a territorial sense as I grew up like a piece of flotsam, washing up here and there and always on the move. My English father was an officer in the Royal Navy, and he with my mother and brother, Tony, happened to be living in Wellington, New Zealand, when my keel was laid (as I was once puzzled to hear my mother describe it). Father, with the rank of 'acting' Commander, was Secretary to the New Zealand Navy Board at the time, an appointment usually held by a full Captain.

Because the nursing home and medical fees in Wellington were more than they could afford, my father very regretfully decided to send my mother and brother, nearly three, across the

Pacific to her parent's home in Canada, for the confinement. Mother, being totally inexperienced in anything to do with infants, had made heavy weather of that first baby, who had colic and feeding difficulties and cried more than was reasonably expected, which distressed her dreadfully. Having no female relatives near to advise and support her, a repeat performance was no doubt expected in Wellington, and, although this is purely conjecture, I can imagine that my father, who deplored any form of inefficiency, could not face another such experience of domestic disruption although he adored her. My grandparents, who had recently retired to Vancouver Island after many years in Burma, were more than willing to render support, so 'we' crossed the Pacific in the Aorangi and I was born in the early hours of the morning of Thursday, 30th August 1928, assisted into the world by the nuns of St Joseph's Hospital, Comox.

Kathleen M. Fletcher (nee Holmes)

Receiving a cable with the glad tidings of my arrival on the other side of the International Date Line, my father insisted that I was born on Friday 31st, and stuck to this rigidly for years. He missed her dreadfully and later heartily regretted the decision, writing her long and adoring letters deploring the separation from her and "the babies", which have survived. It was more than eighteen months before they were reunited.

My mother's name was Kathleen Mary, and she told me she really wanted to call me Jillian Mary. Unfortunately my father had an unmarried sister called Tryphena, with very strong ideas about family names. Mother, who felt rather intimidated by her young sister-in-law, was prepared neither to fight nor to give in over this important matter, so tactfully chose to defuse the issue by confining me to plain 'Jillian'. As it was only employed when my attention was sternly required, I never liked it much and I was more often addressed as Jill, Jilly or Jillywinks, depending on my popularity at the moment. I later felt somewhat aggrieved that Tony had two names, Anthony David, and I had only one, and now I am more aware of family history, I would really have appreciated being the fourth generation, or maybe more, to be called Tryphena, but my mother was not to know that.

I was 14 months old before Father's appointment in Wellington ended and he could return home to England, collecting us from Canada en route and meeting me for the first time. Our vessel, the London Importer, sailed down the west coast of America from Vancouver calling in at various ports en route then through the Panama Canal and across the Atlantic to England. Before the age of five, Tony had now sailed all around the world, clinching his love of the sea.

The story goes that the brand of milk powder, ordered by my mother before embarking, was replaced by a phony brand and I became gravely ill with gastro-enteritis and very nearly died. An unscheduled stop had to be made to consult a pediatrician in San Francisco, where we were hove-to in thick fog for 48 hours with fog horns hooting all around, causing much additional anxiety no doubt. His advice to my mother was to give me only boiled water. Presumably he neglected to put a time limit on this, and Mother later told me that I probably owed my life to a motherly stewardess, with her head screwed on the right way, who, many days (or weeks?) later, was discovered feeding fried bread to me in the cabin whilst she was minding me.

The voyage took several weeks, the ship being half oiler and half cargo vessel, with business to be conducted at nearly a dozen ports of call. As my own survival became more certain, we rolled into Portsmouth in a 'confused sea' accompanied by gale force winds, and half the roofs in our street were blown off, killing a woman below.

Soon after returning to England, Father was sent off to the Persian Gulf in H.M.S Penzance, not returning until 1932, so my parents' married life had hardly been restored when it was

With my mother, Southsea, 1930

disrupted again. This time my mother had to be left to cope by herself without any family support, and we moved around three different addresses in Alverstoke in the next two years, establishing a pattern that was to persist until I was thirty-two years of age.

I can now write mostly from memory, as I have a clear picture of myself sitting on a doorstep in the sun, eating bread and red jam and watching ants running around. Tony attended a small school nearby, and desperately coveted a tricycle belonging to a lucky boy whose house and back garden, surrounded by a tall brick wall, were right next to our rented place. This day, noticing the gate was ajar, he nipped inside, emerging at full pelt on the trike and peddling off down the road and around the block at breakneck speed, head down, shoulders hunched as if the Furies were after him... and they were, in the form of Mummy, sprinting along after him with me in tow, almost airborne and still clutching my bread and jam. Tony's moment of joy was never repeated... but probably reckoned worth it.

Another memory is of a year or so later, when Father returned from 'sea' and took Tony and me to the beach one Sunday morning. Time came to return home for Sunday roast dinner, but there was mutiny in the junior ranks and an undignified chase ensued. Father, who had had very little to do with small children, was a great believer in children doing what they were told, not answering back, respecting their elders, being seen and not heard, and generally conforming, and my insubordination was too much. He upended me, spanked my bottom and transported me under his arm, kicking and protesting loudly, all the way home. Tony trailed behind, hoping no one would recognise him, and I regret to say this was not the last time he would wish to disown me.

Paymaster Commander (later Captain) ENR Fletcher, my father.

Around this time cousins of my mother invited us to Bertram Mills Circus in London. I was only two or three, and remember the clown with Technicolour clarity as he climbed a ladder and then, with much fuss and slapstick, fell head first into a bucket of 'boiling' water, the vapour enveloping his head as his legs thrashed around in the air and his off-sider made fruitless efforts to rescue him. I was absolutely terrified, and refused to be pacified! On the return home in the car I was behaving very badly and Mummy was near to tears. Uncle Ronald decided enough was enough, and stopped the car. He turned to me and said very slowly, "Jill, I have had enough of this behaviour. If you don't stop crying and behave nicely, I am going to put you out of the car."

I didn't believe my erstwhile kindly uncle would carry out his threat, and after a moment's consideration I recommenced my grizzling. Uncle left his seat, opened my door and lifted me onto the roadside. As I remember it, he then drove off into the distance, leaving me in the dark, alone, speechless and stranded, before returning and hoisting me aboard again. Actually, discussing this with my mother years later, she said he did nothing of the sort, but lifted me straight back into the car, in stunned silence, and we continued in peace. It does confirm what I have discovered, that many memories are expanded by imagination rather than being actual experiences.

When I was about four, Father was appointed to Naval Intelligence with an office in the Admiralty, so we moved to north London, and rented a house in Mill Hill. This was in a cul de sac with modern, detached homes and pleasant gardens, and a big improvement for us. There was a large buddleia by the front gate, bedecked with fluttering butterflies and casting a spell of honeyed perfume as one walked up the path.

Here we had a nursemaid, Gwyneth, who lived in, and one of her duties was to take Tony and me for walks each afternoon, in all weathers, unless we were at school. It was easy to find quiet country paths then, and she would grab our hands and run with us, my legs flailing in a knock-kneed circle that always ended up with knees caked in mud, which she would scrub off in the kitchen on our return. When the puddles had frozen over we would slide on them, and look for really long ones we could take a run at.

One day when Tony was giving me a "piggy back" I fell off and came down hard on my nose, which emerged bloody and very squashed. A doctor was called, and he examined me with what I took to be a pair of sugar tongs. The nose never fully recovered, but it doesn't show too badly. Generally a doctor was only called in when things were very bad, with home remedies being resorted to routinely. Before antibiotics were discovered there was little to be done for acute infections except bed rest and something to ease the symptoms like aspirin or cough linctus, and we did spend a considerable time sick in bed.

The medicine chest in the bathroom, during my childhood, held just a few simple remedies. Apart from the tincture of iodine, Vaseline, aspirin, packet of lint, roll of sticking plaster, and bandages of different widths, there was a rusting tin of antiphlogistine which was heated and applied as a poultice to infected glands, bites etc, and smelt really nice like peppermint. A bottle of tasty Syrup of Figs was brought out from time to time, (I never knew why, and didn't connect it with ensuing tummy aches) and the only other items on the shelf were cough linctus, castor oil and an occasional bottle of bitter black Tonic for Mummy. Sometimes a big lozenge of camphor was hung around my neck with pink tape, to ward off colds, and Vick's Vapour Rub was rubbed on my chest when I inevitably caught one.

Later in life my mother would have a day in bed every week, having her meals brought up to her by my father or me, but mostly sleeping. It was then considered therapeutic to get plenty of rest, whereas now we advocate more exercise!

Father hated waste and was a stickler for making us eat everything on our plates, including fat and gristle. I developed a loathing of tapioca, alias Frog Spawn, which I had to sit in front of all one Sunday afternoon, banished to the kitchen in disgrace, (where Father could keep an eye on me as he dug in the back garden) because I could not or would not eat it. I won in the end, as one meal ran into the next and it had to be agreed that it had become too gluey to leave the plate.

On 11th November we were given red poppies to wear. At 11 a.m. the radio was tuned in to the ceremony at the Cenotaph and we stood to attention for two minutes silence in remembrance of those who had given their lives for our freedom in the Great War. The British Legion organised the poppies to help support the servicemen who had lost their arms and legs, whom I saw on street corners with little trays of matches, shoelaces or pencils to sell, often with a sign hung around their necks asking for charity. Later I was told poppies symbolised the battleground of Flander's fields, where the worst fighting occurred, and poppies still conjure up scenes of trenches and barbed wire for me.

One day Father returned from Town - as London was always referred to - looking mysterious, and called Tony and me, putting his hands behind his back.

"Tony first...which hand will you have?" Tony chose "Left" and was rewarded with a little celluloid doll dressed in dark blue feathers, at which he made a somewhat wry face. The other hand produced a similar doll for me, but feathered in light blue, whereupon Father explained about the Oxford and Cambridge Boat Race, rowed annually on the Thames between Putney and Chiswick bridges. He said that Tony could henceforth support dark blue Oxford and me light blue Cambridge, so we always cheered those sides after that.

Tony and I both got whooping cough. I was very concerned at seeing him trying to catch his breath, and lying on the floor kicking, as his face turned from crimson to purple. For my part, I later developed earache, and a stiff neck, and I remember my mother walking with me to an unfamiliar part of town to see a doctor. He referred us to an E.N.T. surgeon, who had me admitted to a private nursing home, where he performed a mastoid operation. All I remember of that is the 'ironing board' they lifted me up onto which presumably was the operating table.

However, some months later it was evident that my mastoid was chronically infected, and the surgeon, an Australian with a name like Mukey, said he must operate again. Father was in a dilemma, having no private means beyond his naval pay. The first operation had cost one hundred pounds, and he had scraped the barrel to pay that, giving up smoking and living as austerely as possible. Now Father had to admit to the doctors that he could not afford more surgery for me, only to be told breezily "That's no problem. Jill can go into The London

Hospital with no charge." He wondered why they could not have said that before.

This next experience was somewhat different. For some reason I was not put in the nice bright children's ward, which I was taken to visit by a nurse when I was convalescing, but in a long woman's surgical ward, with cancer and other cases. I was kindly received, but not encouraged to make my presence felt by playing around and calling out and I envied the other children with their colourful murals and plenty of toys. A friend had given me some mock bars of Cadbury's chocolate, used in confectioner's windows instead of the real thing, and I decided to play a trick on my surgeon, with whom I was getting quite familiar. I grabbed them as the nurse was preparing me for the operating theatre, and, probably hoping to keep me calm, she allowed me to keep them close to my body that was then rolled in a blanket, arms pinned to my sides.

My excitement mounted as I was wheeled into a lift and along many corridors, watching the lights on the ceiling moving past as we made our way to the operating theatre. Here I was confronted with numerous masked faces, and lifted onto a table. With difficulty I wriggled my arms out of the cocoon and waved a chocolate bar around, cheerfully anticipating roars of laughter when the trick was discovered.

"I've got a pwesent for you," I sang out. "Open it... I bwought it for you specially."

The joke fell as flat as a pancake, hostile eyes widened and someone hastily removed the unsterile weapon from sight.

"How was she allowed to bring that in?" I heard, as my smile was wiped off by a rubbery-smelling mask being clamped over my face. Panic set in as my struggling arms were grabbed and held down and I fought for breath before losing consciousness.

Another memory is the dreadful pain of having the packing changed, when a long ribbon of gauze was stuffed through the ear into the raw cavity in the bone behind. First the soiled packing, now stuck to the wound with exudate, had been slowly pulled out. The whole ward must have dreaded these occasions, as I disappeared down inside the bed to the very foot, and struggled, panicking and screaming, until two nurses forced me out and the swathe of bandages round my head and jaw were unwrapped. As an adult of twenty I had to undergo this operation yet again but the first change of packing was done more humanely in the theatre, under a general anaesthetic. Even so the ordeal was excruciating on the subsequent occasions and uncharacteristically reduced me to tears.

I don't remember my mother visiting me, though doubtless she did. Children were judged to be unsettled by home contacts because they cried when the visitor had to leave. Strange logic!

Coward Rd, Alverstoke

Chapter Two

School Days Begin

Soon after recovering from this ordeal my fifth birthday arrived, and I joined my brother at his Mill Hill School, called Earlsmere. This had a big sign, 'School for Girls Preparatory for Boys'. or should there be a full stop somewhere? Tony had a red blazer, cap and tie, he stuck up for me and was my hero. Unfortunately I missed the first day because I was sick all over my new uniform on the way there, from excitement, and had to be taken straight home again.

After another year our home was disbanded and the family scattered. Eight-year-old Tony had already been farewelled on a train to boarding school with a wooden tuck-box containing a fruit cake, some sweets and a few treasured possessions. Father went away somewhere again and our furniture disappeared down the road in a big van. My battered but beloved old toy farmyard was given away behind my back without my approval, and for some reason, never quite understood, Mummy and I took our suitcases on a long train journey, and moved in with her childhood friend, a widow, who lived in a picturesque cottage near Worksop, Notts. Perhaps this was meant to be only until Father found a new house to rent in Portsmouth, but as far as I knew he'd disappeared again for eternity and Mummy and I were all that was left.

If I could have added that 'Aunty Winsome' lived alone, we might have settled down very comfortably and all lived quite happily together. However, Winsome had a jealous companion in the form of an English bulldog bitch called June, who deeply resented the intrusion of this bouncy child, and was not slow in making her feelings known. She waited until we were alone then ran at me growling and barking, scratching my face and terrifying the wits out of me so that I became a dithering mess every time I heard her slobbering and wheezing on the other side of the door.

Aged 6, in Welsh gear

June was rather pampered and hitherto childless Winsome's constant companion, and it became impossible for the two of us to co-habit unless there was always a closed door between us. Obviously this was impracticable and since we could not continue to impose on Winsome, it was decided that I be placed in the boarding school owned by her parents, which is where my mother and Winsome had both spent all their school years. Accordingly, my case was packed again, St Trinian's uniforms hastily shopped for en route, and I found myself, the youngest boarder in the school, in a draughty and cheerless dormitory with lots of big girls. This school was called Birklands, in Harrogate, and I found the Yorkshire winter SO COLD!

My problems at Birklands were in no way due to mistreatment or the fault of the school, which was not large and, looking back as an adult, gave me a good educational grounding and treated me with considerable lenience. My problems were due frankly to being too young to keep up with a programme designed for older girls up to school leaving age, and also from being endowed with rather weak waterworks.

I have some good memories from this time, such as dancing in the annual school concert, held in a theatre in town, when I was dressed in Welsh costume, with a big black hat with a white frill under the brim and did a solo Welsh dance, and another dance in which I was a golden sunbeam with sundry others... but there were also times of great anxiety and mortification.

On Sundays the whole school would form into a crocodile and walk to the Parish church (miles and MILES away). After fidgeting and yawning through an interminable morning service, leafing with frozen fingers through a prayer book whose small print I could barely yet read, and certainly not understand, we would be ushered out into the biting cold wind for the walk back to school. No-one ever suggested a lavatory break, or considered that some of us might need one, and presuming myself to be no more needful than the rest, although with a lamentably poor record, I would start the long walk back with foreboding, knowing from experience that I would probably not make it in time! It never, ever, occurred to me to ask.

I remained at Birklands for over a year, and learnt French from a book about Madame Souris and the mouse family, which I can recall vividly, (later I had a German primer about the rat family, funnily enough) and I made my Shakespearian debut in the part of 'Wall' in A Midsummer Night's Dream. I enjoyed most of my lessons and became a proficient reader and speller, which has stood me in good stead ever since, and I probably benefited from being taught with older children. I still have some letters written in pencil on pink paper that I wrote home from Birklands.

My parents meanwhile re-established our home in a rented maisonette in Ashburton Road, Southsea. For school holidays I travelled down from Yorkshire by train, in the care of the guard (and one trip actually in the guard's van with no seat except when the guard left his corner). This was quite a long trip for a six year old on her own, and I would be met in London by my relieved mother, before changing trains for Portsmouth. One such day she hugged me and said, "Wait till you see what I've got to show you!" She led the way to the car park, astonishing me by putting my case into a waiting two-seater car, a Jowett, and we drove off in style. It was my parent's first car, bought for £9 from a fellow officer who was going to sea and didn't have anywhere to leave it. We named it 'Alf' and Tony and I enjoyed many windblown rides in the open dickey at the back. If something blew away, or we needed to attract the attention of the driver, we had to bang on the little talc window in the canvas cover over the cab, and we huddled under a rug when it rained unexpectedly.

Jowett 7hp similar to 'Alf'

I became aware of the existence of other relations when Mummy and I spent a night with an aunt of Father's, Great-aunt Maude, who lived in Hounslow. She was very tiny, quick and bird-like, and had been a nurse in the South African wars. Aunt Maude once had a husband who had been a Canadian Mounted Policeman but whose preference for the bottle above marital responsibilities made him very unsatisfactory, or so the story goes, and there had been no children. That evening there was a huge red glow in the sky that we watched for a long time, wondering what great building could have caught fire. It turned out to be the Crystal Palace, and I've always wondered how a glass and steel edifice like that could provide fuel for such a conflagration. It must have been the acres of wonderful exhibits inside, or perhaps when it was moved from Hyde Park to Sydenham and rebuilt they had dispensed with some of the crystal?

A couple of times we all went down to Devon to visit Father's other aunt (Great-aunt Lucy) and her daughter's family. They ran a silver fox farm; beautiful creatures, whose particularly characteristic smell, once identified, and not unpleasant, insured that I could always track where a fox has lifted his leg to this day. Those were the days when ladies liked to wear a satin-lined fox pelt around their necks like a collar, the head clasping the tail below one shoulder and the glass eyes staring in unblinking amazement at the perfumed world they were resurrected into. Mother did not have a fox fur, but she did have some orange ostrich feathers in the dressing-up box.

Then there was Tryphena, Father's younger sister, for whom he had taken responsibility after their parents had both died well before she was twenty. Aunty Tryph was a talented actress and singer, who graduated from the Royal Academy of Dramatic Art fully intending a career on the stage. She had not reckoned with my father, however, who considered the stage far too insecure a livelihood in the nineteen twenties, for a girl with a good brain who must now support herself, and he helped her to gain a position in the Bank of England. Here she remained during a long career, eventually retiring as a Departmental Superintendent and the senior woman in the Accountant's Department. I was told she was the first woman to attain a high position in the Bank of England.

The Bank had a flourishing Opera and Dramatic Society and for the ten years before the war she was the leading lady in their productions, which were performed in the Arts Theatre, London, each year. We have copies of a number of articles paying glowing tribute to Tryph who played the lead parts in these productions, and I will quote from the tribute paid on her retirement:

"Miss Fletcher's versatility was outstanding and in all the many and different types of part she played she never put a foot wrong, a simile used advisedly, as her deportment and movements on the stage were always a joy to watch and a lesson to beginners."

Aunty Tryph came to stay, from time to time, closeting herself in the dining room with the piano, and practicing her singing in a very operatic voice which Tony and I thought terribly funny as we sat on the stairs listening. We were accordingly banished upstairs to do our giggling and mimicking out of earshot. We reckoned she did not like children very much, and I found her rather critical and stern when I was little, and a stickler for table manners. As a teenager, when she was very kind to me, and went to great lengths to visit me at my wartime boarding school, I really came to appreciate her and her delightful sense of humour, and quite revised my opinion. Unfortunately she did not marry until very late in life, and had no children of her own.

It was Aunty Tryph who gave me Cubby, my first and only teddy bear, when I was seven. Because he was not yellow, as teddy bears should be, I was desperately disappointed when I unwrapped him and saw him to be a beige colour. Mummy did some quick-thinking diplomacy and quickly had me convinced that this was the Real Thing, and far superior to those common yellow bears. It worked, and Cubby was my beloved and constant bedtime companion until marriage made him redundant. By then he was quite bald, and had unsightly black patches where I had soaked him in undiluted bleach to sterilise him after he had Chicken Pox with me.

Jill (left) at Birklands, Summer 1934

Eventually, to my great relief, I left Birklands and was enrolled at a day school in Southsea, called Byculla, which had the distinction of a light blue cockade on the side of the hatband. I was a nail-biter; so foul-tasting bitter aloes was painted on my nails and the tips of my pencils, to stop me biting them (and it did).

Infectious diseases were an accepted fact of life in those days and over the years I had whooping cough, measles, German measles, mumps and chicken pox, not to mention the usual selection of coughs and colds and (my specialty) bilious attacks. I contracted measles quite badly in the hot summer holidays of 1935 and remember tossing around in a rumpled and crumby bed, all hot and bothered and yelling for Mummy who had gone out for a while, and ten year old Tony lecturing me for making so much noise and disturbing the whole neighbourhood. If I must cry I should do it quietly. This was a totally new idea that I had never even considered before, and it rather decreased the satisfaction of creating mayhem and being the centre of attention.

Tony often took it upon himself to keep me in line, quite effectively too as I respected him greatly and longed for his approval, and he gave me much good advice over the years. Because he was mostly away at boarding school we were not over-exposed to each other, though I think he thought we were, as little sisters were automatically considered brats by his peers and not worthy of notice. At one stage my standing sank so low that I was even referred to as 'It' in front of his friends, and though he loved to tease me, and I always fell for the bait, he made the most of a bad job when he had no-one else to play with. As I grew older and more acceptable, and the age-gap lessened, we became the best of friends, but that was still in the future.

I have a faded snap taken on my seventh birthday on Southsea's shingly beach after a chilly swim. It was my first outing after recovering from measles, and Mummy had made me a cotton frock with yellow and blue flowers (and matching knickers of course). Sitting alone on the shingles was a very nice man with whom I struck up a conversation, eventually involving my mother too. He introduced himself as Mr Atkinson, on leave from the Diplomatic Service in Spain, and for some years following he sent me a present on my birthday, first a delightful necklace of tiny blue/green shells, and then a coral necklace. I guess he had been lonely; we never met again but corresponded for a little while. The world was a safer and friendlier place then and I had a habit of striking up friendships with strangers, which had to be squashed later on. In retrospect it was probably my pretty Mother he was really interested in.

During this period, Father was working at Fort Blockhouse, the Portsmouth submarine base. He usually came and went from the house in civilian clothes, using an elegant walking stick with a bone handle that had been presented to him, and was inscribed with his initials, E.N.R.F. 1914-1918, on brass. Each evening after returning from "the office", whilst Mother was preparing their meal, which they had in peace after we children were in bed, he would go for a walk, looking quite purposeful. When I asked where he was going he would say, "There and back again, to see how far it is." Actually he would visit the local pub, and he liked nothing better than chatting with the locals over the bar, wherever he happened to be living at the time but more particularly if it was a country pub. He was very moderate in his consumption and I never saw him drunk.

We had some memorable holidays in houseboats on the Hamble River in the mid-thirties. The main one was a converted naval motor launch called La Bohéme, moored off Luke's Yard, Hamble, and approached with dry-clad feet on duck-boards over the deep soft mud. She would float and fall with the tide, and belonged to kind elderly friends who were pleased for Father to use and maintain it. Another houseboat we loved staying in was a big three-mast schooner called Norseman, also approached through Luke's yard and stuck deeply in the mud. She shifted when the tide came in, so that it felt like floating, and she belonged to our kind Sunningdale cousins, who sometimes invited us to join them there, and sometimes we stayed there on our own.

Living permanently in Luke's Yard was a colourful old bearded sea dog called Captain Owen, who had retired to his houseboat, H.M.S.Pinafore, with two elderly and decrepit greyhounds. He told wonderful tall stories, which we lapped up, and was always very kind to Tony and me (whom he referred to gruffly as Lop-eared Swabs) and he gave Tony a little dinghy, named Hesperus, which he learnt to scull around the river.

Tony could swim, but as I couldn't I was seldom permitted to embark with him. Efforts to get me swimming were concentrated on tethering me in a rubber ring to a pontoon, moored to the duck-boards but in deep water, where I was able to splash around in safety. Being a skinny little thing with no buoyancy I never became more than a just-adequate swimmer, and I remained psychologically dependent on that ring for some years. Tony tried to wean me off it by letting the air down behind my back, but I could not be fooled. We spent many hours dangling meat on hooks over the mud and catching crabs, or hopefully fishing for bass over the stern of La Bohéme, our lines tangling around beer bottles.

Tony and I used to walk into Hamble to buy fresh bread and a newspaper. One day, in the village, we paused on a curb to wait for two motorcycles that rounded the corner and passed in front of us. They were travelling too fast, and the second one skidded and fell, sliding across the road just by us, the rider tangling with the machine and lying still. I was absolutely terrified and took to my heels and ran all the way back to Luke's Yard. Tony later reported that the rider was not dead after all, but my confidence in the trustworthiness of traffic doing what it was expected to do, was shattered, and I never walked along that quiet country road again without running up the nearest garden path whenever I heard a vehicle approaching.

A rather different holiday is etched on my memory. We were friendly with a comparatively wealthy family whose daughter, Elizabeth, was my particular friend at Byculla. They moved to another district and I was very excited to be invited for a visit in the Christmas holidays. I was loaded onto a train, with instructions as to where to get off, and her parents met me and drove me home, by which time it was well after dark. Elizabeth was at the front door dancing with excitement,

"I've got a wonderful surprise to show you. Quick, come up and see. "

She sped up the stairs to her nursery, with me pursuing in expectation of some wonderful belated Christmas present prepared for me. She danced over to a beautiful doll's crib, bedecked with flounces and ribbons and bows, and lifted out a gorgeous baby doll.

"Her name's Tinkerbell."

I gasped.... the doll was too wonderful for words... and for me!

"Oh! Thank you, thank you!" I managed to get out, as I held out my arms to receive it.

Elizabeth looked at my face and suddenly froze....

"But she's not yours; it's my Christmas present from Daddy and Mummy."... and she clutched the doll to her chest.

I couldn't speak as my throat constricted and my eyes started to water, and disappointment took away all the joy and excitement I had been feeling about this visit. Feeling a dreadful fool at my mistake, speechless and scarlet I managed to choke back the tears until saved by Nanny calling us to supper.

I slept in the parent's dressing room, on a camp bed, and one night I awoke in a lather to find the light on and both parents bending over me looking very concerned. It seems I'd had a nightmare from which they had trouble waking me. All in all I was rather glad to go home again, although they were very kind people and the mother bought me a big picture book at the railway station bookstall for the return journey, instead of the expected comic

In that Christmas holidays Tony and I were taken to a pantomime, Aladdin. This was a wonderful entertainment in which the audience, mostly children, became totally involved with the characters. The Principal Boy had to be played by a glamorous girl, in silk tights and high heels and a very short tunic and I thought 'he' was soppy, as was the Heroine, played by a pretty girl. But the Dame was undoubtedly the highlight, played by a male comedian, and wonderfully naughty. I can remember laughing until I got a stitch in my side.

Chapter Three

Life in Our Street 1935

Ashburton Road, Southsea, where we now lived, was not a very long street, having a continuous row of almost identical four-story mansions on each side, each differentiated from its neighbours by the colour of its paintwork and curtains, and possibly a few scraggy plants or varied railings round the basement steps. Our maisonette occupied the two upper floors and there was no garden except a small rear courtyard, which was the domain of the basement dwellers. When I returned to look for it after the war, I discovered our house had been demolished by a bomb and was one of a number of gaps in the row.

In the thirties many houses were still lit by gas, and though we had electricity in our home, the streets were lit by gas lamps, and I liked to watch the lamp-lighter, with his long rod, work his way up the street at dusk. Not having a garden, I spent a lot of time at the window, as there was always something interesting to see. The calls of the street vendors would draw me to watch the muffin man with a wooden tray of crumpets on his head, ringing a hand-bell, and the Rag-and-Bone Man pushing a hand-cart and singing out "Any old rags and bones;" the black-faced chimney sweep with his array of spiky brushes; the coal man, ingrained with coal dust, humping the heavy sacks on rounded shoulders from his cart to tip down the coal holes, and the window cleaner, with extension ladder, chamois and bucket.

The milkman came round in a humming electric van, collected the day's money and glass empties from the front step, leaving fresh pints, the thick cream risen to the top for at least an inch and probably two, and sealed with a cardboard disc. For a treat the Corona soft drink man supplied big bottles of fizzy orange, lemonade or ginger beer, in returnable bottles with attached china stoppers. The postman delivered letters through our front door three or more times a day, and the paper boy delivered a morning and evening paper which fell through the letter box with a thump onto the mat. Fish, meat, bread and vegetables could all be bought at the door, selected from the back of vans or carts, leaving grocery items to be delivered home by the errand boy on his bicycle. After dark we would be tempted by the smell of roasting chestnuts from the chestnut vendor on the corner of the main road, with red hot brazier and paper bags of piping hot chestnuts.

Spanish onion men rode around on bicycles. They wore black berets and festooned the handlebars with plaits of onions for sale, and there were sometimes swarthy gypsies, with baskets of wooden clothes pegs and bunches of heather which the women sold from house to house. For some reason the grownups checked that the door was locked when the gypsies were around and watched from the window to see when they had gone. On the common we would see their camps and painted horse-drawn caravans with grubby children and dogs playing around. Sometimes the sound of an accordion or violin would make the scene indefinably fascinating and romantic. Mummy told me not to stare, but it was hard not to.

Horses and carts were used extensively, from the magnificently turned out big Shire horses on the brewer's drays to the shiny black carriage horses, with plumes bobbing, pulling the funeral cortèges. I came to know a few of the patient nags of the regular tradesmen by name, and would stroke their soft noses and offer sugar lumps on a flattened palm. Their droppings were a source of revenue to an old woman, bent permanently double, who patrolled with a shovel, and scooped them into a bin that she pushed around in a battered perambulator.

My parents had an old wind-up gramophone, which was sometimes played for a treat. They had very few records, the ones I remember being Charlie Kunz playing the piano, a couple of Gilbert and Sullivan overtures, and Stanley Holloway reciting "Sa-am, Sa-am, pick oop tha moosket" on one side, and "The stick with the 'orses 'ead 'andle" on the other.

A great treat, when Mother took me shopping in Handley's (a department store), was to have a glass of lemonade in the restaurant and watch the Palm Court Orchestra. One day we had to visit the Ladies Room where there was a row of lavatories, with solid wooden partitions between them about six and a half feet tall. Mother put a penny in the slot, took me in with her and shut and bolted the door as usual. When we had finished, the lock jammed and the door would not open, despite all Mother's efforts. We stood waiting for a long time and called "Help" repeatedly, but no one came near. Fearful lest closing time should overtake us and strand us in the dark until morning, my five-foot-nothing mother stood on the seat and hoisted me over the top of the partition. I managed to slither and drop onto the wooden seat below, reach up on tip-toes to unbolt the door, and emerge to find a floorwalker whom I persuaded to listen to my story. Mother was eventually released but I was really anxious lest no-one takes me seriously and I would have no one to take me home. There were three large department stores in Southsea then, Knight and Lee, Morants and Handleys, but I could find no trace of any of them after the 2nd World War, as that area was very badly bombed.

I must have been seven when I first consciously heard the grandfather clock in the darkened hall strike midnight, and I froze in fear lest the fairies, or worse, were afoot. The hall light was always switched off when my parents went to bed, and I was terrified of the dark and often woke with nightmares, too frightened to attend to nature on the 'jerry' stowed under my bed, or even to call out to Mummy, lest something awful grab me.

In some respects I was a very timid child and it took me years to lose my fear of the dark, but I developed strategies that enabled me to cope. One was to roll a rubber ball at speed under the bed so that it hit the wall and rebounded. This way I could test that there was no one hiding there. When I entered a dark room alone, I would fling open the door, switch on the light and say very fiercely "I KNOW YOU'RE THERE IN THE WARDROBE" (or under the bed etc) "Come on out at ONCE!" I could never stand too much suspense, and I still prefer to meet a fear head-on than to delay facing it.

To repay hospitality my parents would give an occasional cocktail party. Father was a very genial host, and most particular in the preparations, making sure that the house was clean and tidy all over, the sitting-room furniture back against the wall to allow plenty of standing room so that people would mingle (Father only expected the elderly or infirm to actually sit down), soft lighting and the house warm and welcoming in time for the first guests. This time I was bathed and fed and tidied out of the way upstairs, with a fizzy lemonade and plate of savouries as a treat, but I crept out to sit on the dark stairs and peep through the banisters as the guests arrived. Father took the furs and wraps and made sure that everyone was properly introduced to someone compatible, and had topped-up drinks in their hands. Mother did her best to keep her end up and was a sweet, if shy, hostess, but I had a chip on my shoulder and as the evening advanced and the noise level rose I started to feel very neglected. My yells for attention passing unheard, I eventually gave up and sobbed myself to sleep, not even responding to mummy's goodnight kiss when they came up to bed. It took days to rid the place of the intriguing smell of perfume and cigarette smoke.

A number of times Tony and I were invited to wonderful Christmas parties given for naval children in Portsmouth Dockyard (H.M.S.Vernon) and Fort Blockhouse (H.M.S.Dolphin). Hundreds of children attended, all dressed up in their best party gear, and a fairground atmosphere under canvas prevailed. It was easy to get lost, and I was always glad to stick closely to Tony... until he was sick, that is, (which was not unusual), and we hovered uneasily by whilst a sailor covered the results with sawdust and removed it on a shovel. We also went to a Christmas party in H.M.S.Hood and I still have the brooch I was given with her crest. She was tragically sunk in the next war.

Chapter Four

Lee-on-Solent.

In 1937 the Coronation Review of the Fleet was staged in the Solent after the coronation of King George VI and Queen Elizabeth. Not only the British fleet but also ships from the world's navies were all moored in the Solent, a strip of water between the Isle of Wight and the mainland. My mother wrote an account for her grandchildren, which tells of Father's responsibility in organising national hospitality for "the largest collection of royalty and heads of countries ever assembled in one place before."

"He was given a room at the Admiralty and a list of all the crowned heads, Chief Ministers, Sheiks etc of every country, about a mile long, and told to work out cabin and table accommodation for a day and a night in P & O S.S.Strathmore, and send out the invitations. To my huge delight I was allowed to attend on board Strathmore and every second was interesting. The Sheiks were dressed in their robes, the Africans in theirs and it was all wonderfully picturesque."

After describing some of the more interesting and colourful guests, Mother writes that as they were leaving the ship "a very arrogant, swaggering, overbearing, monocled man came aboard to escort a most attractive lady; he was Ribbentrop, an unscrupulous Nazi... she was the wife of the German Ambassador, who we had met at a cocktail party when they first arrived in England, the first one after World War 1. At that time she was definitely a homely, solid Frau, and it was hard to recognise her."

Mother mentioned that the guest who caused the most difficulty was the teenage King Farouk of Egypt, who came with his mother. He refused to get up and leave at the appointed hour, and it was Father who had to get through to him that he had outstayed his welcome and it was time to leave.

Father often worked until 2 or 3 a.m. organising this event, and his desk was covered in telephones like a business tycoon's. It was not just logistics that were involved, but an intimate knowledge of protocol and rank etc. so that no dignitary could be unwittingly offended and cause an international incident. He was rewarded with a well-earned OBE. Tony and I were boarded out with friends for a couple of nights, and I remember the wonderful sight of rows and rows of big ships, stretching into the distance, covered in bunting and all lit up at night from bow to stern.

We now moved a little west from Southsea to Lee-on-Solent. Father was to sail to the Far East in HMS Birmingham, after standing by her refit in Plymouth, and he first settled us into a brand new, ground floor flat on the sea front. Tony now became a day student at his school, Edinburgh House, and I was enrolled at a girl's school just along the front called St Boniface. Mummy was so happy, sewing curtains and cushions and establishing a little garden, and she and Father worked very hard turning the builder's rubble into attractive crazy paving, with a rock garden and goldfish pond. My parents were keen gardeners, and always managed to leave a place looking far better than they found it.

The landlord asked us to choose a name for the flat, and after much thought we decided on 'Windover', because the wind did blow right across the Solent over us. From the front rooms we saw clearly across the cliff-top to the Isle of Wight, and would watch the great ocean liners of that day entering and leaving Southampton Waters, such as the Queen Mary, Normandy, Mauritania, Aquitania and Bremen. On the beach we hastily snatched up our towels as the heavy swell of their wash approached the shore, and there were often thick lumps of tar amongst the

'Windover', Lee-on-Solent

shells and pebbles and tumbled pieces of opaque coloured glass, which made a mess of our feet, or worse, woollen bathing costumes.

The Isle of Wight was a few miles over the water. When it looked close and clear, we could expect rain, but on hot, dry days it receded into a haze. On those days I liked to lie on the spray-stunted grass on the cliff-top and look for shapes in the changing clouds, aware of the ripples whispering on the beach below, rolling the pebbles up and back, up and back.

Father was lodging in Plymouth, Devon, during the week, and we spent a few weeks of the summer holidays on a farm nearby, called Leyton Farm. This was full of new experiences for Tony and me, and we were allowed to join in whatever was afoot, having rides on the huge, gentle Shire horse, scratching the pet lop-eared pig behind the ears with a stick, and watching the farmer's wife setting out the great wide pans of cream to scald and turn into delicious clotted Devonshire Cream, some of which would be posted all around the country in round tins.

One day, as I was following the last cow into the milking shed to watch the milking, she suddenly took fright (the farmer later said she'd smelt the caged ferrets which they had been cleaning out) lowered her head and plunged around, chasing me back up the yard. I scrambled over a five-barred gate, tore down to the bottom of the next field, and hid in a ditch because the hedge was too thick to get through. My pounding heart and sobbing breath masked the fact that the cow had not in fact scaled the gate, and probably had no malicious intent towards me at all, and I stayed hidden in that ditch until eventually Father discovered me and persuaded me to accompany him back for tea. A terror of cows, which started then, lasted for many years and clouded the rest of that holiday, as I was sure they were all out to get me.

When the grey and blustery day came that Father's ship, HMS Birmingham, was to leave from Portsmouth for two years in the Far East, Mummy and I went across in the ferry to watch her sail out into the Solent. The entire ship's company was standing to attention on deck, lining the rails, with the officers up on a higher deck. We were not quite near enough to make out Father's face, but as the cruiser passed the closest to where we were standing, he pulled his white hankie out of his breast pocket and blew his nose with a flourish as Mummy knew he would. "There's Daddy. There... with the white hankie!" she told me, and we waved even harder and I yelled "Good-bye, Daddy, Good-bye!" Mummy was wiping her eyes and smiling in a funny way with her mouth closed, and I suddenly felt terribly sad. We went back home to Lee, hand in hand and silent, and the day seemed very flat and grey. Although I was quite used to his absences, and had even found them a relief at times, this was the first time I remember realising that I was going to miss him, and that we were not going to see him for a very long time.

It must have been such a lonely feeling for Mummy, for he was her hero, and the flat seemed somehow dead without the special smell of his presence, his silver-backed hair brushes on the tall-boy, long leather razor strop in the bathroom and bottle of Bay Rum with which he brushed down his hair. He was a big man and his absence left a big hole in our lives. She moved me into the double bed with her now, so that Tony could have the other bedroom instead of the divan in the dining room he had been relegated to before.

Chapter Five

A Happy Period

Meanwhile life went on, and I soon adjusted to the new order. Along Marine Parade West, near our flat, was an RAF base for seaplanes and amphibians, which was later taken over by the Fleet Air Arm. The large planes landed on the water and were then wheeled up the ramp and across the road to the workshops and hangers. I became very friendly with a group of RAF officer's children who lived on the base behind a tall brick wall, and we produced a variety concert in the roomy attic of one family, suitably furnished with a raised stage and curtains which drew across and back. Rehearsing kept us all innocently occupied for weeks beforehand but what was not so innocent was that we would steal cigarettes from our parent's cigarette boxes (and all parents seemed to smoke in those days), cut them in half and share them around. It was not too long before an elder sister turned sniffer-dog and informed on us, and we had to think up other pastimes. Since children of serving officers never stayed in one place very long anyhow, our happy little band was soon split up.

Memories of those few happy years in Lee come crowding in and it is hard to be selective. Around nine and ten years of age I was becoming acutely aware of the world and myself; increasing in confidence, independence and curiosity, delighting in exploring and testing and pushing on the boundaries. With Father away, I ran rather wild, and certainly there was always something exciting to do, unfortunately mostly classified as mischief. As long as we turned up for meals, we could disappear for hours on end without causing parental concern, though officially I was always meant to keep my mother informed as to where I was. This would be a very vague generalisation on my part, such as "I'm going to Yvonne's," not untrue as far as it went, whilst my great friend, Yvonne, would give her mother to understand that we would be at my place, and we thus ensured our complete freedom of movement until the next mealtime.

Yvonne had a bicycle but at first I had only a large scooter with spoke wheels, which meant that my left shoe forever needed mending as I scooted madly to keep up with her. I eventually saved up four guineas in my Post Office Savings account, and bought a gleaming new full-sized Hercules bicycle, which was my pride and joy. I kept it oiled and dried, pumped up the tyres, and rode it around every minute I could. Yvonne and I would explore for miles out into the country, and as there was little traffic in those days, it was relatively safe. It never occurred to us that any ordinary-looking person might wish to harm us, but we did know in theory that we must not talk to 'strange' men or accept sweets from strangers.

No-one ever offered us sweets but our excursions were sternly curtailed after a man had waylaid us in the lonely area of wasteland between Alverstoke and Lee which still had trenches left over from the Great War (or so we thought, actually they were probably from army exercises). He said he had something to show us, and persuaded Yvonne to go into bushes to "look at it" with him. I was distinctly uneasy and said I would stay and guard the bicycles, and we had to get back home, and tried to catch Yvonne's eye to show my alarm, but to no avail.

"It'll only take a minute," he said.

After they had gone I waited a few minutes, growing increasingly apprehensive, and called out, "Hurry up, Yvonne. Come on, we've got to go", and when there was no reply I left the bikes and followed the path through the bushes to find them. Yvonne was being persuaded to remove her pants, and was now getting alarmed herself. Goodness knows what would have happened to her if I had not appeared and said "Come on. We've got to go now." We scrambled back to our bikes before the man could get his act together and pedaled frantically all the way home.

Yvonne's mother must have told the police, who sent a detective to interview us. I was in the bath (of all places) when he came right into the bathroom to speak to me, which, ultra modest as I was, I thought very odd as I took refuge under the nearest face flannel. It was years before the significance of that experience hit me. We must have been nine at the time and totally ignorant of the facts of life and of the real danger we had been in.

We spent many happy hours on a vacant lot up the road where building materials had been dumped prior to work commencing. Yvonne and I 'built' and rebuilt our own house, mapping out the rooms with a layer or two of bricks and furnishing it with bric-a-brac and planks for seats. We always picked a few wild flowers and arranged them in fish paste pots and jam jars, to show we were graciously in residence. Occasionally we would visit a nearby stream and fish for minnows and tadpoles, and I had a small net for the purpose on the end of a long bamboo. I tied string around the neck of a jam jar for carrying on my bike, and took them home to decant into our little pond, spending hours on my tummy, watching frog spawn turn into tadpoles and then grow legs and become baby frogs.

Yvonne's own home was in an apple orchard, and beside the road outside the gate was a good tree for climbing, with plenty of leafy cover. Some very giggly mornings were spent concealed in the foliage, teasing errand boys with a pea-shooter as they passed by on their bicycles. We attached some sewing cotton to a purse weighted with a few pebbles, which we dropped under our tree, and as the infrequent pedestrian passed underneath us and bent down to examine it; we jerked it up into the air. We thought this was SO funny, but it was not something that could be repeated as the regulars saw what we were up to and soon stopped taking the bait.

Another activity I enjoyed was to roller-skate in front of my school, with its big classroom windows facing the sea, and I skated tantalisingly to and fro in their line of vision when I was officially in quarantine for some infectious disease which had broken out in my brother's school, or was convalescing from something myself. Quarantine was taken very seriously in those days, as there were neither inoculations to give immunity against the prevalent childhood infections (other than smallpox and diphtheria), nor antibiotics to help the complications that followed.

An ongoing worry for me was a very aggressive pink and white bull terrier, whose gate I had to pass to get to and from school. Although I crossed to the other side of the road he would work himself up into a lather of frenzy if he heard footsteps approaching, which lent power to my legs but sent my heart into my mouth lest he break out. This dog terrorised the other dogs and their owners in the village, as his mistress would take him out for exercise on a lead that she was generally powerless to keep hold of when he pulled away. For his part he was incapable of seeing anything furry without attacking it. These violent, malevolent dog fights terrified me, and I would forget my errand and flee whenever I saw him approaching, especially after I saw him bite his owner badly when she was trying to prevent him murdering the little Scottie next door. Her blood congealed in a trail of great drops on the pavement, which remained for days and exercised a dreadful fascination until rain eventually washed it away.

Many days of schooling at St Boniface were missed when I suffered from 'bilious attacks' in which I vomited all day until I was retching bitter yellow bile. When I did have a continuous run of good school attendance I enjoyed the lessons. Arithmetic was much taken up with money sums. With calculations involving twelve pence to the shilling, twenty shillings to the pound, twenty-one shillings to the guinea, and crowns, half-crowns, florins, halfpennies (pronounced ha'penny) and farthings to be considered, as well as the obvious sixpence and 'thre'pence'. Understanding money was far more confusing than the decimal system of dollars and cents, or pounds and pence that we have now, and kept our little minds well exercised.

On Saturday afternoons I usually went to the cinema on the pier. Red plush, thick carpets and low lighting with plenty of gold candelabras, transported us into a different, rich and glamorous world. Layers of diaphanous curtains opened to reveal the screen and a large Censor's certificate, and the cinema organ rose up from under the floor as it was being played. You could enter at any time and watch the programme round to that point again, or beyond, for as long as you wanted. I became an ardent film fan and kept a scrap-book that I filled with pictures of my favourite stars. There were always two films, a short and a long one, both black and white, and a newsreel such as Pathé Gazette or Gaumont British News in each programme. Snow White was the first full-length film I saw in Technicolour and I had nightmares about the wicked queen afterwards.

Some of my friends, usually those with bigger houses, held birthday parties, which in those days were highly organised affairs. Often a relative was a conjuror of sorts, and did his tricks, some of which worked well enough to baffle the audience, but mostly we played organised games such as musical bumps or chairs, Pin the Tail on the Donkey, 'Spin the Trencher' and charades, with Sardines (a form of indoor hide-and-seek) after tea, ending up squashed in our hostess's wardrobe with half the other sticky guests.

My own birthday, being at the tail-end of summer, usually attracted gales and rain, which spoilt my birthday treat if we had planned a picnic or other outing. Mummy would place a "W" in the window, and then invite the poor frozen 'Wallsy' man in for a hot cup of tea to thaw him out, whilst we licked our unseasonal ice creams. I don't remember ever having a proper party. Sometimes, for a treat, Mummy would make peppermint creams, pink and white coconut ice or chocolate fudge, and I always asked for a rainbow layered birthday cake (strawberry, vanilla and chocolate), Tony and I competing to scrape the bowl when she was cake-making. I always hoped she had made me a new cotton frock each birthday too (with knickers to match of course) which was necessary as I was growing so fast.

On warmer summer days the Walls Ice-cream man would be surrounded by a small crowd of children waving their pennies. Dressed in a peaked cap and blue striped jacket, he peddled his way around town tinkling his bell, with a large navy blue icebox in front of his tricycle bearing the words 'Stop Me and Buy One'. Most popular were Snow Fruits and Snow Creams, the penny ices in triangular cardboard jackets that you had to fold over or they melted before you could finish, and leaked in a sticky trail down to your elbow as you ate them. The Wallsy man had to keep his eye on people's front windows where they might have stuck a big cardboard 'W' summoning him to call in, which would certainly mean more than a penny sale there. For tuppence one bought the makings of a 'sandwich', a white slice wrapped in paper and two wafers, and for four-pence a choc-bar, in silvery wrapping, which was luxury and utter, utter heaven.

Between the ages of eight and ten my pocket money was raised from thre'pence to sixpence. This could buy a variety of sweets from the Halfpenny Tray at the sweet shop; these included lollipops, gob stoppers that changed colour (needing to be removed from the mouth and checked for authenticity every half minute or so), sherbet in small yellow cylinders, (with a tube of licorice stuck in the top, or a dab stick with a hard blob of butterscotch on the end), licorice coils with an aniseed ball in the centre, or long licorice "shoe laces", and paper-wrapped strips of Eaton Toffee, each just one halfpenny. Alternatively one could buy a pennyworth of aniseed balls, humbugs, licorice allsorts, lemon or pear drops, boiled sweets, extra-strong peppermints, barley sugar twist, Pontefract Cakes, a packet of Wrigley's peppermint chewing gum or a little bag of lemonade powder to dip a finger into. Sweets not eaten up quickly would get sticky in their white paper cone and attract the dust and fluff, which always lurked at the bottom of my Burberry pockets. Pocket money might also stretch to a comic each week,

Mickey Mouse Weekly, Puck, Tiger Tim's Weekly, Rainbow or Comic Cuts and later a film star paper that I could cut out for my scrap-book.

The regular consumption of sticky sweets, coupled with my refusal to drink milk played havoc with my milk teeth, necessitating memorable visits to the dentist and a few extractions as well as much drilling and filling. When my eyeteeth appeared vertically above others , which had crowded them out, the latter had to be removed, but that was not until I was twelve. In the meantime two perfectly good, but crowded, lower jaw teeth were removed under gas in the dentist's chair. He had a drawer full of tiny samples of toothpaste, and I was allowed to choose one to take home 'for being good.' The carrot worked inasmuch as I always tried to be brave so that I would not miss out, but with the old-fashioned drills, dentist's visits could be veritable torture sessions and required heavy bribing. My eyes were also tested and I was prescribed steel rimmed glasses that hooked around my ears, and were my pride and joy for a while, until the novelty wore off. It was hoped these would cure my vomiting attacks, but actually they didn't.

Compared to our grand-children we had very few toys and these were mostly practical such as paints and crayons, playing cards, board games such as snakes and ladders and draughts, jig-saw puzzles, a skipping rope, and roller skates passed on from my brother. Sometimes I had a hoop or a yo-yo and with hopscotch they passed hours of time that often stretched endlessly ahead in the summer holidays. I had one or two dolls, Cubby my beloved bear, and (when our furniture was out of store) a tall, thin, doll's house that had been Auntie Tryph's, for which I spent hours making furniture out of match boxes.

When Mummy was dressmaking I would put a cushion into the upended domed lid of her Singer sewing machine and used it as a cradle for my dolls, otherwise I used shoeboxes and made families of dolls out of stuffed stockings or dolly pegs. Tony had Meccano, a box of conjuring tricks and a Hornby clockwork train set, the engine wound up with a big key, which I was not allowed to touch in case I over-wound it, so I had to content myself with watching longingly or perhaps working the points if I was in favour. My very greatest joy was to be lent a friend's doll's pram, which kept me happy for hours on end as I crooned and fussed over the dolls within.

Attending to my stamp collection, swapping with friends and soaking stamps from overseas relatives, kept me amused, and when I was (quite frequently) sick in bed, I would pass the day sorting through Mummy's big brown malt jar full of buttons of all shapes and sizes, or looking through the box of picture postcards which she had collected since school days, when her elder sister, Mabel, used to write to her from their home in Burma entirely on post cards. Mummy always made me a jug of homemade lemon barley water to sip as soon as I could keep anything down.

Tony was given a really big model yacht called Pallas by Uncle Ronald. This was definitely not a toy, and entailed a lot of responsibility... so of course I was not allowed near it. It could only be sailed on the model yacht lake at Gosport, where enthusiasts would meet to race their immaculate crafts. Transporting it there, and general care and maintenance were really adult matters, and needed Father's presence and cooperation. Very occasionally I was allowed to go too, just to watch, but all too soon Pallas got rammed and her hull splintered, and that was the unhappy end of that. Our family could not afford to repair her and she eventually eked out her life in a furniture store like all the rest of our belongings. Tony was devastated.

I joined the Brownies and gained all the badges I could, so that I 'flew up' into the Guides and added "Be Prepared" to my repertoire of wise advice. Being an avid collector, going for badges suited me down to the ground, and I also found my way to the Parish Church Sunday School with some of my school friends, where we were rewarded with pictures of Jesus and other bible characters to stick in a special booklet. If you didn't turn up you had a disappointing blank on the page for that week, but I seldom missed as I was fascinated by Jesus anyway, and read about him in the illustrated New Testament which my mother gave me on my tenth birthday. I never doubted that Jesus is a living person, and later, at boarding school, easily slipped into the routine of prayer before getting into bed and on rising, and received much comfort from these times. I never actually attended a church with my own family as a child. My parents were believers but not churchgoers, but they didn't discourage me and my faith somehow blossomed on its own.

1937, 9 years old.

Unlike me, who joined everything going, and started my own thing up if no one else had, Mummy was not the joiner type; nevertheless she mustered her courage and joined the Woman's League of Health and Beauty. She made for herself the neat satin uniform of white top and very brief black pants, and they did exercises to music in regimented lines in a local hall, sometimes giving displays to the public. Otherwise her social life was very limited, and she would do a lot of sewing, for herself and me. She enjoyed knitting and listening to the wireless and she would often sing and play the piano; being alone so much, she would listen to classical concerts and plays that were on after Tony and I were in bed. I liked her to sit by me, hold my hand and sing me to sleep when I was sick.

Many contented hours were spent reading books and for birthdays and Christmas my relatives usually sent me book tokens to be spent at W.H. Smith's Bookshops. I would read almost anything that came my way, and was fortunate in having a broad selection of excellent children's books always to hand, many passed on from older cousins, John and Michael Drinkall.

I was sad when a good book finished and I felt I was parting from close friends.

Being a very friendly child, I soon ingratiated myself into our neighbour's lives. On one side was an elderly widow who was a Roman Catholic. She had numerous strings of shiny, black, rosary beads draped around in her cluttered living room, and a big, purry, black cat that I used as an excuse for visiting her. She took me with her to the town library, showed me how to go about selecting my own books and encouraged me in reading widely. Back at her place she fed me elevenses of bread and ginger marmalade. Once or twice, when there was a special festival, she took me to the Roman Catholic church, and I would copy what she did, kneeling, standing, singing and genuflecting, and trying to act as if I belonged, though feeling slightly guilty as if I were eavesdropping, and wondering if my parents would really approve if they knew.

On the other side a childless couple acquired an adorable Scottish terrier puppy, and since I was never allowed to have a pet because we were always on the move, I was unable to keep away and so they acquired me too. The only domestic livestock I managed to collect, to assuage my longing for a pet, was a box full of snails, which would escape every time I turned my back. I kept them in a dress box, which I furnished for them, and made little carts out of matchbox trays stuck onto their shells for them to pull, and raced them against each other. They were hopeless at keeping to the track, forever climbing over the barriers, and were not popular when Mummy discovered their silver tracks all around the front porch. My interest waned anyhow when I got tired of rounding them up all the time. I really would have loved a kitten or puppy.

I had discovered by now that being a child was hard work and a full-time job too, because there were so many rules to be remembered. Certain oft-repeated sayings continually nudged and moulded me in the journey towards behaving in a self-controlled and civilised fashion automatically. Apart from learning table manners, which I never seemed to get to the end of, it was important to look at people and answer when they spoke to me, and to stop what I was doing until they had finished speaking. I must refrain from grizzling, pestering and interrupting, or squabbling with Tony (and kicking or biting); for his part, he must stop teasing me. In public I must never stare, point or make personal remarks, and of course I must not make faces, giggle at people or whisper behind their backs,

Certain things were very definitely Not Done, ever, such as telling lies, taking things that belonged to others, reading other people's letters or poking around other people's drawers or belongings. Answering my mother back and being disobedient were very high on the crime list, especially when Father was around. Then there were the rules such as "Blow your nose, don't sniff...put your hand over your mouth when you cough or yawn...catch a sneeze in your hankie (hankies were tucked up under the elastic of my knickers'-leg) ...wash your hands before meals... brush your teeth properly... don't pick your nose... don't breathe through your mouth." Probably the most irksome was being constantly made to clear up my own messes and keep my room tidy.

As the years went by, more acceptable behaviour gradually became automatic and the rules changed according to my growing maturity. I am eternally grateful to my parents for persevering with me when it would have been so much easier for them to have thrown up their hands in exasperation and let me off. Their concern was always lest we become 'spoilt children', that meant selfish and unpleasant to live with and generally unwelcome socially. I hated being referred to as a spoilt child though I usually managed to act like one, and though I've given the impression my parents were perpetually nagging, in fact this was far from the case, but they were quietly persistent however rebelliously I responded.

Our father was an exceptionally fine man and a good parent, but could seem very stern when we were small, and insisted on a high standard of behaviour from Tony and me. Unfortunately things got a bit out of hand during his long absences, and I would become disobedient and cheeky. His concern was always to protect my mother and he would not tolerate me answering her back, which I was prone to do, sometimes reacting by putting me across his knee and spanking my seat with his slipper. I would start yelling before he had yet touched me, and always felt it unfair that Tony didn't get the same treatment, but I learnt year's later that he did occasionally get spanked too, but bore it in silence like a man. These episodes were very infrequent, and I couldn't feel I was unfairly treated because I knew I had asked for it, and the punishment seemed to clear the air. I would have a good bawl and then start again, briefly determined to turn over a new leaf, or at least to curb my tongue in Father's hearing!

Chapter Six

The End of an Era

1938 was to be the last childhood Easter I remember, when my mother hid little birds' nests around the garden for me and Tony to discover, filled with marzipan bird's eggs. I helped her decorate hard-boiled eggs with painted faces for the Easter Day breakfast table, and boiled others in a pan of onion skins, first tying string or narrow ribbon around them which, when it worked, resulted in a white cross on a brown egg after the ribbon was removed. She made sure we had a chocolate egg or two also, but definitely not to be eaten until after breakfast. (Eating before meals was never allowed in case it 'spoiled our appetite' and we couldn't eat our nourishing meal). On Good Friday we always had hot cross buns for breakfast, and Shrove Tuesday was traditionally celebrated with pancakes, whilst a little cross woven from a palm frond was given to each child who attended Sunday School on Palm Sunday. Thus I became vaguely aware of the festivals of the Church.

The 1938 school sports day at St Boniface was not the happy day it should have been. At the age of 9, I was a fast runner for my age, having been well trained by the nursemaid in Mill Hill. On this day I was selected to be the last runner for my House team in the relay race, and my revered House Captain explained my role carefully, then told me to bring the baton straight back to her after the race. All was going very well, with four contestants at a time running a complete lap of the circular track before passing the baton to the next in their line. As last in my line, I had plenty of time to see what I must do, and when my turn came I successfully grabbed the baton and tore off, overtaking the field to the encouraging cheers of the crowd as I came round to the start again. Alas, I had not been forewarned that a finishing line would be raised across the track behind my retreating back, and as I triumphantly completed the circle all I could think of was that I must return the baton to the House Captain... which I proceeded to do, to the yells of "Keep going! Keep GOING!....... DON'T STOP...GO...GO! GO TO THE LINE!!" And groans of "Oh NOOOOOOO!!!" as I became confused and was overtaken by the other runners. I was undoubtedly the unhappiest and least popular child in the world that day and I still prefer not to think about it.

The second thing about that day, however, was that, because I had gained a place in all the events I went in for, (running, egg and spoon, sack race, three-legged, high and long jump and so on) I ended up with six prizes. These were small trophies like charm bracelets, pencil or paint boxes, fancy notepaper and I forget what else. I was very satisfied with myself, and feeling a little mollified after my public humiliation, but my wise mother, not wishing me to be any more unpopular than I probably already was, insisted that I give away all but two of the six to the other place getters, telling me to choose which I wanted to keep. I considered this most unfair, and consequently sulked all the way home, but in retrospect I believe she did the right thing.

Mother & me, 1938

I guess we lived in that lovely new flat for less than eighteen months, because in the autumn of 1938 Mother and I moved into two furnished rooms in a rather dismal boarding house where the landlady did the cooking and Mother and I shared a double bed. Tony had started as a cadet at Dartmouth Naval College some months before. Children accept life as it happens, and this was just another change of base which I don't remember questioning. Why we had to give up the flat, where it was so nice, I have never asked and I expect it had much to do with my mothers ensuing depression.

Mummy, Tony and I were invited to spend that Christmas with our Sunningdale cousins who we had not seen much of until now. My age fell between Pamela and Alison and I got on well with either cousin, whereas Tony was the eldest and the only boy. It was a memorable Christmas, being the last before the war, and though we did not know it then, it was the end of an age that would soon vanish forever.

Christmas Day, then as now, started in the dark early hours, with the children fumbling at the foot of their beds to see if the big socks had been filled, and feeling around to identify the contents. My parents would always fill ours with any really small gifts that had arrived for us, as well as a silver-wrapped tangerine, big red apple, some nuts, raisins and a cracker. Sometimes there would be some plasticine, coloured pencils, toy soldiers or farm animals, or a celluloid fairy doll or small book designed to occupy us until breakfast, but the rustle of paper, patter of feet and crescendo of whispering meant the end of sleep for everyone.

At the Sunningdale house the whole family assembled around the big Christmas tree in the drawing room after breakfast. The tree had been decorated with coloured lights, tinsel and glass baubles on Christmas Eve, with a huge star on the top. The hall and downstairs rooms were garlanded with paper chains and bells, holly over the picture frames and mistletoe (for kissing under) hanging from a central lampshade. The fire had been lit early and all the house lights switched on as daylight struggled to break through the snow-heavy clouds, and we were impatient to get to our presents.

We had all placed our gaily wrapped gifts around the tree the night before and had done our best to identify our own, rattling and smelling them to have a guess at their contents. Now the presents were distributed by Uncle Ronald and unwrapped; books and games, warm slippers, gloves, knitted scarves and bed-socks, tins of toffees and gold-wrapped chocolate money, writing paper compendiums, bath salts, smelly soap and talcum powder, and hankies, socks, ties, scarves and a hand-knitted pullover for Uncle.

It was all a new experience for me and I loved it after the rather dull and drab life that I was used to. Christmas dinner had all the traditional trappings and the sideboard shone with silver serving dishes and their covers. Roast turkey with stuffing, curls of bacon, tiny chipolata sausages and bread sauce flavoured with onion and cloves; crisp roast potatoes, carrots, brussel sprouts and thick delicious gravy. As usual I was first to volunteer for seconds to fill the odd corners as if this was the last meal I'd ever see.

A large Christmas pudding, a sprig of holly on the top and flaming with brandy, was carried to the table and watched delightedly until the fragrant blue flame gave a final flicker. The pudding had small silver charms and thre'penny bits (when they were still made of pure silver) concealed in it at the mixing, which everyone in the house had had a hand in, so each mouthful was chewed over with the greatest care, and portions were anxiously watched and compared for size as they were served. Brandy butter and cream accompanied it, and then crackers were pulled and examined for trophies, paper hats tried on and jokes read out, whilst the table was cleared and replenished with bowls of mixed nuts, preserved ginger, crystallised fruit, almonds and raisins and silver dishes of fondants and peppermint creams.

After dinner we all collapsed in the drawing room to hear the King's speech. Agonisingly slow at times, and with long silences in which all his subjects mentally egged him on to get the next word out and overcome his stammer, nevertheless George VI was well respected, and was to become even more popular when he and his family remained in London throughout the blitz which, at this time, was but a distant and hardly imaginable threat.

To shake down all that food, Uncle piled those still on their feet into the Dodge and took us for a muddy walk, returning as the light waned for tea with Christmas cake. Later turkey and ham sandwiches and mince pies for supper, for tummies that could still find space, and a game of charades completed the day. What a memorable and wonderful Christmas! I have never had another to equal it, nor ever will.

Once back in the lodgings in Lee-on-Solent, with Tony having returned to Dartmouth, the wet and dreary winter kept us mostly housebound. On top of the wardrobe, gathering dust, were yards and yards of paper chains, stuck together with a flour and water paste, which I had painstakingly made before we knew we would be spending Christmas in Sunningdale, and had never hung. There was something indefinably sad about all that unfulfilled expectation and wasted effort, and I added it to an accumulation of sometimes-irrational disappointments that I carried, often associated with my father. He had sent me back twin Chinese dolls and a set of child's clothes from China, carefully and lovingly ordered from a tailor in Shanghai, and with their own exotic Chinese smell, but they were far too small. He was so disappointed when he heard this, and I was sad for him and could never bear to part with them, carrying them around the world until donating them to the Sydney Power House Museum sixty years later.

Another time he had brought me back a beautiful dressing case from the Persian Gulf, fitted with genuine tortoiseshell hairbrush, comb, mirror, clothes brush, manicure tools and various trinket boxes, all displayed on gold satin within the wooden case. The poignancy for me lay in the fact that the hand-mirror arrived broken and instead of it being left, with the prospect of the glass being replaced one day, a decision was made to throw it away before I saw it, leaving a central mirror-shaped void where it should rest. Apparently Father was so disappointed he nearly didn't give it to me at all! The case itself was abandoned at the next move, with the well-used contents gradually disappearing over the next half century.

Many years later, near the end of the war, he had shoes made for me in Colombo, taking endless trouble to provide the shoemaker with the exact pattern of my feet, and again they were un-wearable, being too small for me. These sound such trivial matters now, in our age of plenty, but in those times such generous gifts were intended to convey all the love that his absences deprived me of. My heart still bleeds for my father's feeling of failure and disappointment, which I always sensed was much greater than my own. I didn't need his gifts to prove he loved me, and he didn't need to tell me in words either, (which would have embarrassed both of us considerably) for I never doubted that he was 100% on my side.

My main memory of the damp and cheerless Lee-on-Solent lodgings is the morning ritual of holding our underclothes in front of the gas fire in the bedroom to air. They were considered dry enough to wear when the mirror above the fireplace failed to fog up when the heated garment was placed against it. Though I had my bike, the public library, school and Saturday's 'pictures' to keep me occupied enough, my mother had little to do, with hardly any domestic responsibilities, and became very depressed. A kind friend must have sized up the situation and she shifted us into her home, where Mummy and I shared an attic bedroom.

I was not at all happy with this arrangement, since Mummy took to her bed and I was mostly in the care of the maid, who insisted on bathing me, which embarrassed me profoundly. After all I was now TEN and quite obsessively modest as well! The family consisted of numerous adults, mostly male, and there was no place for me, however kindly their intent. This situation was not going to improve, as far as I could see, until we had our own home again, which I hoped would be soon but I was not prepared to bet on it. I couldn't help thinking, nostalgically, of the family in Sunningdale, where I had had such a happy Christmas, and one day I suggested to Mummy that she ask them if I could go and stay there for a while until she was feeling better.

Although this was a shot in the dark and I presumed I would have to pester for some time to bring it about, to my surprise and delight she agreed. Mummy was apparently worried about me herself, but feared to suggest it and risk upsetting me with another separation... and so it was that my few belongings were packed into a small suitcase and I was dispatched by Green Line coach to Sunningdale, where I was met by Aunty Iny, installed in the guest room and made a great fuss of.

The Little House, Sunningdale, after the war.

Little did I know it then, but it would be two and a half years before I would see my adored mother again, and a new phase of my life was just beginning which would have an immense effect on my whole future.

Chapter Seven

First Family Breakdown

The situation in early 1939, therefore, was that I was living with cousins in Sunningdale, on the Surrey-Berkshire border, my father was still in the Far East in H.M.S.Birmingham, my mother, deeply depressed, being cared for by friends in Lee-on-Solent, and my brother, Tony, a naval cadet at Dartmouth Naval College in Devon.

Not only my little family, but the whole world, it seemed, was in a state of change and uncertainty which even a ten year old could not help but be aware of, yet I was excited at my personal fortune in being transported from a depressing home situation into this prosperous family home full of affectionate relatives. Although I called them Uncle and Aunty, in fact Uncle Ronald was a first cousin of my mother's (their mothers were sisters), Aunty Iny no blood relation at all, and Pamela and Alison were my second cousins.

As the weeks went by, and I was still in residence, I became rather uneasily aware of long night-time phone calls behind closed doors, with occasional covert references and glances between adults which I felt concerned me. One night Uncle came up and sat on my bed and very gently told me that my adored little mother had had a nervous breakdown and was in a hospital on the Isle of Wight, and he and Aunty wanted me to stay with them until she was better and we could have our own home again. Although I had no idea what a 'nervous breakdown' was, nor understood that her condition was a mental one, somehow this was not unexpected news for me, as I had been getting increasingly worried about mother and her failure to have any contact with me or arrange my return to Lee.

At this time my feelings were somewhat mixed; on the one hand I was grieving for her, as I missed her and longed to see her, especially when I was in bed at night; on the other hand I was receiving so much loving attention, and experiencing a lifestyle of security and comfort that I had never known at home, and so could not help hoping the dream would not end with me being packed back onto the Green Line coach to return to life in the dreary boarding house.

My status now changed into being a permanent member of the household instead of a visitor, and I was treated as an adopted daughter. Pam was away at boarding school, but eight-year-old Alison had a governess (appropriately called Miss Lines) who came to the house each day and held court in the nursery. I was now added to her responsibilities, and entered into the schoolroom with gusto. As far as I was concerned I was on permanent holiday, playing at schools, and since I was two years older than the syllabus Miss Lines was following for Alison, I found it child's play, which gave me ample time to cook up mischief.

For some years I had been running wild at home, with the minimum of supervision from my dreamy mother, and my creative energies were now somewhat stifled, especially since I was confined to the house and garden and could not get on my bicycle and take off on my own as I was used to. I discovered that Aunty ran quite a tight ship, and though the large house and extensive grounds were equipped with everything we children needed to play with and enjoy, I still had a lot of adjusting to do in accepting nursery routine and submitting to a set of house rules that were often not spelt out until I broke them.

Being the elder, I was the one who led into mischief, (and quite rightly, the one who got into trouble), and I doubt if Alison caused any waves until I arrived to lead her astray. She tells me now that I was very naughty. A typical thing I did was to hide us in the Wendy house when Miss Lines came, pretending not to hear as she wandered round the garden in the rain calling our names, and wedging the door so that she could not enter. We were eventually winkled out, but no one (apart from us) was very amused. Another time we hid quite effectively under the enormous leaves of a Chinese rhubarb plant while she passed within inches of us, quite unaware.

Alison, myself and Pamela with new school uniforms, 1939

For discipline I was usually referred to Uncle, and I remember two or three occasions when I had pushed the limits too far, and he gave me a serious talking to. This was a most effective measure as I hated to be out of favour with him, but I think he considered me very brazen and hard as nothing, but NOTHING was ever going to make me cry in front of him, and therefore I was prevented from answering for myself lest opening my mouth released the flood. So I remained apparently obstinate and unrepentant, which was in truth far from the case. My refusal to cry in public started with vanity, I think, after I had once looked at myself in the mirror when bawling my head off! The picture I presented was so ugly that I never, ever, wanted anyone to see me crying again. From then on all my crying (and there was quite a lot of it over the years) was done in the bath, or suppressed in bed after dark, with a hankie stuffed in my mouth.

I adored Uncle Ronald, who was a tall fine looking man whose hair had turned grey rather early. He had a very deep voice and a quizzical smile and he really loved his family, me included. I liked the way he always gave Aunty a big, big hug when he came home each evening. He must have been very brave because he had won the Military Cross in the First World War, when he served in Mesopotamia.

Bedtime at 7.p.m. was preceded by an apple, perhaps a little lettuce, and a glass of milk, which for me verged on a starvation diet, having been used to a substantial supper and a much later bedtime, and I never had liked milk. We younger children had our main meal at lunch-time and did not stay up to dinner with the adults until the age of twelve, so only Pam qualified. My metabolism has always required a lot of stoking, apparently more than my cousins, and when I mentioned to Aunty that I was hungry in the night she made haste to give me a drink of Ovaltine before bed and a full canister of biscuits in my room. She forgot to mention how long the biscuits were to last me however, and the next morning, when I had eaten the lot, decided that this was not in my best interest after all. I seem to remember I was given a sandwich for supper after that, and I soon adjusted.

My health was a matter of some concern to Aunty, and she decided that my bilious attacks and skinny physique needed looking into. The family doctor was called to give me the once over, and he pronounced the diagnosis to be Acidosis, and that regular doses of a brown gluey malt substance called Ostomalt should fix me. I was nauseated by the stuff, which I refused to take, and I don't remember any bilious attacks whilst under Aunty's jurisdiction anyhow. That doctor had acidosis on the brain as he trotted out the same diagnosis for Alison, who had quite different symptoms.

Aunty Iny had very definite opinions on matters of health. If she heard a sneeze anywhere in the house, her antennae would swivel and her voice would come over the airwaves, "WHO SNEEZED?" The guilty party would be ordered to meet her at a corner cupboard in the dining room where she kept a bottle of Langdale's Quinine and Cinnamon. This had a very strong and unpleasant taste and was supposed to ward off the incipient cold, but it never seemed to do much for me.

Aunty was also a firm believer in the ministrations of her osteopath, for which she would regularly travel up to Oxford Street, taking one of us with her if there was anything in our demeanour that warranted it. My demeanour meant that I was a sitting target, and Aunty had great faith that not only my acidosis, but also my (still) discharging ear would be healed this way. Her osteopath at this time was Dr Martesus, a Russian emigré, who had us dressed in a loose white gown and exhorted us to relax "like a sack of potatoes" whilst being pulled about and twisted until something cricked, or more accurately, uncricked. I thus became quite familiar with the dreaded Dr Martesus's waiting room and the accompanying butterflies in the stomach. These visits continued into the war years and I remember one very frightening day in 1940 when there was an air raid whilst we were there, and the building shook from bombs dropping quite close before we could get dressed and organised and find a shelter.

Aunty now bent to the challenge of making me over with a will, and I must have presented a considerable one. Every advantage that her own daughters enjoyed was now my lot too, and I felt like Cinderella being turned into a princess as my hair was set and curled, my boring old navy coat replaced with a lovely new sea-green tweed coat and matching pill box hat (more of that hat later) and interesting clothes handed down from Pam.

The one area that Aunty failed in totally was to get me to participate in Miss Stainer's dancing class. There was NO way that I would expose my skinny legs and bunions to that audience of mothers, and anyway I didn't know how to do ballet. So I was allowed to sit with the mothers and watch, secretly rather envious and hating myself, whilst Alison danced with the others in a pink tutu.

It was a different matter when it came to riding school, which I took to like a duck to water, and would happily have lived in the stables forever more. Alison and I were kitted up in jodhpurs and riding boots and hard velvet-covered riding hats, and driven to Mr Morton's stables for our one hour of pure heaven which cost seven and sixpence. I always knew that I would be as stiff as a gingerbread man next day, and very sore, but to compensate there was nothing I had ever done that I remembered enjoying more.

We often sang round the piano, belting out "There'll always be an England", "We're Going to Hang Out the Washing on the Siegfried Line", "Underneath the Spreading Chestnut Tree", and "You Couldn't be Cuter."

One day we drove past a big empty house with a For Sale sign and Aunty told us a strange story. It seems an agent showed a family around which included a small girl who seemed to look on with amazement. When they emerged, the child tugged at her mother and asked why the people were dancing with no feet. She insisted that they were twirling around the big room with no feet, and surely the parents had seen it. The room was the old ballroom, and when, intrigued, they made enquiries, it was discovered that the floor had been raised a few inches in the recent past. There must have been some sort of a time warp that the child had entered into. We craned our necks and shivered with excitement whenever we passed that house, vainly searching the dark windows for hints of something spooky going on. It remained unsold.

During the Easter holidays, the family took off in Uncle's big Dodge to Newcastle-on-Tyne, where elderly relatives lived in a very large house in Jesmond Park West. They had a loyal old housekeeper called Ditchie, who took Alison and me for an outing to the beach at Whitley Bay one cold and blowy day, and reported back to Aunty that I had been very flirtatious with a man on the bus. I was wearing the new sea-green coat and rather dashing matching pill-box hat perched on my recently curled hair. I must admit I did rather fancy myself, but that my customary friendly manner should be misconstrued as flirting quite amazed me, and since I'd no idea what flirting was I imagined it was pretty bad to have caused such a fuss. Aunty nevertheless felt it her duty to warn me sternly about talking to strange men, and the pill-box hat was removed... for ever.

Shortly before this holiday, because Alison was to join Pam at boarding school at the start of the school year in September, Aunty decided that plans must be made for me too. With Father's permission, she applied for entrance for me to the Royal School for Naval and Marine Officer's Daughters, referred to as R.N.S., at St Margarets, Twickenham. This was one of the oldest, and considered one of the foremost, girl's boarding schools in the country, and one that I'd hardly even dared to dream that I might one day attend.

I was summoned for entrance and medical exams and acquitted myself satisfactorily in the former, but was knocked back in the medical because of my chronically discharging ear. Since the last failed mastoid operation this had needed a plug of cotton wool at all times because the purulent discharge would pool and run out of the ear if not absorbed. Obviously something must be done in addition to Dr Martesus' joint cracking, so my indefatigable Aunt started us on a quest to find a doctor who could come up with a cure. The first two had no helpful suggestions except that my tonsils must be removed, but this threw me into so much of a panic that even Aunty bowed before the storm and returned to the search and I have those tonsils still.

I have lost count of the number of consultants who peered down my ear, only to shake their heads and pronounce that nothing could be done, but eventually we were led to a doctor who pronounced confidently that a course of ionisation would provide the cure, and appointments were booked. Ionisation, as I remember it, consisted of numerous sessions of having to hold my head very still over on one side, bad ear upwards, whilst electrodes were attached and a cold zinc solution poured in. The current was switched on and I had to keep very still and count a predetermined number of wicker baskets (signifying seconds and minutes). It was not painful in itself, except that my ear became very sore and tender. The solution ran down inside my ear and actually into my throat (!) and gave me a bad taste in my mouth, and I did not look forward to the session, which were very uncomfortable. Since anything was preferable to another operation, tonsils or whatever, and I desperately longed to be accepted into the Naval School, I cooperated with a good grace.

A good result apparently eventuated as the ear was at last dry, and I was discharged with a stern warning NEVER to allow any water into the ear, or it might start up again.

That summer holidays, as war clouds gathered, we stayed at a hotel in Cornwall and had a wonderful time playing on the beach, getting as brown as berries and revelling in the freedom of sun and sand. Because of the recent ionisation treatment for my ear, I was not allowed to swim with my cousins, so I was provided with a little blow-up raft on which I paddled around the rocks in a sun hat and bathing costume, enjoying myself hugely and getting quite wet without actually immersing. Eventually an unexpectedly big wave caught me by surprise and soaked the side of my face, and the ramifications of that were to follow me for the next ten years, because at the time I reacted guiltily by jamming my sun-hat further down on my brow and saying nothing.

Well, the ear did start discharging again, and nothing was going to make me admit it, so a life of subterfuge commenced in which I would conceal a tiny wad of cotton wool in the ear and drape my hair over to hide it. For five whole years I kept this guilty secret, silently suffering much pain on a few occasions when a bout of earache could not be reported for fear of discovery and certain (I thought) expulsion from school.

Now able to produce the (bogus) certificate of a healthy ear from the specialist, I was accepted at R.N.S. and Aunty set about organising my uniform with her usual energetic enthusiasm. We drove up to London and spent the best part of an amazing day at John Lewis's, working our way steadily through a Clothes List that did not appear to have been updated since the school's inception in 1840. The only items that she allowed me to balk at were 'Camisoles (plain)' and cotton petticoats, as I had never worn either, and they were marked 'optional'. (I breathed a sigh of relief; what are camisoles anyway?)

We had a slight contretemps over the item '3 prs combinations or vests'. Aunty insisted that I must wear wool combinations as the school was right beside the Thames, and I must guard against chills from the fogs and damp night air. I was horrified at the thought and argued firmly in favour of vests, but lost the battle and later endured the mortification of being, apparently, the only girl in the whole school equipped with 'combies'. The end of the story was that as soon as I became independent of Aunty, I cut the bottoms off and converted them into vests, but clothes rationing prevented me from actually replacing them until they were worn out.

A large cabin trunk and a suitcase were purchased in which to pack all the loot, Cash's name tapes later being sewn onto each piece of clothing by Aunty, with slight assistance from me, and I felt like a film star, combinations not withstanding. Finally, before closing the trunk on the last day of the holidays, my aunt took me aside into her bedroom, closed the door conspiratorially and in a very sober tone, told me that I was growing up and my body was changing, and that one day at school I might discover something in my knickers which looked like blood. I was not to worry, because this was NOT blood, but only a way the body had of expelling bad stuff, so it was better got rid of. When this occurred I should go to the matron and say "Jane's come" (or another girl's name if I preferred) and the matron would instantly understand and tell me what to do.

I was not to talk about this to Alison or other people, though Pam had also been told about it when she had first gone to boarding school. Aunty Iny then handed me a narrow pink elastic belt and a paper package, which I was to pack, unopened, into my trunk, saying that the school required every girl to be thus equipped. Extremely mystified, I filed this weird information away in my mind and promptly forgot about it. This was to prove the only attempt at telling me the Facts of Life that I ever formally received, from anyone, and I remained in total ignorance.

At 11 a.m. on 3rd September 1939, a balmy Sunday morning four days after my eleventh birthday, the whole family gathered apprehensively in the drawing room to hear the Prime Minister, Neville Chamberlain, broadcast to the nation that Germany had invaded Poland and so we were now at war. The air raid sirens were given a trial that set my heart thumping anxiously, but otherwise it was rather an anti-climax as nothing seemed to be happening in Sunningdale, no guns, bombs, fighting or soldiers digging trenches, and as the days went by we all settled down again. Sundays were strangely quiet, with church bells silenced as now they were to be rung only to signal an enemy invasion.

This period was later dubbed the 'phony war' and characterised by sandbags appearing all over the place, particularly around French windows and doors, and sticky tape being stuck on the windows in a lattice pattern in case of blast. The adults had to work out how to black out the windows at night with curtains or screens, and cope with food, clothes and petrol rationing coupons. Sudden unexpected shortages turned housekeeping into a nightmare as one could not anticipate which products would suddenly disappear from the grocer's shelves, never to reappear for the next six or seven years. Backyard air raid shelters were dug all over London, with corrugated iron and instructions being supplied by the government, otherwise we were advised to get under a stout table in the safest area of the house during air raids. When bombing did begin, many preferred to sleep in the cupboard under the stairs along with the coal, rather than freeze in wet and cold dugouts down the garden.

Domestic servants were called up into munitions factories or the women's services, and men too old to be conscripted were given hard hats and became Air Raid Wardens and Local Defence Volunteers, which later became the Home Guard, Dad's Army. After the blitz started, Aunty Iny, too, was rostered as a fire-watcher to patrol at night and report incendiary activity, Uncle was in the Home Guard, and the resident cook and housemaid both disappeared into factories.

Perhaps I should digress here to mention that throughout the six years of the war, Britain was completely blacked out. No lights were allowed to be seen from outdoors, not even a tiny chink, so thick black curtains or screens were used and lights kept to a minimum with low watt bulbs. Air Raid Wardens patrolled the streets on foot or on bicycle, knocking on doors if they spotted any chink of light. There were no streetlights, and any vehicles creeping along at night had hoods over the headlights to deflect the beam onto the ground a little way ahead. Trains were blacked out, signs removed from railway stations, and signposts from cross roads, to confuse the enemy in case of parachute invasion! It didn't seem to matter that the general population were the only ones confused. Travelling around on moonless nights was not to be recommended, and long train journeys were not much better in daylight as there was no clue as to where you had stopped. A porter called out the station's name from the platform as the train slowed to a stop, but that gave little warning. Also trains were never on time as they stopped or crawled whenever there was an air raid warning en route.

Two weeks after the declaration of war Aunty drove me to the Royal Naval School at Twickenham with my new suitcase, and had to leave me, in the panelled hall of Gordon House with other tearful black-stockinged little girls separating reluctantly from their mothers. Trying to put on a brave face I was formally admitted and shown where I would sleep and where to unpack my clothes, my trunk having arrived before me. It didn't seem as much fun as the girl's annuals made out and I felt bewildered, lonely and very homesick as I choked my supper down in the noisy dining hall later. Another new girl, Suzette, a year older than me, was in the same dormitory , which helped, and, thank goodness, I was allowed the comfort of my faithful Cubby when I later climbed into my cold bed.

All along Aunty Iny could not have been kinder to me. On the drive there I hardly noticed that she ducked out to a letter box, and the next morning I received a picture postcard from her, with a large, sad panda, and the words "Keep you're pecker up, it'll turn out nice again!" I still have that postcard. She had truly been like a mother to me, and longing to belong to someone, I had even asked if I might call her "Mummy" like my cousins. Aunty had wisely answered that I had my own Mummy and one day we would be together again, so it was better to stay with "Aunty"

Chapter Eight

World War II and RNS

Although there was as yet no discernible enemy activity, many girls had not returned to the school that term because of its position in greater London. The two main buildings housing the school were Gordon House, the original home of Lord Kilmorey, and Kilmorey House, which he built later. These two large stately homes were in adjacent grounds and included an orangery, now the school gymnasium, a chapel, and a domestic science block, which was now closed for the duration of the war. There were extensive playing fields, and shady gardens that included a rare tulip tree. A freestanding cottage in the grounds of Gordon, known as Canada House, had been the Sick Bay but was now closed too.

The mysteries of all that uniform now became unveiled with three changes of dress on an average school day. All this changing of outfits (presumably designed to train us to dress suitably for every occasion) was quite a strain, especially since all school activities were carried out strictly according to three double strikes on a shiny, brass ship's bell, heard all over the building. There was never time to dawdle. When clothes rationing was introduced, we were permitted to drop the serge day dress but nothing else; it was reasoned that we as spent nine months of the year at school we could wear uniform during the holidays if necessary. As I outgrew my initial outfits I ended up wearing castoffs from Tony's Dartmouth uniform. This was irritating as the jacket, substituting for a blazer, had no side pockets, and I had to stitch up the flies on the pyjamas. For about six years practically the only non-uniform clothes I wore (referred to as 'mufti' rather pompously) were handed down from unidentified others, but this didn't worry me at the time as any change of outfit was exciting.

At first I found the daily routine at R.N.S. one long and rather anxious scramble. At bedtime, junior girls went up first and had half an hour before lights out to get to bed, in silence. The duty mistress checked that all was in order, and switched off the light, and we had hardly got to sleep before the bell was sounding for the next wave at eight o'clock. On went the lights again, and the clatter of girls drawing the cubicle curtains, filling their wash basins, brushing their teeth, and then emptying water into slop pails, made it impossible to sleep, even though talking was forbidden. The most senior girls switched on the lights and repeated the whole process an hour later again, removing the blackout screens from the windows after switching off the lights for the last time, so that windows could be opened to the fresh air and starlight.

By this time I was so wide awake that I had to pluck up courage to ask to go to the lavatory, always my Achilles heel, or hang on until the screens were down when I could tiptoe out unnoticed in the dark. I had soon learnt one should not ask to 'be excused,' but to 'go along', and this was taken to strange lengths as the word had become a noun and lavatories themselves were referred to as 'alongs'. Permission had to be obtained from the bedroom captain unless the lights were out and I then had to creep along the darkened gallery at the top of the Grand Stairs, shivering with fear at the black, silent hall below, filled with the resident ghosts and unimaginable horrors ready to creep up and grab me. The W.C's were at the far end of the building, and dimly lit, but when you gotta go, you gotta go, and my fear of wetting the bed triumphed over my dread as I tiptoed nightly along the creaking boards, knowing that I must face the horrors again as I returned.

I was impressed by the teaching staff, who nearly all wore their black academic gowns. Before each lesson, a girl was posted outside the classroom door, and as the staff member approached she flung open the door and yelled "Stand!" which was the signal for much scuffling and banging of desk lids with everyone expected to be standing silently by her desk as the 'staff' entered. It was not done to refer to them as 'teachers' or even 'mistresses'.

Autumn 1939 was crisp and cold, and one consolation was to collect chestnuts from under the trees, and toast them in the flame under the gas radiators, stuck on the point of a pair of compasses. Horse-chestnuts, known as conkers, abounded too, which we hung on string and had fights with, and another favourite game was Dibbs, or knuckle bones, soon replaced in popularity by Jacks. Marbles were traded and swapped, and we played hopscotch and skipped, and competed in making cat's cradles.

One day we were all issued with gas masks, and had a happy hour or so being fitted and getting accustomed to the feel and rubbery smell of them. Each came in a square cardboard box, with a tiny piece of soap and bit of cloth to rub on the talc window to prevent fogging. We all looked like pigs with snouts, and the air snorted past our ears as we exhaled. These became our personal property for the next six years. We enclosed the boxes in waterproof carriers with a strap over our shoulder, and had to take them with us whenever we left the house, and our Identity Card too. I only actually wore mine again once, for peeling onions for pickling one school holidays! When the sirens signalled an air raid we all had to file down to the basement. If it was nighttime and we had been woken up, we sat in rows on the narrow benches, each leaning to the right and resting her head on the hips of her neighbour, like a millipede.

The girls were divided into Houses named after Admirals Drake, Nelson, Rodney, Grenville and Hawke. Grenville and Hawke were housed in Gordon, and I was allotted to Hawke, finding myself the youngest girl in the dormitory (always to be referred to as a bedroom) with about twelve other girls, graduating from Third Form to Upper Sixth. This was all that remained of Hawke House, and before the year ended we were informed that Hawke was too small to be viable and must be disbanded and spread among the other houses.

My new house was to be Rodney, and I was pleased that one of the daygirls in my form, Lizzett, the daughter of the school doctor, also ended up in Rodney. Although the few daygirls missed out on most of the interesting life of the school, which started after lessons ended, and were considered third class citizens as their fathers were probably not naval (yes, we were snobs) yet Lizzett was very popular because of her sunny personality, and we became firm friends for life.

Knowing how I longed to play the piano, Auntie Iny arranged for me to have lessons and I now started with Miss Cotter. She had a piano in her bed-sitting room in Kilmorey, whither her pupils visited her for instruction, and I enjoyed having new pieces and practised diligently. Her bedroom was a high ceilinged, gloomy and cold room on the ground floor, rather dark and probably lacking a power point. Miss Cotter evidently disliked getting out of bed on winter nights to turn off the light, so she had rigged up a Heath-Robinson-like contraption using hooks, cotton reels and string which travelled from over her bed to the light switch by the door which she could then switch off with a good tug from under the blankets. This contraption was a source of furtive wonder to me for weeks... wondering what on earth it was there for, until I managed to get a better look at it and work out its purpose.

Eventually, after an eternity of cold, dark mornings and gloomy afternoons when our games were often replaced by damp walks along the tow-path in long chattering, navy-clad crocodiles, the Christmas holidays arrived and I was fetched back to Sunningdale again. Monopoly had now become the rage, and parties generally were smaller and more subdued, often with progressive games and quizzes. This year's Christmas season was very different to the previous one, with the blackout keeping travelling around to a minimum, shortages of goods beginning to be felt, and the new food and clothing rationing cutting out all extravagance, but thick snow added to the fun and excitement.

I have a photo of the huge snowman we made and dressed up as Hitler, with characteristic black forelock (a sock), a carrot nose, and gloved broom-handle for an arm outstretched in a Heil! But it seemed we had hardly settled back into the luxury of soft, warm beds and home cooking, when we were packing for school again.

Chapter Nine

German Measles and Cornwall 1940

This first winter of the war was a memorably severe one; snow lay on the ground for weeks and the ponds in the parks were frozen solid. Very shortly after our return to R.N.S. all Third Formers were isolated because one of the daygirls had developed German Measles and it was hoped to avoid its spread throughout the school. In hindsight I feel it was a pity it's spread was not actively encouraged, but medical science had not yet recognised the danger of Rubella to pregnant mothers, and girls were shielded from it instead of gaining immunity.

In order to make our isolation complete, a Governess was brought in from outside, who taught us our lessons, read to us, taught us to knit and crotchet, and took us for long walks in the snow in the Old Deer Park across the river. We had a lovely time for a few weeks, and wished it would never end. On the very last day of the quarantine, when we were apparently all going to escape infection, and the school saved, I developed a headache. By the evening I could feel two little peas at the back of my neck, just under my hair, and when I tremblingly removed my combies and examined my chest, there was a pink rash all over it.

Matron Pullen went into crisis mode, bundled all my goggling supporters out of the danger of my presence, whisked me into a small room marked Out of Bounds, brought me my meals and a comic or two from the little shop opposite the school gates and isolated me from the living world. Alone and bored and hardly sick, I was entertained only by the cheerful school doctor, Lizzett's father, who would visit daily and sit on my bed. Fortunately for me the others discovered that there was a secret entrance into my bedroom cupboard leading from the Alongs, and they would creep in guiltily after lights-out, in ones and twos, to sit on my bed whispering and giggling. In a short while most of them came down with Rubella also, and then the whole school, which augured well for the next generation when you come to think of it.

We used to sing a song to the tune of the British Grenadiers:

> *Some talk of Mussolini*
> *In Stalin's name turned blue.*
> *But Stalin is a ninny*
> *And Mussolini too.*
> *But of all the world's great tyrants*
> *There's none you can compare*
> *With bad old Adolf Hitler*
> *And his German Measles scare.*

We greatly enjoyed singing or reciting nonsensical songs and verses. Goodness knows where they would originate.

R.N.S. Gordon House

For the rest of that term the Third Form remained together in one large dormitory in Gordon, instead of returning to our Houses. We were under the supervision of the elderly Junior

House Matron, Mrs Harris. I think she found us quite a handful as we had little respect for her, and got up to all sorts of mischief. One bone of contention concerned the Tick and Cross Book displayed outside the Sick Bay. This was an R.N.S. institution in which every girl had to line up and record a tick or a cross every evening, regarding the current state of her bowels. The fact that no-one ever bothered to put a cross was not lost on Mrs Harris, who was not fooled by a page full of ticks, but took steps to keep it that way by lining us up every Saturday night and popping a sugar-coated Cascara Sagrada into each mouth, swilled down by half a glass of water under her beady eye. At least, that's what she thought.

It was not difficult to hide the tablet under one's tongue, and spit it out later into a spare washstand jug we reserved for this purpose. Unfortunately we were not as clever as we thought, as every week or two we would tip the accumulated contents out of the window onto the gravel driveway below. Imagine our horror one day, to see two of the staff stop in their tracks, bend over the evidence, look up at the windows above, and put two and two together. Mrs Harris went into clucky hen mode, and we were hauled over the coals by the Head Mistress, but this did give us the opportunity to explain that we were not permanently constipated and didn't need tablets that were being forced on us. Mrs Harris was asked to cut out this routine to everyone's relief.

As the year progressed the war really hotted up and things were not going well for the allies. When France fell, Britain was standing alone and June saw the evacuation of the British Expeditionary Force from Dunkirk. An armada of small ships and vessels of every shape and size heroically sailed across the English Channel to Dunkirk, from British ports, to rescue an astounding 300,000 troops off the beaches.

We were very aware that Hitler had conquered Europe and was poised only 20 miles across the channel, so invasion seemed inevitable. The country rallied to Winston Churchill, who had replaced Neville Chamberlain, and we gathered round the wireless to hear the first of his memorable war-time speeches in which he promised "nothing but blood, toil, tears and sweat." Hitler's failure to keep up his impetus must rank as one of the biggest military blunders in history, but for us it seemed nothing short of a miracle as the anxious days passed and the church bells remained silent.

Some weeks before war was declared, Father had been prematurely recalled from the China Station on compassionate grounds because of Mother's illness. As the ship he was returning home in passed HMS.Birmingham, the sailors, of their own accord, lined the rails and gave him, their erstwhile Purser, three cheers. This was practically unheard of and showed how remarkably popular he was with the men.

His captain's report states.... *I have an exceedingly high opinion of him and could not want a better Paymaster Commander. His wide experience and sound judgment are of great value, as is the excellent influence of his strong, straightforward and kindly personality. Unusually well equipped for any service required of him and I assess him as excellent.*

In the summer of 1940 he was appointed Supply Officer to the Royal Naval Air Station, St Merryn, and rented 'Trescore', an old stone house in Porthcothan Bay, between Padstow and Newquay on the north coast of Cornwall. Tony and I joined him there for the long school holidays and Father installed a live-in housekeeper for their duration. A friend from Dartmouth, Jimmy, came to stay and the two boys allowed me to join them in cave exploring and cliff climbing, though I must have been a drag as I could never keep up with them. I vividly remember my terror at being stranded hanging by my finger-tips half way up a cliff, unable to find a toe-hold either up or down, and having to be rescued by their joint efforts.

One day they went off to the beach with fishing gear, failing to return for supper. Father was beginning to get quite angry and after we had waited for about half an hour, and the housekeeper was showing annoyance at the food getting spoilt, he said we would go ahead and eat, and they could do without for failing to turn up at the proper time. Underneath he was getting worried, and this increased when darkness had fallen, with no moon, and there was still no sign of them. There were all sorts of possibilities to account for the boys' disappearance, and after Father had alerted the coastguards and Home Guard, he took a torch and disappeared into the dark, leaving me to get to bed, wakeful and anxious, and with my imagination, as usual, working overtime.

With brother Tony, Trescore 1940

Wandering around the cliffs and beach in the dark was not to be recommended. All the bays on the coast were protected by land mines, with barbed wire and warnings to keep inhabitants out. We "locals" knew a path through the minefield, so continued to get through to the beach safely, but that would not be practicable at night. That the mines were not to be taken lightly was brought home to us when, on two occasions, dogs wandered over the area and ended up as bits of hair, flesh and bone strewn around the neighbourhood. Windows were broken and we all thought we were being invaded! Father must have had an extra worry lest the boys might not have the sense to wait till daylight before attempting to cross.

The adventure ended at dawn, with the boys climbing back up the cliffs safely. They had been stranded on a large rock to which they had jumped across at low tide. Absorbed in fishing on the seaward side, they did not notice the tide rising until waves surged through the passage between the rock and cliff, preventing them from jumping back and climbing the cliff before darkness fell. A long, cold, wet and hungry night was spent on the top of the rock, Tony knowing full well what must be going on back at home and was doubtless awaiting them on their return! Actually I seem to remember that Father considered they had been punished enough... he was too relieved at finding them safe to want to add to it.

My meagre store of information re the Facts of Life received a boost one day later those holidays, when Tony and I called on a friend's wife to deliver some home-grown eggs. I had met her before and was struck by the way she had recently put on weight.

"Gosh, she's got FAT," I remarked to Tony when we were out of earshot.

He gave me a look, "Well, you know why, don't you!"

No, I didn't know why... how could I?

"She's expecting a baby of course."

I thought this through. Although nearly twelve I had never seen a newborn baby, nor had anything to do with babies of any size, and though I knew where they came from in theory, I had never thought that one's presence inside a tummy would actually show.

Chapter Ten

The War Hots Up

The long summer holidays were cut short that year because many girls had no parents at home for them. The blitz had started and as fewer girls were now at the school we were all moved into Kilmorey, dormitories closed, and the beds crammed into the big basement, with hardly room to move between them. Air raids might come day or night, and our sleep was disturbed each night by the big ack-ack guns in the Old Deer Park across the river, protecting the many bridges over the Thames. The nights were now lit up like day by searchlights combing the sky, and every morning we would search the drive and lawns for interesting bits of shrapnel that had rained down during the night's bombardment. This was the time of the Battle of Britain.

It was a very different school we now found ourselves in. Routine was continually disrupted by the sirens when we had to stop anything we were doing and head for the basement. We would sit close to each other on the crowded beds, listening to the roar of heavy planes, and try to judge if they were 'theirs' or our own and if the crunches of bombs were getting closer or going away. Some beds were in the outer rooms of the basement, each with a window below ground level opening into a light well. These windows had internal wooden shutters that were closed at night for blackout and security, and it so happened that the head of my bed was right under such a window.

From Germany, Lord Haw-Haw, the British traitor who broadcast propaganda messages into Britain, was heard to target RNS and a number of staff in the school heard him on the wireless in September 1940.

"Gairmany calling...Gairmany calling! We are sorry to have to bomb the Naval School.... so upsetting for the fathers at sea."

No one took him very seriously.... why would they target a girl's school?

As the school chapel was closed, a small windowless room in the basement was whitewashed and dedicated as a chapel, with just space for a table with a cross, a few rows of chapel chairs and padded kneelers. This was for personal prayer and quiet, being too small for services, which were now held in the main hall, and I loved to go there, finding it a haven of peace and tranquillity. Candles burned continually, giving a comforting light, and I felt a loving Presence, which was almost palpable, as if the air was velvet.

The Head Mistress at this difficult time in the school's history, and for the whole of my own six years at the school, was Miss H.M. Oakley-Hill, always called O.H. One day at the end of September, she called me up to her study, and told me that my father had phoned. He was concerned at the danger the school was in, and wondered how I was handling it and if I would like to join him in Cornwall. Without thinking, I hotly denied any anxiety, and said I preferred to stay, but when I told my friends they looked at me in amazement.

"What! Stay at school when you could get off and have a holiday in Cornwall? You're mad!" I agreed that I had been foolishly hasty, and hot-footed it back to OH to say I had changed my mind.

She looked at me quizzically for a moment, then said, "Very well, Jill. I will inform your father and see what travelling arrangements he wants made for you."

I felt I had gone down in her estimation and slightly guilty, but that decision may have saved my life as within a day or two of my leaving, incendiary bombs hit the school, fires started and then all the windows were smashed by blast, including the one over my now-empty bed. Lizzett, by now a boarder, later told me that in spite of the shutters, glass showered down onto the end of my bed where my head would have been. As a result of this damage all the girls were sent away and Kilmorey was closed on 30th September 1940, a few months after the school had celebrated its centenary, and sadly was never fit to be occupied again. The school had first moved into Kilmorey in 1857, having been established in 1840.

Meanwhile a member of the staff deposited me on a morning train from Waterloo, equipped with suitcase and sandwiches in a brown paper bag, with a ticket to Okehampton in Devon. Father had arranged to meet me there and finish the journey by car, but instead of taking the expected few hours, due to enemy air activity along the route the train crawled and stopped, crawled and stopped all day, with me sitting on my suitcase in the corridor or leaning against the window to stretch my legs. All the compartments were full of troops with their unforgettable odours of stale sweat, cigarettes and boot blacking. They were friendly enough, and watching and listening to their banter helped the time to pass. At least the corridor, though draughty, was less stuffy than the compartments, but my light suitcase developed a concavity from which it never recovered.

It was after dark before the blacked-out train drew in to Okehampton, where my increasingly anxious father had been pacing the gloomy platform for four or more hours, wondering what on earth might have become of me. There was no chance of driving to the north Cornish coast in the blackout, so father managed to get us a shared room in a local hotel and we drove on in the morning.

I remember bowling along in light rain through golden autumn leaves falling gently from an avenue of trees, and father saying that autumn always depressed him, and he thought he would die in the autumn. He had rather a melancholic streak. He eventually did die in Australia on the first day of autumn, thirty-four years later, but it was March, the antipodean autumn, and not September. I have often wondered since if he was aware of the new season on that, his last day.

For the next two months I lived a lonely life in the big grey stone house with Father, the housekeeper having left after the summer holidays. He left for work early each morning after writing out the day's programme for me to follow, and returned after dark each evening. He wisely insured that I passed the days busily, going from one task to another, and taught me how to cook and prepare our uncomplicated meals, and to do the personal hand washing and ironing. I was responsible for sweeping, mopping and dusting the house, using a carpet sweeper on the rugs, making my own bed, and washing up after breakfast. I cleaned out and laid the fire and filled the coal scuttle, and kept the kitchen fuel stove going on the days we needed hot water or were using the oven. Otherwise we cooked on a two-burner paraffin stove.

'Trescore' lay in the valley, down a very steep, rough lane, attached to another house and above an old mill house, now a farm. Drinking water at Trescore was pumped from a well in the scullery with an old-fashioned iron pump. However, the main well was located at the top of our terraced vegetable garden, some way up the steep hill above the house, and we had to spend hours up there pumping water by hand into a tank, from which it was run down by hose into a tank in the attic. It was another of my jobs to keep the attic tank from running dry, and father, too, spent many cold hours pumping in the pitch dark on moonless nights.

Some nights when out pumping we saw tracer bullets out to sea, and knew there was a sea battle going on out there, and one afternoon one of our planes chased a German plane down the valley with machine gun fire, right over our heads. Father and I dived for the house, and heard a racket in the roof as they passed over, which turned out to be a shell ricocheting around the attic.

Another of my tasks was to cycle to the village of St Merryn for the rations, or else walk along the valley to the little Porthcothan Bay shop, that somehow managed to keep open without much to sell. Groceries were never pre-packed, but weighed out for each individual order, the sugar, tea, rice and dried fruit dispensed into stiff blue paper bags; dollops of butter, lard and Stork margarine carefully weighed and patted into shape before being wrapped in greaseproof paper; cheese cut off the big round or slab with a wire, and one's few bacon rashers sliced off the piece with a vicious circular blade turned by hand.

A bottle of Camp Coffee and Chicory substituted for coffee, milk was collected from the farm in a can and we grew our own eggs and vegetables, surplus eggs being preserved in a big ceramic jar of waterglass. Bread, unwrapped and unsliced then, was not actually rationed until after the war, and was made of a mandatory but healthy mixture of white and wholemeal flour. There being a paper shortage and plastic bags not yet invented, we had to provide our own bags or newspaper wrapping, so paper bags were saved and re-used until they disintegrated and one never went shopping without a basket or string bag to carry the food home in. We got used to wasting nothing, and I became an ardent squirrel and recycler.

At the shop I could talk to a friendly soul, otherwise I could go for days without seeing anyone except father. In the summer holidays I had made friends with two boys, who came down to their holiday cottage from London with their mother, but now there were very few residents left, and they kept to themselves, and most of the cottages were boarded up for the duration. I had difficulty walking through the valley because of the cows, who still terrified me, but the alternative route to the bay was to push my bike up our lane to the top of the hill and then descend by road, with the same long climb back, which would take hours longer. I compromised by skirting around the very edge of the field, ready to jump up on the wall when a cow so much as looked at me. In the summer there were sometimes adders to be seen sunning themselves on the warm stones of the stile between fields, which was another cause for anxiety.

Trescore house (centre) and field (with cows!).

Living in the country had many advantages, apart from being out of the blitz, as there were many ways to augment our rations. Father would occasionally shoot rabbits; we kept chickens and a few ducks, all raised from eggs under a broody hen, grew our own vegetables, collected mussels from the rocks and sometimes caught small trout in the stream running along the valley floor. In autumn we picked blackberries in the valley, the fields were a source of mushrooms for the picking, and If we had no greens we would don gloves and pick stinging nettles, which were like a coarse and furry spinach, that Father insisted were good for us. We ate quite well as long as we could give the time to it, which was not always easy for Father, who had a very time-consuming and responsible job without being a hunter-gatherer also.

I loved the chickens, and would spend hours on sunny days just watching them feed, collecting their warm eggs and talking chicken language back. I even got out my paint box and painted their portraits! What I detested was the periodic task of cleaning out their house, with accompanying flea infestation, and the other awful job was plucking the cockerels for a special birthday or Christmas treat. I would hold my breath as I put my hand up inside the carcass to draw out the warm and slimy innards, which I could hardly bear to look at as I sorted out the edible giblets from the intestines.

Father always did the neck wringing after which they were hung up by the feet to drain the blood out of a slit in the throat. He also slit open the rabbits and pulled out their entrails, but it was my unpleasant job to skin them and cut them up for the pot. Sometimes we tried to cure the skins with salt, but they always ended up hard and rather smelly. Father was a great one for offal of all sorts, which one could sometimes obtain off the ration if you were friendly with the butcher, which he made a point of being. He taught me to eat tripe (quite tasty with onions), sweetbreads, ox hearts, brains, pig's trotters, and of course kidneys and liver which were delicacies on any table.

My extended holiday from schoolwork was certainly not leaving me in an educational void, though of a different nature, and I became quite self-reliant and more practical and self-disciplined as a result of my father's training, though increasingly more shy, a characteristic markedly lacking before. Father was a very orderly person, and would write me out a time table each day, itemising the chores he expected me to have done by his return so that I would not be bored and idle. I always had the best of intentions but invariably ran out of time after I had dawdled over the fowls at feeding time, wandered up the valley to the bay, spent too long over a book or cycled into St Merryn for the week's rations, all infinitely preferable ways of passing time than housework.

A great highlight, that bleak winter, came in the form of a cardboard box of little treasures from my mother at Christmas, the first contact she had made with me for two years. She had collected together a number of small craft items she had made in her therapy time, and I was utterly enchanted with them. There was a cross-stitched belt, a needle case, key ring and little woollen dolls, and a number of other small objects, all of which became my best treasures bringing her close to me again. I would lie on my bed and take each one in turn and examine and play with it before replacing it in the box for safe-keeping.

Apart from this I had not been told anything much about her, except that I knew she was now at a hospital in Salisbury. Tony had visited her the year before but I had no communication from her, though I was encouraged sometimes to send her a letter. I really didn't know what to say except a rather stilted run-down on what I had been doing lately. I had learnt it was best to put her out of my mind as I had so little information to work on, and get on with life as best I could in her absence, always trusting that one day she would recover and everything would be just as it used to be. I had absolutely no concept of the suffering that she was herself experiencing during these years of forced separation from her family. Later she was to express very strong resentment at those who had subjected her to it, primarily Father, though I knew that he was totally devoted to her and would have done anything to have prevented the hospitalisation it if had been possible.

Father took his responsibility of sole parent very seriously, and undertook the daunting task of trying to turn this awkward tomboy into a gracious lady. "Poise" was the catchword, and he drilled me in social graces like a debutante being prepared for a royal ball. I clearly remember him coaching me in how to enter a room in a dignified manner, to sit down elegantly, and how to make introductions and look after guests. Whenever he could, over the next few years, he would bring a guest home for afternoon tea, having drilled me carefully in their correct titles and order of seniority. These would usually be visiting senior naval or WRNS officers with time to fill in, and they were always very nice to me, and probably rather intrigued by our ménage.

The old house itself was interesting, being built of local grey stone and roofed with Delabole tiles. Some walls were reputed to be six feet thick, especially in the kitchen where the floor was of huge stone flags, and local folklore had it that there was a secret smuggler's passage running up from the bay, which was about half a mile down the valley. Though the cliffs were riddled with caves and passages, Tony and I never did discover one of any great length, but it gave me a spooky feel when I was in the house alone, and I was still scared in the dark and very uneasy after sunset until I heard Father's car arrive. Next door was another large house, which was later occupied by a mother from London with her two little girls, but this winter it stood locked and empty, with bleak dark windows.

It was at this period that I commenced sleep-walking, and woke up in pitch darkness quite a few times, not knowing where in the house I was. One time I could hear the kitchen alarm clock ticking very close to me... I must be in the kitchen. All the windows were blacked out, so there was not even starlight to show me where the window was. I felt around for something familiar to give me my bearings, but nothing felt like the kitchen at all and somehow I was on foreign ground. Eventually I gave up despairingly and sank to the floor with a sob... I heard a scrabbling noise, and then a torch picked me out, and then Father's voice, " Hello! Whatever's the matter?" I was in his room, not the kitchen at all. He'd taken the alarm clock to bed with him and as usual left the door open for ventilation.

R.N.S., Kilmorey House

Chapter Eleven

Mother Returns, Treyarnon Bay School

At the end of November we were notified that R.N.S was to reopen in temporary quarters, in a stately home belonging to the Schuster family called Verdley Place, near Fernhurst in Sussex. This place had been taken over by the Admiralty for the duration of the war and could just accommodate the small school of about 70 girls that R.N.S. was now reduced to. We reassembled there, looking around for familiar friends and staff, and trying to identify with the school we had known. The owners had been required to move out, leaving beautiful carpets in place and valuable furniture shrouded in dust-sheets and stacked to one side as far as possible. Every room was now brought into use as a bedroom or classroom, and ink was forbidden because of the carpets, so all writing had to be done in pencil (no biros in those days).

The house was deep in the country, and had extensive grounds with a long winding drive hedged with rhododendrons. There were no playing fields so instead of lacrosse and netball we skipped with ropes, ran cross-country races (Hares and Hounds) or went for long country walks in crocodile. The worst feature was the lack of modern plumbing, which provided only a couple of majestic brass and mahogany thrones upstairs, supplemented with Elsans sited wherever a small room or large cupboard permitted, and too few bathrooms. The former lack led to agonised queues of dancing girls in the early mornings, and the second meant one's turn to immerse completely came round too seldom for good hygiene, and we had to rely on the ubiquitous chilly wash basin and slop pails even more. As we did much of the domestic work, such as emptying the slop pails from the bedrooms, an accident that had to happen, did, and a girl tripped at the top of the grand staircase, letting go of her slops that cascaded all the way down to the bottom, while she came tumbling after. [In response to my grand-daughter's horrified question, I hasten to add that 'slops' were just soapy washing and tooth water, and nothing more ominous.]

Three days after we arrived, the dining room doors burst open as we were tucking into our breakfast porridge, and the Headmistress with two senior staff staggered in, their faces streaked, clothes awry and hair unbrushed. We were appalled, and more so when we were told that they had been back to Kilmorey to collect school belongings and had been caught in a very bad air raid that had scored a direct hit on the building. Luckily a warden had earlier persuaded them to go to an air raid shelter nearby, which had saved their lives, but they were unable to salvage anything and had come straight back just as they were. So Lord Haw-Haw had not been joking and it was very sad and sobering news for the school. We wondered if and where the school was going to survive after the war, when this temporary home would have to be returned to its owners.

The next term we knew better what to expect, so came more suitably equipped, at least with gumboots, skipping ropes, pencil sharpeners and large knitting needles for knitting oiled wool into sea-boot stockings and Balaclava helmets for sailors. For ourselves we knitted mittens to try to keep our hands warm. The cold was intense and many of us remember bloodstained exercise books from our bleeding chilblains.

A new English mistress now took me in hand because I was still not pronouncing my R's correctly in spite of Father's remonstrations. I had to roll my tongue on my palate umpteen times a day with "R-round the r-rugged r-rocks the r-ragged r-rascals r-ran", and I suppose it did the trick because I was not teased about mispronunciation from then on.

The next infectious disease to empty the classrooms was mumps. It so happened that I had read somewhere that each mouthful of food should be masticated thirty times in order to be properly digested. Lizzett and I put this into practice one day, and by supper-time I, for one, could hardly open my jaw. So much for that silly theory, I thought. The next day it was no better and I reported for sick parade, feeling rather sheepish. Of course, it was not mastication but mumps, and I joined the small but festive band in the mumps ward, where we all looked like Louis X1Vth but enjoyed ourselves once the worst was over. We formed the Mump Band with combs and lavatory paper, performing a particularly classy calypso among other items, and by the time we were released it was the end of term and start of the long summer holidays.

I returned to Cornwall to find that everything had changed. Father had written that my mother was coming home, and I was very excited to see her again but the meeting was rather an anti-climax as we were now virtual strangers. My well-remembered Mummy of thirty months ago now looked different, dressed differently and of course, was a stranger in our house. As for me, I had grown taller and matured from a rather wild ten-year-old to nearly thirteen, and I was now the capable one on home ground. My mother, on the other hand, had been protected from all responsibility, in an institution, since before the war had changed everything, and was now faced with a situation totally strange to her. Also I was now fiercely independent and didn't take to being mothered. We both had a lot of unexpected readjusting to do.

Tony had just recovered from measles at Dartmouth, whilst I was malingering over mumps, and now he broke out in chicken pox, which had also been rampant there. I caught it too, and had a very bad attack, and Mother had her hands full, nursing us with all the difficulties of living so far from shops and having to produce meals out of rations without prior experience. When the school holidays ended Father decided that I must remain at home to help her, so once again, I was severed from my school and friends, not knowing if I would ever see them again.

The empty house next door was by now occupied with a London doctor's wife and her family of two little girls, an old nanny, and three Scottish terriers. I became very friendly with Anne, the mother, and spent a lot of time over there, even earning pocket money by cleaning her windows and willingly volunteering for odd jobs, rather than doing the same at home where I was actually needed much more. Somehow the grass is always greener on the other side of the fence. I sensed my parents were unhappy, and I used to have long, serious talks to Anne about the family situation, feeling rather disloyal at the same time. It helped me having someone sympathetic to talk to, and Anne, in turn, shared her marital worries with me which made me feel very adult, which I really was not! Wartime must have thrown together many such inappropriate liaisons.

A small school of about twenty children had been established in a private home in the next bay, Treyarnon, to cater for children like myself who found themselves marooned in the area because of the war. I now cycled over there each day, kitted out in oilskins and sou'wester when the winter gales were blowing. It was another pleasant interlude, rather like having a governess, as there were only three of us in my age group.

Treyarnon Bay school, 1941 (me at top left)

Mother was going through a period of ups and downs, mentally. Father had to take her back to the hospital in Salisbury from time to time, where she was given Electro Convulsive Therapy. When he collected her and brought her home the first time, she was very vague and had lost her memory, though it came back eventually. Father was very short with me because I had not managed to get the fire lit and the house warmed and cheerful to greet her, as he'd most carefully instructed. I'd been unsuccessfully trying to get the poor-grade coal to flare for ages and he didn't notice that I was fighting the tears back or give me credit for trying, which I thought he might have done. It showed how worried he was about poor Mummy... we all felt out of our depths with her, and this was particularly testing for father who made it his business to see that everything ran efficiently and happily.

For some weeks after these treatments my mother would sit staring into space, with her eyes unfocussed, and I formed the habit of waving my hand in front of her eyes to capture her attention when I urgently needed an answer to a much-repeated question. I had to shoulder quite a lot of responsibility in keeping her in contact with reality, as well as doing much of the housework and cycling into St Merryn for the rations. I really didn't have a clue as to what was going on in her mind, or what her needs were, and now feel that she must have found me impatient and bossy when she so longed for the warmth and love we had always shared before, and which would have been so therapeutic for her.

A consolation for me was that Father asked the village greengrocer at St Merryn if he would like his horse exercised, since it was no longer being used in the cart, and offered my services. I borrowed a saddle and bridle and set out to catch the horse, which had the run of a very large field. Eventually it allowed me to approach it, aided by carrots, but would not agree to function in any bridle other than the one it was used to, which of course had blinkers! My preliminary attempts to ride in a normal bridle resulted in the horse being startled by every object that moved, and choosing to look anywhere but the direction in which we were meant to be headed, progressing along in a crab-like manner that was not at all reassuring. However, once blinkered again we got on fine, and I spent many happy hours trotting around the (fortunately) empty lanes, fantasising that I was National Velvet, or grooming its shaggy and neglected coat after first getting my own exercise in catching it.

That Christmas, cultural monotony was relieved by the production, in St Merryn village hall, of a Nativity Play involving all the village children, whose numbers had been swelled by evacuees from London, and who, apart from the lucky few at our little school, all went to the Council School. Because their Cockney accents sometimes needed an interpreter for the Cornish audience, it was decided it should be mimed, with a narrator telling the story. I was cast as the Angel Gabriel, and was garbed in voluminous white cheese-cloth, with enormous wings and a large lily, which I had to brandish over Mary. When the make-up was being checked in front of the lights, before the curtain went up, the producer yelled out,

"Gabriel's got too much rouge. Can you wipe it off and make her a bit paler?".... But actually Gabriel just had her usual rosy cheeks and had no make-up on at all so had to be whited-out to make her more ethereal.

And so another year ended, with blackout and rations, fuel shortage and war news tightening their morbid grip on us all, seemingly with no end in sight, though another scene change was looming for our family.

Chapter Twelve

Somerset, RNS Haslemere

Father was next appointed to the Royal Naval Air Station at Yeovilton, Somerset, and he and mother settled into rooms in Higher Farm, West Camel, leaving me to finish the first term of the year at Treyarnon Bay where I now moved in with a friend, Carol, and her nanny. Being relieved of all my domestic responsibilities, I felt as if I could be a child again and it seemed like a holiday for me, and a very happy interlude. When term ended I was really sad at having to leave the little school to join my parents in Somerset, but life on the farm turned out to be great fun, and provided a host of new experiences.

Because all the local able-bodied men were called up for the war, the farmer had to rely on any unskilled labour that presented itself, mainly old men and in my case, young girls. He milked about 30 cows twice a day, and I lost my fear to a certain extent as I came to know them for gentle and patient creatures that tolerated my amateur squeezing and pulling unflinchingly. I was allotted four quiet cows as my own responsibility, whose udders I struggled to empty whilst the farmer did the other twenty six and then stripped mine too, but I gained strength and confidence in time and took my work quite seriously, being rewarded by a daily jug of milk for the house.

I even came to enjoy calling the herd up from their fields and following them down the road to the yard and into the milking shed, and liked to think of a future career as a real Land Girl. There was one fly in the ointment, however, in the form of a very large and untrustworthy bull, of whom I was terrified. In the English tradition he did not run with the herd, but was kept in a field of his own, which had a notice on the gate "Beware of the Bull" for good reason. One day he had been moved to a field next to the farmyard, and being filled with lust at the sight of his harem, he crashed through the gate and tore around the yard bellowing and making mayhem. After a while his nose ring became snagged on a piece of farm equipment and he was brought to a sudden and painful halt.

The cows had been safely tied up in the bails, with the door hastily slammed and reinforced as the bull approached, and I was mercifully still near the house. I rushed upstairs, half expecting the bull to burst in after me and chase me up the stairs, and watched through the window as the farmer and his wife managed to catch onto the nose-ring with a hooked pole, and eventually get him tied up. I decided against a career as a Land Girl after all. Years later I learnt that my father's grandfather, Henry Summers, who lived in Hillesley in Gloucestershire, was killed when the bull he had tended for years knocked him down and knelt on him. Bulls in England always had a reputation for unpredictability and I, for one, was not prepared to test it, keeping as much distance and as many gates as possible between us from then on.

Calves and lambs were being born, and I had my own little curly orphan babies to feed from a ketchup bottle with a rubber teat. The lambs quickly accepted me as mother and had to be forcibly shut out of the house when I went inside. One day I was in the apple orchard when a pregnant ewe started giving birth. This I had to see, but I felt so guilty that I hid in a shed and watched unseen through a crack, feeling like a voyeur.

The farm-house was very old and the plumbing primitive, and we shared it with the farmer and his wife and two year old daughter, Anne. They had two bedrooms and otherwise lived in their large stone-flagged kitchen, which had a curved wooden settle round a huge open fireplace. There was no electricity. We had the rest of the house, comprising of oak panelled sitting and dining rooms with two bedrooms upstairs. We did the cooking on a two-burner paraffin stove, and washed the dishes and clothes in an outhouse, where the farmer's wife made cheese when milk in the churns turned sour (for which it was occasionally given a little surreptitious help). The bathroom was shared, with cans of hot water being carried up from the farmer's kitchen, but the pièce de résistance of that establishment was the three-seater family privy, situated over an open cesspit in the back garden, and able to cater for three members of the family in line at once, the seats mere holes in a scrubbed pine bench graduating from infant to man-size.

The question of school reared its ugly head again and my pleas to return to R.N.S. bore fruit, rejoining it at the third address since I enrolled less than three years before. This was my ninth school change in all, involving seven different schools (one being the governess) and it is a wonder to me that I ever passed any external exams as most private schools followed different curriculums. I was still 13 and although I didn't know it then, this was fortunately my last change.

We were told that Stoatley Hall, Haslemere, in Surrey, where the school was to be re-established, had been a luxury girl's school. Being war-time, with no central heating, we did not consider it at all luxurious, though there was a gracious old house and lovely grounds, a drive lined with huge rhododendrons, and, Oh Boy! an indoor swimming pool. It seemed very isolated being at the summit of an interminably long hill lined with stately homes in generous grounds, with no public transport, and was frequently enveloped in cloud. Somewhere on the other side of the hill were Hindhead and the Devil's Punchbowl, and fairly lonely countryside. I now found myself in Upper Fourth Form, old friendships were quickly re-established and we all made a new start.

The Head Mistress, O.H., still held the reins firmly in velvet gloves, and discipline remained very strong. Probably around fifty, very dignified and reserved, she kept herself rather aloof in her own spacious quarters, not appearing to fraternise much in the staff room. With a very fair complexion and pale blue eyes, she wore her soft white hair drawn back in a bun and always wore an immaculate blouse and skirt, or costume, under her academic gown. Apart from the one occasion after the bombing of Kilmorey, I never, ever, saw her ruffled. O.H. never joined in any fun and just had to appear on the scene for there to be an instant hush and scrambling to feet, Though she never raised her voice her authority was absolute and respect for her unquestioned.

Back at the farm in West Camel for the summer holidays Auntie Tryph paid us a visit and was given my room, so I had to sleep in the dining room on a camp bed. Tony had been sleeping there and complained about mice, and now I found they were only too real, not only running over my bed, which kept me awake and on edge as I slapped at them hysterically in the dark with only a torch or candle to light them up, but they nibbled away the utility labels on the precious food tins in the cupboard, jealously hoarded for emergency use or Christmas. Now we couldn't tell if we were opening baked beans, jam or tinned peaches. What is more, the mice smelt, and we tried eliminating them by trapping and by shutting up the yard cat in the room, but they kept returning, and the cat caused even more trouble than the mice.

Alas, the holidays ended but not before Father had cajoled Tony and me into peeling basketfuls of onions for pickling. After weeping our way through the first pound or two we decided to try using our gas masks, which helped but a little. I never trusted my gas mask again after failing that test, and it was fortunate I didn't need to.

Tony had a very unpleasant experience when he was out hunting rabbits in the fields, which lay between the farm and the naval airfield. Two planes collided just overhead, and the pilot from one, in midshipman's uniform, fell clear and landed near him, being at too low an altitude to open his parachute. Tony was the first to reach him, but he was already beyond help. This was his first experience of death, and he was very shaken. A couple of weeks later, Tony, now 17, was sent to sea as a midshipman in H.M.S.Sussex. I missed his company and we worried about him as we seldom had any idea where he was because of censorship.

A week or two after Tony had left for sea, Father had a dreadful motor-bike accident in which he was thrown over the bonnet of a car that suddenly turned right, without indicating, just as he was passing it. He was thrown across the road, his face and a leg getting deeply lacerated and with severe gravel rash, and his nose fractured and half torn off his face along with his left eye. When Mother and I were taken in to see him in hospital, he looked like a cartoon character, being totally wrapped in bandages except for one eye and a slit over the mouth for tube feeding, and a cage over his legs. We were horrified and could only understand his attempts at communication with great difficulty. A local Naval Hospital had been set up for the duration of the war in a large country house, and the RNVR surgeon, who was a gynaecologist in civilian life, did a great job of rebuilding Father's nose by moulding it over a wax shape. Although he always looked different and rather lost his good looks, the eventual result was passable, but Father was to carry those scars on his face, and patches of discolouration, like bruises, for the rest of his life.

Such was father's courage and dedication to his job, that as soon as he had recovered from the anaesthesia enough to communicate he continued to fulfil his duties from his hospital bed. I will quote his commanding officer's report exactly a year later, still in the same appointment:

"2nd September 1943.

This is to certify that E.N.R.Fletcher has served as Paymaster Commander O.B.E. R.N. in H.M.S. 'Heron' under my command, from the 5th day of June 1942 to the 2nd day of September 1943, during which period he has conducted himself to my entire satisfaction. It is due to his thorough knowledge of his duties, abundant energy and 'drive', with splendid leadership, that has enabled him to organise and maintain his department in an excellent state of efficiency. Keeps himself very fit and devotes his whole energy to his duties. Strongly recommended for promotion and for an award for devotion to duty."

It is signed by the "Captain H.M.S. Heron", though I cannot make out the signature. Father was 46 at this time and was promoted to Captain (S) soon after.

When he had recovered from his injuries, Father managed to rent a small, furnished house on the outskirts of Ilchester, which was a relief for my mother after the primitive conditions on the farm. Farmers were always looking for extra (and unpaid) help with harvesting, and I worked hard the following summer of 1943, building stooks, pitching the sheaves of wheat, oats or barley up onto the wagon, and working as hard as any man. The old men would share their flagon of local cider with me at lunch-time as we sat in the shade eating our bread and cheese and pickled onions, passing it from hand to hand (the cider flagon that is). There was no fuel for tractors, and everything was done with big carthorses. Unfortunately the work proved too heavy for me, and I hurt my back to the point of coming to a complete stop in bed, unable even to turn over, for a week. This was to come against me on and off until 1980 when it was permanently, and miraculously, healed.

Talking of horses, a sight that always excited me when cycling along the quiet country lanes, was of the magnificent Shire stallions, which were individually led around to service the mares of the district. Their preparation was immaculate, having been washed and brushed and polished until their coats shone, their tails and manes plaited with bright coloured ribbons and their harness gleaming and festooned with bells and brasses, showing them off to the full!

It was this summer that I had my first permanent wave, a Wella. My straight locks were moistened with a strong smelling potion, rolled up onto rollers and strung up to a fearsome electrical apparatus, which applied heat, not only to the rolls, but to patches of scalp as well. This had to be endured whilst the attendant tucked in wads of cotton wool as near as possible to where I was gesticulating in agony whilst waiting for the timer to ring. The next week was spent picking scabs out of the hair roots as the burns healed. From then on I had to roll each curl up with my fingers and fasten it with a hairpin before going to sleep... such a chore, but worth it as the result looked shiny and natural and not frizzy, which was then considered the ultimate no-no and give-away! The tomboy was changing into a girl at last.

One balmy night that summer, I stayed up alone after my parents had gone to bed, sitting by the open French windows and listening to a performance of Ibsen's Peer Gynt on the radio. Grieg's atmospheric and eerie music so absorbed me that the long twilight gradually deepened without my noticing, until I was sitting in darkness. Too scared to draw the blackout curtains before switching on the light, I scooted upstairs to the safety of my room, pursued by imaginary trolls. Years later I mentioned this to my husband, who also remembered listening to it at the same time in the spooky summer twilight, many miles away.

Father managed to obtain a discarded white parachute, greatly prized at a time of strict clothes rationing, and Mother and I made it up into petticoats. My grandmother in Canada sent food parcels from time to time, and they sometimes concealed a pair of nylons, unobtainable in England, in a chicken noodle soup packet, to fool the customs. The first time this occurred we were looking forward to the soup, and had the water boiling before realising we were not going to flavour it after all.

Before Christmas each year I would get busy making inexpensive gifts for family and friends. This year I had found sticks of sealing wax in gay colours, and was pleased to have found some that had a wick, so that by lighting it like a candle the little round drops of wax could easily be controlled, and I decorated match-box covers and pencil tips. The next year I made sprays of flowers out of felt, attached to safety pins to make brooches, and I knitted tea cosies. Later I learnt to make knotted string bags, which made very useful gifts and I always enjoyed making things.

Unfortunately, Mother was not well again, and life for us all was a great strain, not knowing what she was going to do as she was rather unpredictable and occasionally became quite aggressive. Once again Father had to have her admitted to a mental hospital, which he hated doing, but there was no medication or treatment that could help her in those days before tranquillisers, and as she had attempted to harm herself in the past, he dared not leave her alone now I was back at boarding school.

On his own again, Father gave up the house and moved into rooms in the historic, oak panelled old Manor Farm where the scientist and philosopher, Roger Bacon, had been born in the year 1214, on the edge of the ancient little town of Ilchester. The farm still belonged in the same family and the following summer I became friendly with the son, Roger, and his mother. Roger was the same age as me and also on holiday from boarding school. They lived in another part of the big old manor and we used to have long and noisy sessions of three-way Racing Demon every night, and laughed ourselves silly, whilst the rather elderly farmer dozed in his chair.

Father now continued my lessons in social etiquette and 'poise' and, after he returned from work on the long summer evenings, I would cycle with him to the local pub. He'd chat with the locals and buy me a small glass of Vermouth, which he called my "giggle mix", before we pedalled back to the farm and cooked our supper. He was very firm in his instructions as to what drinks were suitable for me, and how much, and particularly warned me about the dangers of liqueurs. Opposite the pub was the site of a gibbet where Judge Jeffreys used to hang people during the 'bloody assizes' of the 17th century.

Chapter Thirteen

Confirmation, Doodle Bugs, School Cert

After four years of war, now fifteen and in the Upper Fifth, I was feeling the strain. England was being subjected to V-One's, otherwise known as Doodlebugs or Buzz bombs, and Haslemere appeared to be directly under a route between their launching sites and London. These uncrewed flying bombs were powered by a pulse- jet with a distinctive deep-throated roar but at night I found myself unable to sleep if anything at all flew over, listening lest the motor stop, and diving under the bed if I thought it had, before the crunch. The nasty thing about them was that once the motor cut they crashed, so if you heard them stop you were in the danger zone, and froze until the explosion resolved your fate either way. I was showing symptoms of stress in other ways too. One day, for no discernible reason, I decided to see what would happen if I kept blinking my eyes. What happened was that I couldn't stop, and it went on for months without me regaining control, until I was quite exhausted.

The time was approaching for Confirmation into the Church of England for my group, and our preparation was undertaken by the Reverend Ritchie, Rector of Haslemere parish. He came up to the school weekly in order to teach us the things we should know and he was very much liked by the girls, kindly and accepting and speaking to us in a way we could understand. He was to have a most profound effect on my life, though not in the way one might have expected.

When his classes were nearly finished, and The Day approaching, he asked if any of us would like to confess anything we had on our consciences, so that we could feel we were really ready to make a fresh start before God. Oh Yes! Yes! Yes! I thought. He suggested that we might see him individually if we chose and he welcomed me with a kindly smile when I entered the room and sat down opposite him. Eyes down, I started to tell him about my ear, discharging pus illegally for all these years, and my cover-up and lies and the whole ghastly thing. I knew that this would mean expulsion and shame and create dreadful problems both in school and family circles, but the relief in confessing it and getting it out in the open was so great that it was more than worth it.

I looked up at him when I had finished, waiting for stern words of condemnation, pursed lips, a shake of the head and indrawn breath, but none came. He appeared quite unimpressed with my guilt, but practical and sympathetic about the problem and suggested that now I should speak to O.H. and explain it to her. I begged him to tell her for me, and he said he would do this, and I must not be fearful, he was sure she would be understanding and helpful. And indeed, not really surprisingly in retrospect, she was.

O.H. contacted Father and it was agreed that she would arrange for me to see an ear specialist in London. Accordingly, an appointment was made and one of the staff accompanied me to London on the train. I was seen by a specialist who shook his head over the problem, but set me up with a metal probe on which I had to fix a screw of cotton wool, dip it into methylated spirits and wiggle it through the hole in the back of the ear canal into the bony cavity behind (which had been formed by the mastoid operations). This had to be done two or three times a day initially, and was intended to dry out the cavity and stop the purulent discharge. I was so relieved at that stage that I would have done anything, and I soon got the hang of it. It was not painful in itself, except that the meths stung. The only snag was that it did not stop the discharge, but at least it was now legal! I felt as free as a bird and realised then what a crippling and weighty thing a guilty conscience is, even when it is actually false guilt.

On December 5th, 1943, I was confirmed by the Bishop of Guildford in St Nicholas Church, Haslemere, along with most of the other girls in Upper V. Although it was freezing winter weather, we wore our cream summer tussore dresses (being the nearest thing to white) becoming thoroughly chilled, and had to walk down the steep miles-long hill of Farnham Lane, and back up it again later in the gloaming. Although it was a very special occasion for me, I was unable to retain much spirituality due to coming down with tonsillitis during the night, and spending a very miserable week in sick-bay with a few others. Antibiotics were not yet heard of but sulphonamides were trickling through, and I was given some, which possibly helped, though I felt terrible.

Anne, our Cornish neighbour, sent me a small leatherbound copy of 'The Imitation of Christ' by Thomas a'Kempis, which I would dip into each night before lights-out for years. I must have had quite a serious side to me, and really desired to be a good Christian but although I was very sincere in my approach to religion, it was to be many more years before my relationship with God become a living experience, and that breakthrough was unfortunately still over thirty years away.

Early on 6th June 1944, we became aware that something big was afoot. The sky overhead was filled with formations of wave after wave of four-engined bombers towing huge gliders, sometimes two at a time, all headed eastwards. The gliders were full of soldiers and equipment and we wondered how they were all feeling up there as they faced such uncertainty, first with the landing and then the battles to follow, knowing for sure that many of them would never return.

It was D-Day, the invasion of Normandy by the Allies to liberate Western Europe from the German occupation, and the thunder of heavy engines kept up for hours, followed by hours of a pregnant and anxious lull. The returning planes were less orderly, some limping back with signs of shrapnel damage. Many never made it home. We gathered round the radio that evening to hear the news about the landings and how many aircraft were missing, and all our thoughts were with those men battling just across the English Channel.

Some time before this we had been puzzled to find the top of the hill behind the school strewn with what appeared to be strips of silver paper or fine aluminium foil. We later learnt this was called 'Window' and was to confuse the German radar. Unfortunately a decision had been taken to delay its use in case the enemy learnt of it and used it back!

That summer my class sat for the School Certificate, occasionally having to break off, put down pens and retreat to the basement for the duration of an air raid. This happened to me twice, the second time in the middle of a long and involved arithmetical calculation, which I had to abandon. I doubt if it made much difference, and I did manage a pass in mathematics, though it was the only subject out of seven in which I did not gain a Credit or better.

That summer holidays, when the results came through, Father and I were staying with friends of his in Somerset as he had given up the rooms at Manor Farm. He was pretty well at the end of his tether with worrying about Mother, especially as he knew he was due for an overseas posting again, so we were both most relieved to learn that I had gained Matriculation exemption and university entrance. It was decided that I would return to R.N.S. for another year or two before deciding on a career, to which I had not yet given serious thought. As I left him, Father waited with me on the station platform and brought up the question of my future; it was the first time that subject had been put to me and I was quite unprepared. With my usual impulsiveness, I clutched at straws and said "A missionary doctor... or go on the stage."

I really don't know why I said that, but I was perfectly sincere on both counts, and looking back, perhaps they reflected the different sides of my personality. Father was decidedly taken aback and mumbled something about my needing to get an exhibition (a form of college funding like a scholarship) if

I wanted to do medicine. I knew he would never agree to my going on the stage anyhow, which was just as well really.

The train came in and there we had to leave the matter, and I didn't see him again for nearly three years, though we wrote to each other every week or two. I went into the Lower Sixth intending to work towards an exhibition for medical school, but I became attracted to another career prospect later in the year, about which I felt enthusiastic enough to change direction completely.

Father was now appointed to the staff of the Flag Officer (Air) East Indies, in Colombo, and he asked Miss Oakley-Hill, to stand in loco parentis to me during his absence overseas. Tony was involved in a submarine course in Blyth, followed by a posting as navigator to H.M.S Vanquisher, a destroyer operating from Sheerness, and Mother was now in a very good private mental hospital, the Holloway Sanatorium, at Virginia Water, Surrey. This left me with no home base and I had to organise the school holidays to fit in with any friends or relatives who invited me for a week or two. Fortunately I had two special friends at R.N.S. whose families often made me welcome, Lizzett's in Richmond and Annie Edmond's near Basingstoke, and with my Sunningdale cousins, I never lacked somewhere to go. It wasn't the same as having the security of my own family and home behind me, as well as the inconvenience of permanently living out of suitcases, with unseasonal clothes left in different locations around the country during term time, but I owe a great debt of gratitude to those families who took me in so kindly.

Lizzett and I were taken to the theatre by her father to see John Gielgud in Hamlet. I was totally enthralled with the power of the performance and nothing on stage has so affected me since. I walked around in a daze for the next week, sent a letter to Gielgud asking for a photo, and wrote a long and dreadful poem about the performance, which I've mostly forgotten (I used to write a lot of poetry!).

I had some very happy holidays with Annie's family too. We had much in common as far as family went, as her father and older brother were also naval officers. The big difference lay in our mothers, hers being tall and capable, and mine being small and dreamy and not able to cope with life. The unfortunate but logical result was that one family had their own comfortable and charming home, and the other didn't have a home at all.

By 1945 Germany had discovered that the Doodlebugs were rather inaccurate, and replaced them with the V2. This was a rocket bomb and the first long range ballistic missile; It was 14 metres long, and carried a 1 ton warhead. I found it much less nerve-wracking than the V1, as by the time you were aware of it you were either alive or dead with no agonising wait for the crunch. Again, it inflicted devastating damage on London in particular, and many thousands more civilians and children were killed.

One of the things that transformed the senior years for me was the choir, in which I had the position of leader for my last two years at school. After VE Day (Victory in Europe) in May 1945, the R.N.S. Special Choir was invited to join with the local choral society and orchestra in Haslemere, conducted by Anthony Barnard, in a Victory Concert. This threw me into a state of great excitement, judging from my letters to Father, which he kept and later returned to me, especially since I was chosen to sing a small solo in a setting of Psalm 130. We were later told we sang 'like angels'.

Another compensation of boarding school life lay in the dramatic productions that were a regular feature of the school year, which I loved being involved in. In my final year the School Play was 'The Barrett's of Wimpole Street', and I played the lead part of Elizabeth Barrett Browning, mostly languishing on a chaise longue and fading away with something very like Chronic Fatigue Syndrome. As usual, I entered into the part with such enthusiasm that I practically became E.B-B for the duration, floating around school in a dream and more or less giving up on eating too. Nowadays I might have been suspected of having anorexia nervosa, but at the time no one seemed to notice, and I soon built up to normal again after the final night! The critique in the school magazine, written by the usually very down-to-earth science mistress, put it thus:

".... and in the centre of the room, looking so delicate and fragile, was she who throughout was the centre of the play. Elizabeth maintained through the first two acts, that air of transparency as though, in the words of Bella, she "already saw the angels". Even in the smallest of her movements she gave the impression of a really sick woman, and yet she showed the alertness of mind, and the personality which drew all her family to her room. What a difference in the last two acts, when we saw that side of her which loved life and freedom, and her growing impatience with her father and all that he had stood for, as she became more independent. I do congratulate Jill Fletcher on a really finished performance."

Yes, I can't help feeling that if it had had a longer run it might have finished me off too!

Many years later I came across some newspaper cuttings referring to my Aunt Tryphena performing the same role in The Arts Theatre, London. The Daily Telegraph stated

"...The standard of acting in general was on a high level for amateurs, but what made the production outstanding was the sensitive interpretation of the part of Elizabeth Barrett by Tryphena Fletcher. Her poise and her ability to suggest underlying emotional intensity would have called forth praise on the professional stage."

Another said *".....The Elizabeth of Miss Tryphena Fletcher is a beautiful and memorable study."* And another *"...Miss Tryphena Fletcher, for instance, displayed a wistful beauty, and in the scenes with Browning and with her father, her acting was strikingly good."*

I really loved this side of school life, and gained much satisfaction from another criticism that commended my performance in 'The Romany Road' in which I had played a gypsy girl, wandering around barefoot, with coffee-stained skin, singing mournfully.

".... There were some moments which I enjoyed enormously; far and away the best of it was the effect of Jill Fletcher's characterisation and singing and Pat Bradlaw's dancing, which had both verve and atmosphere. I should like to have seen Pat given more room to dance in, and more time to dance, and I should have liked more of Jill's singing voice, which was the most artistic asset in this production." Boot ended, "And now I think I cannot close this without telling you again how much I appreciated the performances of Jill and Pat. These were excellent. Jill recalled to me all the charm and mystery of gypsy lore, and I easily imagined the 'ting, tong, tang' of the gypsy guitar; and yes, I shall remember Patricia; I shall remember the 'twirl and the swirl of the girl gone chancing, glancing, dancing, backing and advancing, out and in!' Between them they made that meadow a milestone along the Romany Road. Thank you, Rodney House."

Patricia's father happened to be the RNVR gynaecologist who had patched up Father's face after his accident!

With the joy of the war being over, at least in Europe, the exciting choir rehearsals and concert in Haslemere, and the incredible relief of my guilty secret now revealed and forgiven, I ended my six years at R.N.S. on a high note, even sharing the Music Prize, much to my amazement, and being awarded an unsolicited scholarship towards my tertiary education. I had made some close and loyal friends, some of whom still keep in contact over fifty years later, and I have nothing but gratitude for having been so privileged as to attend that school, even at that unsettled time in history. It was probably the making of me.

Earlier in this, my final year, an Occupational Therapist had given a talk at the school which really interested me, and I felt it would be a good career for me and a shorter and easier training than medicine. Lizzett had not yet decided on a career, and liked the idea too, and though neither of us had even heard of it prior to this talk, we went forward for more details and in due course were both accepted to commence training at the London Occupational Therapy Centre and Training School in Hampstead. It was agreed that I would board with Lizzett's family in Richmond from then on, so we left school together, and I was very happy with the arrangement and excited about the future in general.

It might be of interest to note that the following year, 1946, R.N.S. celebrated its first formal Speech Day since 1939 and O.H. gave a résumé of the difficulties of the war years, which had taken us from Twickenham to Fernhurst and finally Haslemere. Her remarks addressed to the girls were typical of the leadership she gave, and as relevant now as then. I quote from the School Magazine:

"I may have appeared to emphasise our academic successes, but I feel very strongly that much more will be demanded of you than intellectual ability. What is wanted in you is grace of heart and mind that can only come by growth of the spirit. Every year makes new demands on the spirits of men and women. You have all to prepare yourselves to meet these demands and your greatest obstacle will always be yourself. The Great Freedoms are claimed as essential to man. I want to put it to you that all these freedoms will be valueless to keep the peace of the world without one more-... freedom from self.

"I think that here the value of boarding school can be seen. It is quite true that home training counts for much, but at home the circle is small, and natural affection comes into play. The child is considered at every turn, and it is affection that prompts any return a child may give. During the war years so much emphasis has been laid on the importance of the child and its needs that, as far as character is concerned, it is almost a case of killing by kindness. At School, a child meets many different characters each with its own circumstances and peculiarities, its wishes and, I hope, ambitions; and life is planned for the good of all alike. Each child must accustom herself to realising the needs and feelings of others, for some of whom she may have no natural affection, to showing forbearance and toleration, to giving as well as receiving, to obeying and to taking responsibility, to fulfilling duties as well as claiming rights; in fact cooperating for the common good. Unless she is willing to do this and make herself a living part of the community, she will gain little.

"... I say to you Seniors, realise, here and now, your seniority. Don't cling to a self-centred and belated childhood. Come out of your shelters,

and be up and doing. Take your full share in your homes. Give to your parents real companionship and understanding of their problems. Don't go on taking all that is done for you for granted. Don't be guests in life, taking all the care and love as if it cost nothing. Give back now something of what you have received at home and at school; the more you will give of yourself, the more you enrich your personality - so prepare to go out into the world, not to please yourselves, but to share in building up a society which can live in harmony and peace."

[In the 1990's The Royal Naval School was combined with a local school, The Grove, to become 'The Royal School' and so no longer retains its exclusive connection with the greatly reduced Royal Navy, though Her Majesty, Queen Elizabeth II remains the Patron.]

Chapter Fourteen

Student Days

I note that my height at this time was 5ft 4 3/4 ins and my weight 7 stone 12 lbs. I was growing up to be very adaptable and managed to fit into any situation that I found myself in so that outwardly I probably appeared self-reliant, confident, helpful and friendly, but inside I frequently felt lonely, isolated and diffident and there was nowhere, other than school, that I felt I really belonged, even though I was made welcome.

Sometimes I wondered 'who am I'? Where did I really belong in the social order? The person I projected was not the real me, but a composite of other people's expectations of me and my own imaginative creation. Who was the real me? I was a chameleon, changing to suit the environment. There was an inner voice I strained to hear, struggling to be understood over the demands of those other voices, but I couldn't grasp it. I felt different from my peers, lacking substance, a nobody, much needing to exert all my energy to make myself into what I appeared to be but probably was not. I was always the visitor, never in my own home. I saw my value, my identity, largely through the eyes and expectations of others, and I must not fail to be liked and to be successful or everything could come crashing down.

Part of the cause may have been that at that time I was unaware of any tangible heritage, no family history, nor foundation that I could stand on. No flesh and blood grandparents with homes that I could relate to, with tastes to accept or reject, stories to tell me, or voices to hark back to, that comforted, instructed and connected me to any roots. We had no established home of our own, however humble, that remained constant and was not just a roof over our heads, to change unexpectedly every year or often less. Although undeniably English, I could identify my family with no particular community or even county. Add a fragile maternal role model, which I daren't accept; too gentle, sensitive, retiring, to handle this world's demands. No consistent presence of even one parent to provide that undergirding of support that I needed. Although I had good parents who I cared about, they couldn't help me in this. The very fact that it was circumstances that brought about this family situation and that no-one could really be blamed, increased the necessity for each of us to pull our weight and not let the others down, always hoping that one day everything was going to come right. After the war is over!

These feelings of isolation were to remain and grow, never verbalised, scarcely rising into consciousness, but deeply rooted and threatening always to destabilise me. I compensated by taking control of my life even more, distrustful of any other's ability to make right decisions for me. Independent, energetic, always willing to jump in and prove myself, apparently the know-all, needing to be noticed, accepting challenges and often having beginner's luck, refusing to give in to the haunting self-doubts which years later I was to recognise as a warfare between my maternal and paternal heredity - the hard working, high achiever and sensitive, dreamy non-coper.

Physically I resembled my mother, though I was taller and less pretty, and it was generally expected, and in some quarters feared, that I resembled her emotionally too, but this I was unable to accept. Quite unconsciously I set out to deny that side of my genetic heritage and prove myself superior. I could cope. I must cope, for all our sakes. This gradually set up a barrier between us in which I became more the mother and she the daughter. There later developed an unspoken family conspiracy that she should be forever protected from any decision-making or responsibility and she came to accept this role quite passively, especially after deafness cut her off even more from normal socialisation.

The war officially ended in August 1945 with VJ Day (Victory in Japan) and much dancing in the streets, and I moved in with Lizzett's family in Richmond, Surrey. They lived in a lovely William and Mary terrace house at 32, The Green. The elderly Dr Matthews, our school doctor of Kilmorey days, appeared to live a quiet and contented life, visiting his patients in the local hospitals or reading in front of the gas fire in his large consulting room, where his old grey dog, Gunner, slept and twitched at his feet. He continued to conduct a small private practice, and we sometimes met his patients in the hall. He still laughed a lot and Lizzett resembled him in many ways. After a bad bout of 'flu, I had a series of unstoppable nosebleeds, and it was so reassuring to have a resident doctor to pack the nose and take charge. Another time I had violent diarrhoea and vomiting all night, and he cured me with a dose of chlorodyne when I was discovered next morning having nearly given up the ghost. My perception of doctors as pain-givers to be avoided like the plague, changed to seeing them as highly desirable to have on tap.

I decided to apply for an audition to the only big London choir that had kept going through the war, the Goldsmith's Choral Union. It had survived by having a number of branches in different London suburbs, all rehearsing the same works under the conductor, Frederick Haggis, on different nights of the week, and coming together once or twice before each concert in the Royal Albert Hall. This saved the suburban choir members from the risks of travelling into central London for weekly practices in the blackout and blitz, and attracted members who would otherwise have been in former major London choirs that had gone into recess. Haggis also formed the Goldsmith's Symphony Orchestra that usually accompanied the choir.

My audition was held in the Royal College of Music, and I was very nervous but sang a solo from Handel's Messiah, and handled some sight-reading well enough to get me accepted.

Rehearsals were held weekly in Westminster Cathedral Hall, after which I would catch a late train back to Richmond, arriving home exhausted and aching for my waiting supper, having had nothing but a sandwich since an early breakfast.

The first work I sang with the Goldsmith's was Bach's B Minor Mass, in the Royal Albert Hall. It was a very cold November night, with buses looming out of silent shrouds of thick fog, including one bringing my mother, allowed out on leave from her Virginia Water sanatorium for the occasion. Her last words to me were "Good luck, Darling. I hope I don't hear you!" Such confidence!

Lizzett and me, 1945

Her allocated seat, with Lizzett, was on the far side of the enormous circular hall, and the fog had penetrated the building sufficiently for us to have trouble picking each other out from the crowd. Nonetheless it was a wonderful experience for me, being carried along in the body of sound, and I can still remember much of that most wonderful of works by heart.

A month later, on Boxing Day, we performed Handel's 'Messiah', which the Goldsmiths did annually, and every month or so there would be a new work performed, always in the Albert Hall. That summer we put on a Handel Festival, performing different works on five nights in a row, and each year we were invited to sing in the Sir Henry Wood Promenade Concerts. My first year, we sang extracts from 'The Mastersingers' by Wagner, conducted by Sir Adrian Boult, and Constant Lambert's 'Rio Grande', conducted by the composer, and in 1947 Beethoven's Ninth (Choral) Symphony. Other works I sang with the Goldsmith's were Haydn's 'Creation', Mendelssohn's 'Elijah', 'Sea Drift' by Delius, 'The Dream of Gerontius' by Elgar, (specially memorable as Kathleen Ferrier sang the part of the angel), 'Hiawatha' by Taylor-Coleridge, 'The Hymn of Jesus' by Holst and others which I have lost track of.

A result of our performance of 'Rio Grande' was that Constant Lambert asked for a small choir to be selected to perform it as part of a programme in the Cambridge Theatre, under his baton, and I was lucky enough to be selected and have another exciting experience I shall never forget.

Since neither of us had a sister, Lizzett and I were now enjoying each other's company to the full, and revelling in freedom from the restrictions of war and boarding school, although rationing and shortages were to continue for many more years. In September 1945 we had started our training at the Occupational Therapy Centre in Hampstead, travelling up daily from Richmond by train. Ours was the first intake after the war, and contained many older students who had been de-mobbed from the services, including, I believe, the first two men to train, one of whom had been a sergeant major. It was quite a shock for them to be thrust among all these giggly girls, but they coped well, and both men were to make their mark on the profession in later years. Lizzett and I enjoyed working together on our projects, sometimes going out to Virginia Water by train to visit my mother. I also had my life in the Goldsmiths, with extra rehearsals and monthly concerts constantly interrupting the flow, and it was a full life without any need for other social outlets.

It was a great time to be in London, returning to life after the war as it was, and I went to as many concerts as I could afford. I went to the B.B.C. concert studio to hear Benjamin Britten and Peter Pears in recitals; to the Albert Hall for Yehudi Menuhin, Myra Hess, Eileen Joyce, Jacqueline du'Pre and a young Ida Handel, with her hankie tucked up her puffed sleeve also Verdi's Aida.

On a lighter note some relatives took me for a lovely night out to see Ivor Novello's 'Perchance to Dream' and I went to 'Oklahoma' and 'Annie Get Your Gun'. From time to time over the years I was taken to the repertory theatre at Windsor with my Sunningdale cousins.

1945 finished on a glamorous note with the excitement of the end of the year Student's dance, my first formal dance. Tony nobly brought a party of Naval friends and Liz and I gathered a few of our friends, and we all turned out in the very best we could manage. My first long dress was of recycled light blue satin, with a soft pale blue net overskirt looped up with an artificial rosebud. Slightly puffed sleeves were also covered in the soft dotted net.

Responsibility for this vision of delight must go to Auntie Iny, who took a slinky blue satin pre-war ball gown with a train, (passed on to me by my Aunt Mabel but which I was unable to squeeze into) to her dressmaker, along with a length of net she 'just happened to have'. Together they concocted something that would fit me, and I really felt very satisfied with my appearance, as it had been a long time since I had dressed up in anything so pretty. I look back on this otherwise happy period with some remorse though, owing to fits of moodiness, which often resulted in me relapsing into total silence for days at a time. These descended on me with no reason; it probably mystified my kind friends, and I've always felt ashamed at my apparently churlish behaviour.

Chapter Fifteen

Training Hospitals

By February 1947 I was considered ready to start the practical side of my training, and was appointed to Bethlem Royal Hospital near Beckenham in Kent, a private mental hospital (originally Bedlam) that had moved from London to be re-established in the country. That was a particularly cold and bleak winter, the coldest since 1893 in fact, with fuel shortages and frequent power failures complicating life in struggling post-war Britain. The temperature plummeted to 16 degrees of frost, and 14-foot snowdrifts were reported in the country.

I was decidedly apprehensive as I alighted from the coach and plodded through thick snow, stopping frequently to rest and change my heavy canvas bag from hand to hand. Arriving at high wrought-iron gates, I rang the bell, and the gatekeeper emerged to unlock a side gate for me, clanged it shut behind me, and pointed the way to the nurse's home. I would be here for three months and had said good-bye to my room in Richmond. I had never even seen an O.T. Department, knew no one and had very little idea what to expect, but was anxious to get on with it nevertheless.

The three months passed quickly, and I enjoyed the challenge on the whole, though facing a few tense moments when left alone in the wards. As in all mental hospitals, the daily supervision and provision of activities for the patients was left to the O.T's, the nurses otherwise being responsible for their personal hygiene, meals, medication and general physical care. A qualified O.T was meant to be on the ward with a student, but the system often broke down when shortage of staff, or sickness, meant staff were spread too thinly, and I occasionally found myself coping on my own and locked in without a key or means of retreat. Those were the days before tranquillisers and other more sophisticated treatments had arrived, and shutting the mentally ill away in the acute phases was often all that could be done to confine the wanderers and ensure their safety.

1947

A few days after I arrived, the regular social dance was held, which the voluntary patients and staff were expected to attend. The idea was to encourage socialisation and normalisation, and I was surprised to find that I could not tell who were members of staff and who weren't, and in fact was quite likely to get it wrong! The psychiatrists in particular seemed far loonier than many of the patients.

My father at last returned from Ceylon and was appointed first to Chatham Naval Barracks in Kent, and then to administer the Naval Hospital at nearby Gillingham, and he rented a furnished house where Mother now joined him. In May I had left Bethlem and gone to my second resident hospital appointment, the Ministry of Pensions Hospital at Stoke Mandeville, Bucks. This was housed in rows of huts to rehabilitate servicemen with war injuries, and Doctor Guttman was pioneering work on spinal injuries. The patients were all ex-servicemen suffering mostly from spinal or head injuries, the former being mostly paraplegics in wheelchairs, but sound of mind, whereas the head injuries as often as not appeared to be normal, but had personality changes, emotional volatility or depression, that made them very difficult for us, young students as we were, to relate to and deal with. This was accentuated by the fact that they were starved of feminine company, and were attracted to the nurses and O.T.s like moths to a candle.

I moved in with my parents shortly before my 19th birthday, in August 1947. Still a student, by this time I was 'working' in the York Clinic, Guys Hospital, leaving home at 7.20 each morning and travelling up to London, getting back home over eleven hours later. After a meal, I would have to settle down to my studies before Wednesday came around again with another gruelling day of lectures and note taking at the O.T.Centre.

York Clinic was a private clinic for voluntary psychiatric patients, and somewhat different to Bethlem as there were no locked wards, and the patients were all presumably quite wealthy. Some of the patients were celebrities; others needing a complete break from war strain and overwork. In those days one referred to mental illness as 'nervous breakdowns', and my experiences with my mother, in different mental hospitals, had prepared me well for the scene in general. In this I had an advantage over my fellow students for whom the conditions they met with, particularly in the large institutions, came as a rude shock. However, the York Clinic provided no such shocks.

The Head O.T. told us about her brother, who was very clever at reading palms and such-like, and could even do it from a handprint without meeting the owner. Predictably, the other students and I decided we just had to know our futures, so we made the hand prints with black ink, and waited for the readings, for which he was kindly not charging us. When they came, we were rather impressed and decided that his discernment was spot on, each reading well fitting the individual named, although he had never met us.

There were quite a few generalities in my own, that I would marry and have a family, travel and so on, but one that stuck in my mind ever after was that I would have a 'more or less serious illness in my early forties, from which I would recover.' The unfortunate effect this had on me was that I thought, "Did my hand really say that I would recover, or was he just saying it so as not to get me worried?" I waited until I was 43 for the matter to be resolved, when I had a radical mastectomy for breast cancer, and yes, I did recover! All the same I can see dangers in this game and would never recommend it.

Shortly after moving in with my parents, Father remarked that a very good friend of his from Colombo days was now the Senior Naval Stores Officer in nearby Chatham Dockyard. One of his four sons was my age, a medical student at the Middlesex Hospital and travelling to London daily on the same train as me. Accordingly we were introduced over the phone, and as my station, Gillingham, was a stop before his I said that I would be in the last 'no-smoking' compartment, that I would be wearing grey rabbit gloves (made from two of Father's recently consumed Chinchilla rabbits) and that I had a squint. The poor boy was stuck with this blind date and with some misgiving kept the unwelcome tryst next day, being very relieved to discover that my squint, at least, had vanished overnight and we found plenty to talk about.

And that is how I met Robin, my future husband, although it was some years before we would have believed anyone who read that into our futures! We were both nineteen and had no intention of 'going steady' with any one in particular. We both had our own interesting lives , which we enjoyed sharing with each other in our twice-daily hour in the train, and we became very good friends, also sharing the crossword puzzles in the Daily Express and Evening News. Later, as my exams approached, he coached me in anatomy and my other medical subjects, to good effect.

After three months at the York Clinic I was sent to the Middlesex Hospital, so now entered Robin's territory. His two older brothers had both qualified there before him, and one, Tony, was now a medical registrar. Dick, the eldest, had specialised in tropical paediatrics, and was presently on leave from the Sudan with his wife Pat. I met them at Chatham one Sunday when Robin had invited me to come to tea and meet his family.

When I arrived in early afternoon, the door was opened by his young stepmother, 'Tim', who showed me into the drawing room and introduced Dick and Pat, then disappeared, saying she would inform Robin. Time went by and there was no sign of him, so, finding me rather shy and heavy going, Dick and Pat passed me a Sunday paper and settled back in their chairs by the fire with their books. Eventually I found the courage to ask where they thought Robin might be.

" He'll be in his room at the top of the stairs, probably building a model aircraft."

I climbed the stairs, knocked and turned the handle and there indeed he was, quite unconcerned that his invited guest had been waiting downstairs for half the afternoon. His room was festooned with small balsa-wood models of aircraft, all made with the greatest accuracy and painted appropriately, and he was engaged in pressing a tiny perspex windscreen out of a home-made mould, tongue slightly protruding through closed lips, utterly oblivious of the time or of any social obligations.

Robin's mother had died when he was six, and in addition to Dick and Pat here on leave, and Tony in London, the household consisted of their father, his second wife, 'Tim', and four year old half-brother, Adrian. I became very fond of Adrian, and often baby-sat over the next few years. He was an engaging little fellow, an only child living in an adult world, and loved books and dinosaurs and having rather serious discussions.

Robin participated fully in the different activities of the Middlesex, from the Christmas Concerts in which he played a variety of comic roles to the Hospital Orchestra in which he played timpani. One day it occurred to him that as I could read music, and as he was also responsible for a variety of percussion instruments, which there was never anyone to play, it might be a good thing to introduce me to them. So I found myself crashing enormous cymbals in The Hall of the Mountain King, and playing the triangle and side drum on occasion. The conductor was a lecturer from the Royal College of Music, Rita Sharpe, and the orchestra was largely, but not solely, Middlesex Hospital personnel, from consultants down.

The first programme being rehearsed when I joined included the Mozart Clarinet Concerto, which captivated me since I had long held an ambition to play the clarinet myself, (an ambition I eventually realised forty years later) and the concert was given in a nearby hall on a Saturday evening. It so happened that Robin was playing rugby against an army team at Aldershot all afternoon. I had asked him what the orchestra wore for concerts, wondering if I should wear my long black Goldsmith's dress (a hand-me-down from Aunt Tryph) but as he said "Nothing special" I turned up in my only decent warm dress. Unfortunately it was red, and so was my face as orchestra members drifted in to set up their stands and tune up, all attired in black dresses or dark suits and black ties.

Our partnership really made its mark that night, as Robin barely made it into the hall before the opening bars, and found his three timpani had been positioned incorrectly. What was worse, he had no opportunity to work out which was where, and the opening number was unfortunately the Overture from Ruslam and Ludmilla by Glinka, which involves frequent loud and prominent bangs on two drums. The difficulty was 'which two?' His first guess was not the right one! Neither was the second, though he crossed his hands over and feigned nonchalance. The conductor's face expressed disbelief turning to horror, but the musicians kept playing with great self-control, taking care not to catch each other's eye.

From my seat next to Robin, right at the back and keeping a low profile, I watched the drama unfold with a desperate desire to giggle. Unfortunately the cymbals are always played standing, and when my time came to play, having silently counted about three hundred and thirty three bars and three beats rest, I could sense surprise in the audience as eyes focused on this upstart in a RED DRESS suddenly rising up and crashing a large pair of cymbals. Later Rita was surprisingly forgiving about our unfortunate performances. There was no other timpanist in the offing, and no other off-sider either, which definitely helped our cause. Apart from our pathetic showing that day it really wasn't a bad orchestra.

Weekends were often spent together and we would cycle miles out into the Kent countryside, explore the dockyard (locked and deserted at weekends) where Robin's family lived in a large terrace house, play tennis or listen to classical records on Robin's 78 rpm gramophone... when he could be levered away from his model aircraft construction that is. On my twentieth birthday he treated me to my first flight in a plane, a joy-flight in a local Proctor, in which he accompanied me in case I should feel nervous.

Although I spent quite a deal of time with Robin, I also had other friends, and one of these was a Naval Lieutenant whom I shall call Tom. He was seven years older than me, and I can no longer remember how we met, except that he was not one of Tony's set. Unfortunately, I gained the impression that he was longing to settle down with a wife and family and decided, I believe, that I was the girl for him. This was a pity as I was not at all ready to abandon all for him, though he was very kind and attentive and I liked him well enough as a friend.

Tom loved music and theatre, and took me to innumerable London concerts and shows, often finishing with an expensive dinner and a night-club. One night in a theatre after a play, I embarrassed both him and myself by losing a high-heeled shoe, which I'd slipped off to give my bunion a break. Since I couldn't leave without it we both ended up grovelling anxiously around on the floor and getting dusty and flustered, which did little to help the sophisticated image that I tried to project when with him. It eventually turned up under the seats two rows ahead, some one presumably having kicked it down the slope.

When I realised how serious Tom was getting, in spite of (what I intended to be) no active encouragement from me, I started refusing two out of three of his invitations, hoping he would get the message that I was not wishing to deepen the relationship. Alas, he never did, quite the reverse. One day he invited me to meet him for dinner in Chatham, knowing that I would be returning from London on my usual train, and, I thought, allowing time for me to walk down from the station to the hotel where he had booked a table.

To my surprise he was not at the hotel to greet me, which was most unusual for Tom, whose manners were impeccable, but he came in a few minutes later looking very dour. When I commented that he was very silent, he asked me why I had walked right past and totally ignored him at the station, where he had gone to meet me with the car. Oh dear! Not expecting him to meet the train I had indeed not seen him, but what was worse, I had walked past him engrossed in conversation (and hand in hand) with another man, who had left me further down the road!

This, of course, was Robin, though we were not yet formally engaged. Tom was very, very hurt, but still failed to get the message that our friendship was only that, and not an exclusive relationship. My attempts to remain friendly but discouraging continued to fail dismally until eventually I wrote him a letter, thanking him for everything, but saying that my heart belonged to another, or words to that effect. He was very cut-up but wrote me back a very nice letter all the same, and I have never heard anything of him since. I have always hoped that he found a wife who appreciated his many excellent qualities and was worthy of him, and who returned that spark that I was unable to.

My final hospital appointment as a student was to St Bartholomew's, Rochester. Here the O.T. in charge was Vera Lynden-Bell and I was given a wonderful practical grounding in orthopaedic rehabilitation. I also appreciated working so close to home and Wednesday was now the only day I needed to travel up to London for lectures. This was my fifth and final three-month practical appointment before a term back at the Centre and then Final exams, after which I looked forward to a real job.

Chapter Sixteen

Ear Surgery and a Real Job

All these years my 'bad' ear had continued to discharge, and the hearing on that side was now slightly affected. After more than fifteen years and many specialists' failures, I presumed I was stuck with it for life, and did the best I could to minimise its effect with little hope of a cure ever being found. However, Robin persuaded me to see C.P.Wilson, a top ear, nose and throat surgeon at the Middlesex, in whom he had the greatest confidence.

C.P.Wilson apparently found my ear quite unique. Every three months I would have to give a fresh batch of medical students the privilege of queuing up to peer into it through their auroscopes. As to actual treatment, that was another matter, and C.P.W. said he needed to think about it carefully, as the dangers outweighed any possible benefit. I really appreciated his reluctance, and was personally not in the least anxious to be a guinea pig on the operating table only to end up with a facial palsy, or worse. On the other hand I soon became heartily sick of having ham-fisted students breathing heavily into my increasingly sore ear, whilst they manipulated a too-large, cold and sharp, metal instrument into a very small entrance, and then round the corner some.

There came the day when I said I had had enough, and if he did not want to touch it, that was all right by me, but if he felt confidant of a reasonable chance of success, then let's get on with it. C.P.Wilson had a very good reputation, and I trusted him, so that when he eventually agreed to operate, albeit without glossing over the possible complications, I felt apprehensive but really quite relieved that a decision had been made. Auntie Iny had exchanged her faith in her Russian émigré osteopath for a Christian priest with a healing ministry, and she now persuaded me to accompany her to visit him. I was not averse to accepting any help from any quarter and knelt down whilst he laid hands on my head and prayed a quiet prayer. Later I was to feel this had been answered, though at the time I soon forgot about it.

I was admitted to Burner's Ward in the Middlesex Hospital, shortly before my 21st birthday, with Robin looking forward to attending the operation as a student spectator. He was hovering around as I was wheeled out of the ward, and wished me luck. Many hours later, as I drunkenly opened my eyes back in the ward, there he was, sitting by my bed looking very concerned. When he judged I was compos mentis enough to hold a conversation he told me that he had unexpectedly found himself quite unable to enter the theatre as it suddenly hit him that it was ME about to be cut into, with an uncertain outcome, and all of a sudden he realised that he cared very much and wanted us to get engaged.

I guess he didn't time it to catch me in a romantic frame of mind, though I was very touched by his new-found sensitivity (which I must admit I had considered somewhat lacking heretofore). I turned down his intended proposal, pointing out that before I got engaged to anyone I would want a proposal of marriage, and I was not quite ready for that. "Let's just carry on as friends the way we are."

I think he should have been relieved, in the cold light of dawn, as he still had another year before qualifying, and no hope of supporting a wife. Meanwhile, according to the post-operative methods of the day, I was kept in bed for a whole three weeks, without being allowed to sit out or put foot to floor, returning to the theatre once for the first change of packing under general anaesthetic. When the day came that I was allowed up, I was amazed to discover that my legs refused to hold me up, and returning to normal strength was obviously going to take some time.

I gratefully accepted an invitation from Carol to convalesce in Cornwall, where I had been so happy as a thirteen year old. There was quite a large family party staying at the house in Treyarnon Bay, including Carol's mother, grandmother and two boy cousins around our age. The weather was fine and warm, my strength soon returned and, joy of joys, the operation seemed to have been successful. Not only did I not have any of the possible complications but also the discharge had cleared up and the area seemed to be healing well. After a blissful fortnight, when Cornwall worked its usual magic, I returned to dowdy Chatham in a dismal mood, which quickly infected Robin too, and we spent innumerable monosyllabic hours on the phone to each other, with nothing to say, but somehow, loathe to break up.

As my depression lifted I felt as if a new life stretched before me now that I felt confidant my ear was at last healed, and by my 21st birthday had recovered my spirits enough to have a night out in London with Robin. We went to the Cambridge Theatre to see Jessie Matthews in "Sauce Tartare" and then on to Maxim's, for dinner and dancing. The evening was interrupted between the venues when I got a painful foreign body in my eye, and we detoured to the Middlesex Casualty Department for Robin to remove it, causing me to finish the evening with one very dilated pupil.

The year before this I had passed my exams and gained the Diploma of Occupational Therapy. I applied for an Assistant's position at St Bartholomew's, Rochester, in what I considered the best run O.T. Department I had encountered, and I was very excited to be accepted. The other qualified Assistant was a friend from student days, Norma Fraser. Both of us were keen and interested in our work and we made a good team, always encouraged and nurtured by Vera Lynden-Bell, who nevertheless controlled the department with a firm hand and watched over us like a rather stern broody hen. We dealt with a varied cross-section of patients, both as Out Patients treated in the O.T. Department, most of whom were orthopaedic or arthritic cases, and in the wards, where we also treated children recovering from what was to be the last serious epidemic of polio before the Salk vaccine.

I particularly remember one little girl, badly paralysed and very weak. Every day we carried her to the bleak, old fashioned bathroom, put her in a deep warm bath, with a sling around the bath which supported her head (modern baths would not have suited) and I played water games with her to encourage movements in her floating limbs. I was thrilled to see small results at first, and very gradually her limbs began to respond and a little strength returned.

Occupational Therapists in those days used crafts as treatment, carefully selected to get the desired range of movement needed to exercise stiff and damaged joints and build up muscle strength. Weaving was used extensively, and a loom could be adapted to be worked using almost any joint in the body. I enjoyed working out 'set ups' for individual patients, and found I had quite a creative talent using a Balkan beam, pulleys and blind cord. It occurred to me one day, when reaching up to pull the plug in the W.C., that a certain patient's stiff elbow would benefit greatly by regular plug pulling. Since I could hardly treat my patient in the lavatory, I set up an arrangement using a beam and cross bar that raised the shed (shuttle opening) of a loom with just that action of the arm, and the patient recovered her elbow movement in double quick time, also producing a colourful scarf which helped take her mind off her (considerable) pains.

Another problem that exercised my ingenuity was how to treat bed patients in the ward who were recovering from hip surgery. Non-weight bearing exercise was ordered in those days, to maintain muscle tone and joint function in the unaffected limbs, mobilise stiff joints, re-establish neuro-muscular coordination and build up strength and morale in general. I invented a strange looking device to which the patient was attached with a variety of cords and pulleys, whilst lying on the bed, and which was basically an upright loom. It worked really well and I named the prototype "Pegasus", as it had two wing-like pieces, and it soon evolved into the Fletcher Orthopaedic Bed Loom. Eventually I improved it to the point of being able to interest remedial-minded O.T.'s around England, and then overseas.

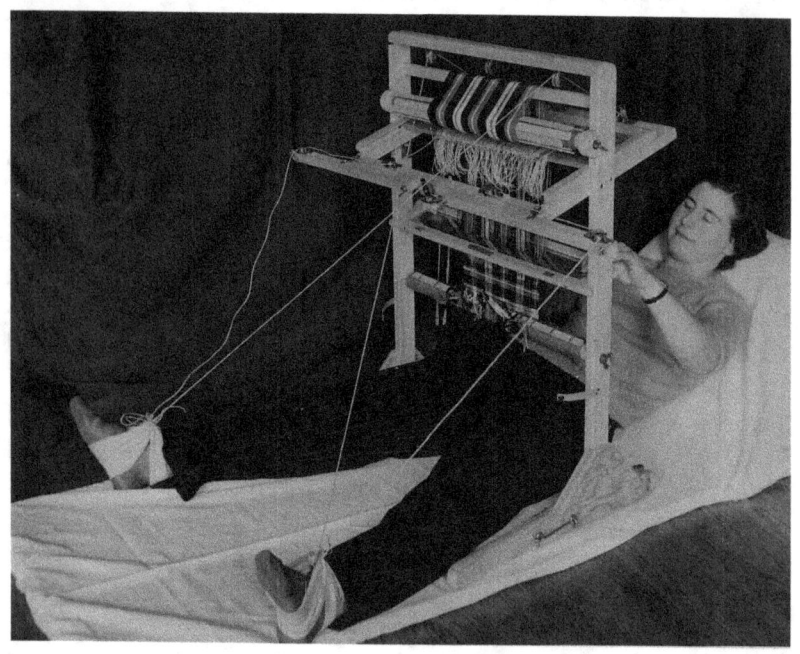

Demonstrating my Fletcher Orthopedic Bed Loom.

In the early days I made the string heddles, did the publicity and marketing and paid a carpenter to build and crate up the looms. After my marriage, when I went to Nigeria, my father, by then retired, did the business side and Mother took over the heddle-making. Some years later I found a professional loom-maker in Kent who was interested in the therapeutic side of weaving, and I handed the whole enterprise over to him. I never bothered with a patent as the small market was soon saturated and I was not in a position to invest any money or time in it. I also couldn't see it as potentially generating much profit and was just pleased to see it being available to any O.T.'s who wanted to use it.

The loom was now improved again and took on the name Fletcher-Wiltshire. There are probably quite a few still existing around the world, though O.T.'s use different methods nowadays, which are certainly far less labour intensive both for themselves and their patients! Orders came from Switzerland, Holland and New Zealand and, some years later, Mr Wiltshire sent me a copy of a small glossy booklet entitled 'Fletcher-Wiltshire Orthopaedic Bed Loom' written by a Swiss O.T. who had used the loom extensively in hospitals in Basel, Davos and Zurich and found it invaluable. Her 'Conclusion' pleased me a lot:

'The Fletcher-Wiltshire Orthopaedic Bed Loom soon became a very important piece of apparatus in my career as an Occupational Therapist. With it I was able, for example, to treat tuberculosis patients in such a well graduated way that would not have been possible with any other loom. It did in fact provide me with the first realistic method of treating these patients remedially. Moreover, I believe that many Swiss patients have this loom to thank for a shorter stay in the sanatorium, for overcoming the pain more rapidly, for better posture, and for more courage to face life. It made my work considerably easier and I hope that it will give my colleagues as good, or even better, service than it has given me."

Patients were retained in hospital for long periods in those days, particularly with tuberculosis, gastric ulcers, fractures and orthopaedic surgery and so on, and another part of an O.T.'s job was to provide them with activities which helped recovery both physically and emotionally, now called diversional therapy. We spent long hours cutting out and preparing slippers, soft toys, macrame, cross-stitch, weaving, leather gloves, raffia work, and anything that could be done in bed, and in sorting out their muddles later. All materials had to be measured and accounted for down to the last thread, and the patient billed and receipted, which of course, added to our working day that just went on until we had finished. The concept of paid 'overtime' had not been discovered, as far as I remember.

V.L-B, as we called our head, had once been a dancing teacher amongst her other considerable accomplishments, and she had the bright idea of producing a Christmas concert, scraping around for a bit of talent among her staff and patients. It was decided that the regular O.T. out-patients would perform the first half, and the O.T. staff of five the second half (this included two others working at nearby All Saints Hospital, Chatham.) Norma and I were keen singers in a small madrigal group that met weekly in an old Thames barge on the Medway, and volunteered to sing together. We were joined by one of the others, and rehearsed a bracket of songs in triple harmony, dressed as gypsies with a gypsy caravan backdrop.

V.L.-B. practised up a tap-dance, I had a Gilbert and Sullivan song, and we had a few more items to kick around, but not enough... UNTIL V.L-B looked ruminatively at Norma (short and plump) and me (taller and thin) and asked us what size shoes we wore. The next day she said mysteriously that she wanted to see us in the gym after we'd finished work, and to our utter horror, she produced two pairs of red tap shoes and put forward the monstrous suggestion that she would teach us a dance for the concert. We reacted with one voice "NO WAY! Anyhow we can't dance!"

Vera Lynden-Bell was nothing if not determined, and eventually persuaded us to give it a try, and to trust her, that if we were not up to scratch, she would not let us make fools of ourselves (and her). So training started, and for weeks, Norma and I tap tapped to 'The Heather on the Hill' from Brigadoon, until we were managing, after a fashion, to keep our faces straight and our feet tapping rather more than less in unison.

Did-er-ley-dum, did-er-ley-dum, did-er-ley-dum-de-dum-de-dum we went, trying to keep in exact time with the record, whilst V.L-B called out instructions and wound up the gramophone.

The next hitch was the question of wardrobe. We were totally unmatched in shape and size, so this was circumnavigated by making Norma a girl Bell-hop, and me a boy. We wore identical blue tops and round bell-boy hats, with Norma in a skirt and me trousers, and the dance was designed around these characters. From the start I insisted that I would not throw my arms around as tap dancers do, and the least moving parts I had to control the better. After a while our coach was forced to agree that I had a point, and kindly added props of large parcels, behind which we could hide at least part of us, and the delivery of which formed the story behind the dance, as it were.

The concert, called 'OT Pot', was performed on consecutive nights, with an audience of hospital staff, patients, friends and families. So successful was it that there was no standing room left on either night, and our tap dance got a huge ovation. Norma and I were gratified at being the source of so much pleasure, but were never quite sure... Oh well, never mind!

One day V.L-B asked us if we would like to accompany her to a London west end musical. Of course we would, though we had not actually heard of it and she refused to say any more than "Wait and see." When the curtain went up we noticed that the actors wore no stage make-up, and it soon became evident that the entertainment was very cheerful and wholesome, and full of edifying messages. In fact, we discovered, it was staged by members of Moral Rearmament, and V.L-B later introduced us to a group which met in Chatham with whom we became very friendly. I was immensely drawn to the philosophy, which is to base your life on the Christian virtues of Absolute Truth, Absolute Honesty, Absolute Purity and Absolute Love.

Some years later I met up with a group of them touring Nigeria, and was always impressed with their simple lifestyle and rather Quaker-like practices of 'quiet times'. Unfortunately my good intentions (to be good) never managed to stick long enough to feel I was worthy enough to be a member, and I drifted out of contact after a while.

Since the two O.T's at All Saints Hospital, Chatham, were also officially Assistants under V.L-B's covering, she considered it only fair to give them experience in the mother department at St Bart's. For this it was necessary to rotate us, and she asked me to exchange places. I had no option but to agree, especially since it was meant as a compliment in that she considered me capable of running the Chatham show by myself, but secretly I was not at all happy at leaving St Bart's, with the good company and its stimulating environment.

Shortly before this, in January 1950, Robin and I had formally announced our engagement to a not-very-surprised world, having decided that we really cared only for each other and could not visualise a future with anyone else. I had been pressing my nose against the window of a second hand jeweller in Chatham High Street for some time, and eventually we went in and asked to see a lovely sapphire and diamond ring, which I had been anxiously watching. It fitted perfectly, but the price was £25 and Robin's entire savings totalled only £12.

I was now earning and saving a bit, so made up the total, and we walked out with it on my finger, ready to face the world together. The next day I wore it to work, and flashed it around under V.L.B's nose, only to be told quite curtly that jewellery was not allowed (as I well knew) and please take it off. I should have known she was not one to compromise. Shortly after this she suggested the transfer, and I could not but wonder if the two events were connected in that she no longer saw me as a career O.T. and weaned me before I wound down, as it were. I could be wrong.

I was sorry, too, to be separated from Norma, who had been such fun to work with. Thanks to her I was able to graduate from the agonising burnt-scalp Wella perms to Toni Home Perms. These used cold chemical solutions and involved a very wet and smelly few hours, but Norma was adept at the rollers, and very generous in her help, and the results were soft and natural. Since Norma had natural curls, I was not called upon to reciprocate (for which I was very thankful). Both she and Lizzett went on to have quite illustrious careers. Norma eventually became the Principal of the Occupational Therapy Training School in Cardiff, and Lizzett later was to have a term as Chairman of the Association of O.T.'s and for twelve years would be the O.T. Officer and Adviser to the Secretary of State at the Department of Health.

The work at All Saints Hospital was not the remedial orthopaedic work I loved, and I spent four days a week there, providing craft work for long-term pulmonary T.B. patients whose beds were mostly on an open balcony. I had to wear a mask at all times, but was handling craft work that they had coughed all over, so there was little I could do to avoid the bacillus. The other day was spent on alternate weeks at a geriatric hospital in Gravesend, where I travelled by a dismal slow train, and a geriatric hostel in Milton, ditto in the opposite direction, which had been an old Dickensian-type workhouse. Both places were unutterably depressing, and I took the smell, a mixture of urine, disinfectant and unwashed craniums, back home with me. It was so hard to think of anything to uncover the skills that I presumed lay dormant in these pathetic old souls, and simple knitting, raffia-work and occasionally crotchet were about all they did.

I was no longer feeling fulfilled and happy in my work, and decided I would apply for a job in a mental hospital to assist in gaining the psychiatric qualification, which would boost my pay packet. A vacancy came up at Napsbury Hospital, a large psychiatric institution outside St Albans, Herts, in beautiful grounds surrounded by a high brick wall. There were 1,000 male and 1,000 female patients and here I joined the fairly large resident O.T. establishment concerned with the female side.

We were housed in single rooms off one of the first floor wards (called galleries), the nurse's home being full of nurses. My room had a small coal fire on which I would warm up milk for Ovaltine at bedtime, having carried the coal up myself, and I enjoyed making it quite cosy. Everywhere I went I had to unlock a door with a big key hanging from my belt, and lock it behind me. Our own corridor was in such close proximity to the female galleries that on nights with a full moon we were often disturbed by screams and strange sounds. There were few available treatments other than Electro-Convulsive Therapy (ECT), which was still in its fairly barbaric days, an operation called pre-frontal leucotomy and Insulin Shock Treatment, when the patients were given high doses of insulin, which sent them into a temporary coma. We had the care of these patients in the afternoon, usually taking a group for a walk around the extensive grounds and stimulating them as much as possible to stop them from lapsing back into a coma, for which we had to carry a large bottle of glucose with us.

For the rest, agitated patients were sedated with unpleasant smelling paraldehyde or locked in 'the pads', a windowless cell with padded walls covered in soft chamois leather, a mattress on the floor, a flat light high in the ceiling and viewing panel in the door. This was only resorted to if they were too violent and aggressive to be controlled but I found it very disturbing. There was really no alternative other than to knock them out with sedatives until they calmed down, or wrap them in a straight jacket.

Apart from the predominantly British doctors, nurses and O.T.'s, Napsbury was staffed by 'D.P's', Displaced Persons who had come across to Britain from eastern Europe as refugees after the war and had no homes or country to return to. Many of them were professional people such as doctors, lawyers or pharmacists, but they now had to work as domestics or porters, before requalifying, and mostly spoke little English. I was taken to visit one young wife, befriended by the head O.T., who lived in a bare single room with her husband, their furniture appearing to be just a mattress on the floor and a gas ring for cooking. She was heavily pregnant. Compared with the horrors they had fled from in war-time Europe, they were not complaining, but we felt terribly sorry for them. She expressed a desire for books, to help pass the time and improve her English. Rather insensitively I lent her 'Gone With the Wind,' which I was raving over and had just finished, only to be berated by the other O.T. later, who pointed out that it had not cheered the girl up at all!

My duties at Napsbury often extended into the evenings and Saturday mornings, when I would take groups for country dancing or exercises to music, but as soon as I had a day off I would take the bus and train up to London to see Robin. My parents by now had moved to Somerset, following father's voluntary retirement for the sake of mother's health, for which he gave up promotion to Rear Admiral (S) and head of his department in the Admiralty. They bought a picturesque old thatched cottage at Knighton, near Stogursey, and set about modernising it, installing a bathroom and eventually electricity.

Robin and I decided we would visit them one Bank Holiday weekend, and hitchhiked by what turned out to be a tortuous route and about ten changes of conveyance, including a pantechnican whose driver alarmed us by taking a high-speed detour across a deserted airfield. We ended up at dusk trotting romantically along a country lane in a pony trap.

Napsbury, 1950.

One Friday, back at Napsbury, a van visited the area with posters urging all those who were blood group 0, Rhesis negative, to donate blood. It had only recently been discovered that severely jaundiced newborns, whose parents had incompatible blood, could be saved by transfusions of 0-ve. blood and I had already given one donation, a month or so earlier, without any ill effects. After work finished I rode my bike to the local hall and gave my pint of blood, staying long enough for a cup of tea and a biscuit before riding back to Napsbury. I was the only O.T. rostered for Saturday morning, and the others had all left for the weekend so there was no-one else at my table in the dining room. I found suddenly that I didn't fancy supper and so turned in very early, feeling sweaty and strange, to toss and turn fitfully.

Around midnight I woke feeling desperately ill. I was craving a drink, yet couldn't summon the strength to get myself over to the wash-stand where the water carafe was. Eventually I rolled out of bed and fainted on the floor, alternately vomiting and fainting in between attempts to clean things up. My ears were ringing and I really thought I might die. I vaguely wondered how long it would take them to miss me and who would tell my parents and whether anyone would know how to contact Robin, but I was really past caring.

I spent the rest of the night like this on the floor, until the sound of a broom sweeping the corridor outside my door alerted me to the presence of the 'trusty' patient who swept each morning and would not return until Monday. I crawled to the door and gave her a terrible fright as I emerged at knee height and in a ghostly voice begged her to go and tell someone that I was ill and needed help. Her broom and her jaw dropped simultaneously, and she backed away before disappearing at the double, to return shortly behind a nurse who got me back to bed and summoned a doctor. I was told to stay in bed for a day or two and given a bottle of iron tablets. The nurse brought me a cup of tea and some toast and flickering life gradually returned. Apparently I had given the blood too close on the heels of the last donation, and had acute anaemia.

Robin had often talked about his granny, widow of a regular army R.A.S.C major, who had moved in and kept house for the family after the death from breast cancer of her daughter (his mother) when Robin was six. She lived at Castle Gresley, near Burton-on-Trent. Robin was particularly fond of her and wanted us to meet, so we travelled up that Easter on the train, for the long weekend. I remember the comfort of sinking into the feather bed, which rose up around me like a nest, and her house was rather like a time capsule of the previous century, which continued to slip back as the rest of the world progressed. Water was still heated in a copper and carried up to the draughty bathroom in a can, and much cooking was still done over the open grate in the kitchen, but Granny Hebb was warm and welcoming, and we took to each other straight away. We both loved Robin, so how could we not?

Unfortunately I had developed a bad cold and cough, which took ages to shake off, and an Xray showed a shadow, diagnosed "Atypical pneumonia or Primary T.B." The cough seemed to clear up eventually, and the Xray was not repeated. Shortly before this, soon after I'd started at Napsbury, all medical and nursing staff and O.T.'s had been given Mantoux tests to see if we had acquired a resistance to T.B. (as most people in England had in those days). Those who tested negative, as I did, were given a new vaccine, B.C.G. which was being trialled on hospital staff only. Because of this no one seemed to worry that my Xray might need following up later, as it was presumed I must now be safely immune to T.B.

In August, I was standing in a crowded bus when I felt something trickling down my shin and into my shoe. I was unable to check on it until I arrived back in my room, and found a huge bleb, like a blister, full of clear serous fluid was leaking down continuously from the front of my shin. Very curious. This was repeated on other occasions, and I formed the habit of carrying a large hankie to wrap round when I became aware of another bleb leaking. Over the next few months blebs and abscesses kept forming, mostly over small long-bones such as the back of my little finger, back of hand and finally in my 'bad' ear, which had been giving no trouble at all since the last operation. Twice I ended up admitted to the Middlesex, as an abscess needed opening and I was running temperatures and obviously not at all well.

Just before all this I had sat for my psychiatric qualification, very much helped in studies by being allowed to attend lectures with the resident M.O's who were also working for psychiatric qualifications, and when my results came through I found I had gained a distinction in Psychiatry. Unfortunately by November I was really quite ill, and was again admitted to the Middlesex for investigations to try to get to the bottom of my weight loss, pallor, abscesses and 'pyrexia of unknown origin'. Previously the diagnosis of T.B. would have been considered, especially in the light of the earlier lung X-ray, but faith in the new B.C.G. apparently ruled this out, and I was left wondering if in fact I was vaccinated just in the nick of time to have stimulated my immune system sufficiently to cope with the invasion. It was some years before such cases were documented.

All my systems were now subjected to investigation (except lungs, as mentioned) and I had various surgeons and physicians scratching their heads over me. With my head still full of psychiatry, I came to the conclusion that I must be neurotic, since my symptoms didn't fit any expected pattern, and probably they all thought so too, though none was so unkind as to voice it in my hearing. Every attempt I made to return to work and live normally resulted in my temperature going up again, my pulse racing, and back into hospital again I would have to go.

Meantime Robin had been awaiting the results of his finals, and came bursting in to the ward to tell me that he had qualified, and with honours. He deserved a good holiday, and took off to Italy with three friends, to celebrate the end of their long haul. We had decided that he had better complete his first appointment of six months as House Surgeon before we got married, because a resident in those days could find himself on call virtually 24 hours a day. Then he would apply for a non-resident position for his second House job. This later worked out well as he was offered a job in the neuro-surgery dept. at the Middlesex first, and then, after our honeymoon, went to St Mary's, Portsmouth as House Physician.

Chapter Seventeen

Marriage 1951

It seemed unlikely that I would be able to hold down a job until I had recovered from whatever it was that was dragging me down, so I officially resigned from Napsbury and took the train down to Somerset to convalesce with my parents. A quiet life and plenty of rest eventually restored me somewhat, though my problem never was diagnosed to anyone's satisfaction. When an urgent phone call came to me late in February, begging me to return to London and work for three months as locum at the Royal Northern Hospital, where they were desperate for an O.T. in Charge, I felt I really should get cracking again, and accepted the challenge on the spot on the end of a long distance phone line, rather to the consternation of my parents.

Back in London, I found lodgings in an attic room in Eaton Terrace. The position suited me well, but I was again beset with coughing all night, and found that travelling by tube and bus to the hospital in Holloway Road, leaving the house in darkness and returning in darkness, often wet and cold, left me little spare time and little energy, though I did some more sewing for my trousseau.

The job at the Royal Northern was very challenging, and my ingenuity was stretched to the full. I endeavoured to ooze confidence, but I never knew what contraption the orthopaedic surgeon was going to ask for next. Evidently he expected me to have all the answers like my very experienced predecessor, so I made sure to appear as if I did, and worked it out later! Luckily the training made us quite versatile, and much of my work as an O.T. has necessitated putting on a bland face whilst underneath my mind is racing like a duck paddling against the current.

Now I was back in London I was able to plan our wedding and look around for bargains in blankets, bed linen and household necessities. Most goods were still in short supply, with little choice of design. Rationing of clothes and food still made shopping difficult and articles carried the Utility label to show they conformed to set economical standards. I was delighted when Auntie Iny invited me to be married from their house in Sunningdale. None of our friends lived in Somerset, and Sunningdale was easily reached by train from Waterloo, so this would be much more convenient for all. She was a great help with planning the reception and I combed the big stores for a wedding dress and going away clothes, finding just what I wanted off the rack, white chiffon, long-sleeved and full skirted. I spent hours deep-hemming by hand all around a long piece of tulle for my veil, which was later worn by Tony's bride, Jean, and it ended up as a mosquito net for my tropical babies.

As expected, Robin's job scarcely allowed him time to sleep, and I would try to see him at week-ends by sitting in his room at the Middlesex with a book or knitting, hoping he would be able to get a little time off. I would wash his socks and spread them to dry on the radiator, mend his frayed clothes, and if it was getting late, leave a note and catch the bus back to my digs.

My parents travelled up from Somerset for the wedding in Sunningdale Parish Church on 2nd June 1951, and my father gave me away. Tony, who looked particularly handsome, escorted Mother, looking her sweetest in a smoky pink dress. We were married at 2 p.m. by the Middlesex Hospital chaplain, assisted by the Rector of Sunningdale, and the church organist and a choir of gowned choirboys provided the music.

Reginald "Jelly"   "Tim"   Best man Martin Sawday Robin(groom) Jill(bride)   Tony Fletcher   Captain Lyn Fletcher   Joan & Tony Jelliffe
(Robin's father) (Robin's stepmother)   Bride's brother   (Bride's father)   (Robin's brother & sister-in-law)
    Front row :- Grannie Hebb(Robin's grandmother) ....Kathleen Fletcher (Bride's mother) .... Adrian(Robin's brother)

2nd June 1951, Sunningdale, Berks, England.

I had arranged for the organist to play the Prize Song from Wagner's "The Mastersingers" whilst Robin was waiting for me in the church, because it was favourite of ours, and we returned down the aisle to Mendelssohn's Wedding March. I carried a huge bouquet of white carnations and lilies of the valley, which spread their perfume over all, and we emerged from the church to the recorded bells of St Margaret's, Westminster, pealing joyfully from the belfry.

Our 50 guests gathered at The Little House afterwards. It was such a beautiful early summer day that the reception was moved outside and tables and chairs were set up under trees in the garden where the guests could wander around and chat. Light refreshments, champagne and wedding cake (for which we had had to supply the ingredients out of family rations) were served, the toast to the bride was kindly spoken by Lizzett's father, the doctor, speeches were informal and kept to a minimum, the sun shone from a clear blue sky and Auntie Iny had filled the house with flowers. All our closest family members and friends were there, except for Dick and Pat, now in Nigeria, and Robin and I later reckoned it was undoubtedly the nicest, most natural and unstuffy wedding we had ever been to.

A few hours later our plane touched down in Paris, and we checked in at Le Grand Hotel du Globe, Rue Croix des Petits Champs, which was the start of a magical four days in which everything, from the weather down, seemed to favour us. We walked and climbed and explored and photographed, sat outside in boulevard cafes, and took a yard of bread and a bottle of wine on the train for a picnic at Versailles. I ate grilled rump steak for the first time in my life, and meringue glacé, and experienced the intricacies of French hotel plumbing.

Never having seen a bidet, I was uncertain how to use it; was it for the feet... but the occupant of the next room evidently had no such problem, the water glugging and bubbling up and down our shared waste pipe on and off all night.

We asked the concierge if we could use the bath, and where was it? She consulted a book and made us an appointment for the next morning when a maid with clean towels knocked on our door and escorted us down the corridor. The large bathroom had innumerable doors opening into it, I presumed with innumerable guests waking behind them, just about to enter, but I was too shy to rattle the knobs and test if they were locked. The deep and antique iron bath, parked in the middle of the room, had taps and plug-hole situated in the centre, instead of at one end, and we were now handed over to a uniformed male, who started to run the water for us.

At this stage Robin decided this was all too public for him, and took off to the safety of the salle de chambre with its wash basin and bidet, leaving me shivering in the care of Monsieur

Paris, June 1951

du Bain, and wondering if my very English modesty was about to be seriously affronted. After filling the bath to his satisfaction, Monsieur left the room, but left no key in the lock, so I performed my ablutions as fast as possible, handicapped as I was by trying to keep my private parts covered at all times by my flannel, not knowing from which side a door might be flung open and I would be exposed. For the rest of our stay we resorted to R.N.S. type 'strip washing' and the bidet, which was much easier on the nerves and required less organisation.

After a wonderful time in Paris we took the night train to Austria, alighting at Landeck and arriving at the Gasthof Patznaunerhof in Galtür after a hair-raising mini-bus trip high up into the Silvretta Range of mountains. This being a small ski resort there were only two accommodation houses open in the summer, and we virtually had the place to ourselves, meeting no-one who spoke English. The locals wore lederhosen and the cows had bells round their necks, and we were enchanted, going for wonderful walks beside clear mountain streams, often above the snow line. I was surprised at getting dreadfully sunburnt so that I couldn't bear even the feather-filled duvet on me (which was unfortunate on our honeymoon), but all in all we had the best holiday ever.

The Gasthof cost very little for the two of us, including three excellent meals, but we fell into a trap with our insistence on a daily bath, as this cost us an extra schilling a day and entailed being late for breakfast as we had to wait for the fire to be lit under the chip heater in the communal bathroom. We considered it a necessary luxury, and had a great system going whereby I bathed, Robin bathed, Robin shaved in it, I washed the smalls, then the socks, and then we let the water out. I objected to washing the smalls in water that had whiskers and shaving cream scumming on the surface, but Robin refused to rinse his face with water that the socks and smalls had polluted, so he won, after which we hurried down to hot chocolate and caraway and other assorted breads with apricot jam, and planned the day's hike with a packed lunch. Our last day was spent exploring Innsbruck before returning to Paris.

We both agreed that it had been a wonderful honeymoon, everything had gone well, even to the weather which held up until the last two days spent back in Paris, but after three weeks we were back in dowdy, rain-soaked, post-war England, still rationed six years after the war's end, and a BIG anti-climax. Robin went straight to St. Mary's Hospital, Portsmouth, as a resident House Physician, and I was left waiting for news at his parent's place in Raynes Park, missing him dreadfully, with no role and little to occupy me.

It was not long before Robin found a flat in Southsea, at 54, Heyshott Road. This was the next street to where his grandparents had lived, where he and his brothers and cousins had spent many childhood summer holidays. I joined him then and we established our first home together where he was able to sleep two weeks out of three at home, which was so much better than his previous job. I set about looking for temporary work, totally without success as all the O.T. positions were filled. We knew that we would be moving on again after six months anyhow, but badly needed to supplement Robin's very meagre salary.

I decided to make good use of my shiny new hand-powered Singer sewing machine, bought with wedding present money, and answered an advertisement which promised big money for stitching together triangles of leather into a round-based knitting bag. It looked well within my capabilities and I parted with the money for a sack of leather off-cuts, templates and instructions, with high hopes. I was told that my first efforts were to be sent in as samples for them to assess, before I would actually be paid. When they judged that my work was up to standard I would be paid so much per bag and I could then produce and send in as many as I wanted.

There ensued weeks of slavish labour and blistered thumbs while I cut out fiddly little triangles from the templates, stitched them into strips, stitched the strips together, stitched the round base on, added two covered rope handles and proudly posted off the results for judging... and they were always below the standard required. Robin helped with the cutting-out when he was at home, and our joint efforts produced a formidable line-up of two-tone blue bags, but nary a one perfect enough to pass the test. I stopped sending them off after many rejections and eventually gave them all away as Christmas presents to bemused friends and relations (who are probably still wondering what they are supposed to do with them) and ditched the rest of the sack of scraps into the dustbin. So much for the Gina Knitting Bags scam!

Our flat was actually the upstairs in one of a long row of terrace houses opening almost straight onto the pavement. Downstairs lived the kindly landlady, a Salvation Army widow with appalling varicose veins and a fascinating black straw uniform bonnet that had a hole for her bun at the back. She shared the bathroom, which was in our territory, and we had a tiny kitchen, a bedroom and sitting room. The bath water was heated by the ubiquitous gas geyser, and in the bath I had to do all our washing, including towels and sheets (with no mangle to help me wring and reduce the weight of water) which must then be carried down the stairs and through the house in a heavy galvanised bucket to be hung out in the little back yard. Nonetheless we remember our first home with much affection, and spent many night hours in the kitchen, blacked-out against the street-lights and moonlight, developing and printing photos, which was Robin's enduring hobby when he couldn't be building model aircraft.

I discovered quite a few old R.N.S. friends living in the district who were also newly married and unemployed, and I enjoyed having them round for lunch or tea and exchanging recipes, and I made a little money by sewing nighties for friends after the Gina Knitting Bag failure. Since I made nearly all my clothes, as my mother had always done, I always had some project on hand that I was altering, patching or creating out of something else, so I was never bored. Food rationing and shortages still made planning menus quite a challenge, but Robin was not hard to please and we ate pretty simply. We were very much in love and the months passed very happily.

Shortly after our arrival in Southsea, Robin heard he was accepted into the Colonial Medical Service for two eighteen-month tours of duty in Nigeria. He had applied for this instead of the obligatory alternative of two years National Service in one of the armed services. However, his wife, as supposedly non-productive accompanying baggage, had to obtain special permission from the Nigerian Governor General in order to go with him. One of the questions I had to answer was "Are you pregnant?", to which I quite truthfully answered "No."

This being the case, and other answers also proving satisfactory, I was cleared to accompany him, albeit feeling that had I answered in the affirmative I could possibly have missed out. For that reason, when I did fall pregnant a short time later, although we were delighted, we kept it to ourselves and I submitted to numerous mandatory vaccinations and inoculations, and even pelvic X-rays. In this more enlightened day that would be considered very threatening to the foetus in the first trimester, but the danger was not then appreciated and it seemed necessary to establish that my small pelvis would not cause a difficult birth, possibly in a remote area. Fortunately Michael, the resultant baby, has shown no ill effects.

We paid a visit to the recommended tropical outfitters in the West End of London, F.P.Baker's, which would supply all that we would need for life in West Africa. Heavy furniture was provided in the M.O.'s houses, but we must take with us such things as pots and pans, china and glass, cutlery, linen and any personal effects that we felt essential. We would also need camp beds, mosquito nets, Aladdin or Tilley lamps, water filters, mosquito boots, khaki shirts and shorts for Robin (including two Palm Beach Suits for best), broad brimmed hats, strong shoes and so on. We added a vinyl carrycot for the baby and two dozen nappies. These were all packed by F.P.Baker's into tin trunks, wooden chests and a lidded enamel bush bath, and shipped out for us.

Portsmouth, 1951

Although we were heading out into that part of the world known as 'the white man's grave', with no training course or any advice to prepare us, and though we knew nothing about the living or working conditions we would face, or even the climatic conditions, we headed out full of confidence that we would be able to manage. Robin was a doctor and he was being employed to practice medicine, so all would presumably fall into place when we got there and fitted in to the slot allotted to us. My imagination for once was not permitted to work negatively overtime, and I was looking forward to a great adventure, which was fortunate as it turned out, or I would probably never have gone.

Chapter Eighteen

To Nigeria, January 1952

I had been slightly troubled with morning sickness, but by embarkation date on a snowy 3rd January 1952, I was feeling really well... until we went aboard M.V. Apapa at Liverpool, and I had to rush out of the dining saloon before the evening meal. We had not even left the Mersey and here I was feeling seasick! It was a bonus for us that Robin's brother Dick, and his wife Pat, now working in Nigeria and returning there after leave, were also on board.

Once horizontal I remained there for days as every time I attempted to join the social scene on the now rolling deck I was forced to retreat, pallid and retching, to the haven of my bunk, where a sympathetic steward, who had seen it all before, kept me alive with Bovril and water biscuits. I did make sure, however, that I took my daily tablet of Paludrine, which I had dutifully started the day we embarked, two weeks before entering the malarial zone.

One sortie I had to make, however, was to the Sick Bay to have three tiny stitches removed from an eyelid where a wart had been removed a week before in London. By now we were in the Bay of Biscay. It was rough and the ship's doctor turned out to be rather drunk. Those two factor's alone were enough for me to want to keep my stitches and clamber back to bed, but when he produced an unsuitable pair of scissors to do the job, and approached me unsteadily, with whisky-laden breath, Robin decided to halt proceedings until a more suitable instrument could be found. He returned to the cabin and came back with our pointed nail scissors, which he dipped in spirit then insisted on doing the job himself. The M.O. comforted himself (though not me really) by holding my head steady, pumping whisky fumes at close quarters the while, and Robin managed somehow to extract the stitches between rolls without blinding me.

A few cabins away, another of the steward's charges was needing personal room service, and he would inform me of her progress, or lack of it, presumably to encourage me. After a week or so we entered calmer, tropical seas and I summoned enough strength to rise and dress for the gala dinner and make a wobbly appearance in the world of the living. Emerging from our cabin I was confronted by an apparent mirror image of myself, similarly skinny and pale, and dressed in an identical long cotton dress, of red and blue flowers on a white background, supplied by the same tropical outfitter in London. This was Mary, and our paths were often to cross again later, and our destinies remarkably similar for a few years. I often wonder what happened to her after we lost touch.

MV Apapa

One day Mary's husband, Jim, an Assistant District Officer, was pointed out to us as having spent the last tour (his first) in a particularly isolated and arid station in the Northern Region of Nigeria, called Azare, mid-way between Kano and Maiduguri. It was looked on as a punishment station, and was considered rather tough. Now he was returning for his second tour,

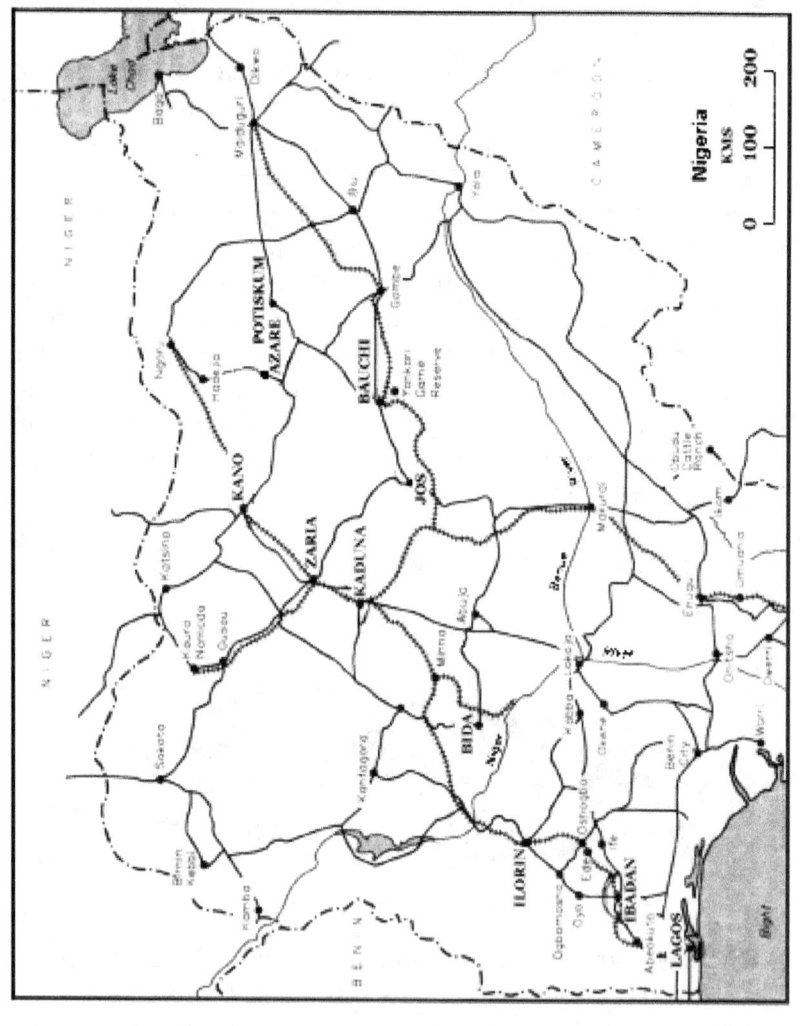

Places in Nigeria, West Africa, mentioned in my story.

this time with his new bride, and was anticipating a pleasanter posting, especially since she was already pregnant. We looked on Jim with interest, and struck up a friendship with them, but hoped that we ourselves would be posted nearer Dick and Pat in Ibadan, in the south of the country. We knew hardly anything about the Muslim North except that it was sub-Saharan, very hot and dry and thinly populated.

After a week at sea, we had our first sight of Africa, and anchored in the river off Bathurst, Gambia. Robin and I went ashore in a small boat and wandered round the unimpressive small town taking in the strange sights and smells. Two days later we anchored off Freetown, Sierra Leone, and here the heat and humidity hit us with a vengeance. I was so fascinated with watching all the comings and goings from shore to ship, and the small boys in canoes diving for money, that I stood too long at the ship's rail in the sun, and by the time we had embarked in a launch for shore, with standing room only, I blacked out. Pat, who was a nurse, pushed me down with my head between my knees, and I managed to pull myself together and control my ever-present nausea enough to have a cold drink at Kingsway Stores and wander around Freetown with the others, seeing the slave steps with evidence of past slave trading.

The flies, open drains, squatting food vendors; colourful backdrop of palms, hibiscus and bougainvillea; perspiring Africans with loads on their heads and teeth stained with betel nut; sleeping babies carried on the backs of the women, heads lolling without support; graceful, bearded Muslims in long robes and turbans; mangy pye-dogs scavenging around the food stalls; such overwhelmingly strange sights, sounds and smells, coupled with the unaccustomed tropical heat and humidity were nearly too much for me, and I was relieved to board the Apapa again and make it to my cabin without disgracing myself.

After a stop at Takoradi Harbour, Gold Coast, (later Ghana), we disembarked at Apapa Wharf, Lagos, on 16th January, after queuing for hours in stifling heat as we slowly made our way through Immigration and the bedlam of the customs shed.

Dick and Pat left us for Ibadan, 125 miles north, hoping that we would be able to call in and see them en route to wherever we were posted. It had been a real bonus for us to travel with them and we had gleaned some useful information. Eventually a young African from the Medical Department introduced himself and transferred us to the Bristol Hotel in the centre of Lagos, with another new doctor and his wife who had voyaged out with us. He told us that the Medical Inspector General, with most of the H.Q. staff, were on tour up-country in the Northern Region, and that no-one was left in the Lagos HQ who knew where we were to be posted. We found this suspense not at all encouraging and hoped they would decide what to do with us before too long.

The Bristol Hotel in 1952 turned out to be awful. It was situated in the Moslem quarter of town, so we could not avoid regular calls to prayer from right outside our window... except that I don't recall there being a window, only a wooden shutter supported on a stick. Our first floor room was basic, but had the saving grace of a grey-stained bath and a toilet, which could be flushed if it was in the right mood, for which we were thankful. The worst part was the dreadful smell emanating from the lumpy kapok mattresses and pillows, of previous perspiring guests over many decades, with consequent build-up of mould, odour and exotic insect life. I spread my kimono over both pillow and sheet, and sprinkled it with Chanel No.5 (remains of a wedding-present), but the mixture proved as nauseating as before.

That night I didn't sleep a wink and was utterly miserable from the noise, heat and high humidity that had sweat pouring off me. We didn't trust the hotel drinking water, the lumpy mattress and pillow smelt so foul I was feeling sick and grossly uncomfortable, and to cap it all an enormous cockroach, the size of a mouse, ran over me in the dim light. I screamed and chased it with a slipper but lost it under the bathtub. Robin fared little better and was seriously wondering what he had let us, and particularly me and the baby, in for. A continuous din in the street just outside our window continued until the early hours, and by the second night we had both developed diarrhoea. The beds had no mosquito nets, neither were there fly screens and Robin was bitten by a mosquito on his eyelid which became painfully infected and by the end of the week needed penicillin and a daily visit to the hospital. Not the most auspicious start to our new life and I looked back at the hygiene, order and predictability of the life we'd so recently left, with some nostalgia.

On the assumption that, having transported us so far, the Government would eventually discover some purpose (and destination) for us, we pressed on with attending to what came to hand. Iris, the other wife marooned with us, and I managed to fill the days with opening accounts in Kingsway Stores and shopping for strange things like charcoal irons, in between long drinks in the hotel courtyard, and getting what rest we could, to make up for the sleepless nights, whilst our husbands haunted Medical H.Q. for news of their postings and sorted out what official matters they could.

On the third day they came back from Medical H.Q. with the news that there were chalets available at Ikoyi Catering Rest House, where government officers were accommodated and where we should have gone in the first place. We piled our luggage into taxis and transferred ourselves to what seemed to us to be Paradise, clean and mosquito-proofed, the only noises at night being the croaking of frogs and the swish of the ceiling fan, surrounded by lawns and flower beds... and the food was good too, with wonderful curries featuring around 20 or so side dishes, and tropical fruits that we had never tasted before. I reckoned my chances of surviving had shot up 100 %.

Robin and Humphrey each took possession of blue Standard Vanguard Estate cars, and we drove to Victoria Beach to cool down, first getting hopelessly lost in a bewildering maze of back streets full of Africans in festive mood. Many streets seemed to be 'one way' but lacked identifiable signs, and people kept shouting and waving us to go back. Over the next few days we were to discover that driving in Lagos is pure hell, with people, donkeys, cyclists and pye-dogs heedlessly walking and riding all over the narrow streets, and no pavements or appropriate attention to safety.

Eventually our marching orders came through to report to Kaduna, capital of the Northern Region, whilst Humphrey and Iris were posted to Benin City in the Ibo, Eastern Region. We would not see them again for over four years. At last we could set off on the road north, spending the first night at Ibadan and having a meal with Dick and Pat, who showed us around the new University site. I was still being sick, usually after breakfast each morning, and was looking forward to exchanging the enervating humidity of the south for the more intense but dry heat of the north which was reputed to be easier to adjust to. We pressed on next day to Ilorin; 103 miles of dusty, corrugated, laterite road, arriving in late afternoon at the Catering Rest House.

A word of explanation about rest houses, of which there were two types. Catering Rest Houses (C.R.H's) were really the forerunners of motels in a country where there were few navigable roads and very long distances between towns. These towns usually offered no hotels, safe food, convenient petrol pumps or other facilities necessary for travelling government officers, who were mostly British expatriates. C.R.H's were government run and usually had a European supervisor, such as an under-occupied District Officer's wife, who endeavoured to see the standards were adhered to as best she could, usually without any training or experience. They were strategically placed in most of the major towns, a day's comfortable drive apart, and we found them to be clean and pleasant on the whole, with a cold drink, welcome bath and meal after the glaring heat, dust and bone-rattling of the day's drive.

The other type was the bush rest house, which I found better to avoid, especially once the baby arrived. These were to be found near every town and village, and were built of bush materials, mostly one circular room with mud walls, thatch roof, dirt floor and perhaps a wooden shutter propped open on a stick for a window. The loud buzzing of flies enabled one to locate a dark and smelly little outhouse some yards away, with (in the five star model) a wooden seat of sorts suspended over a hole in the ground, and possibly a ragged hessian bag shielding the occupier from any interested onlookers gathered outside. The rest house would also have a basic fireplace outside, for cooking.

The traveller must bring everything with him, preferably starting with a competent Houseboy. While the officer was attending to the business which had brought him there (such as a medical line-up in Robin's case), the Houseboy would set up house, light a fire, put water on to heat in a kerosene tin for the bath, unpack the lidded tin bath containing clothes and bedding, sweep out any resident snakes, scorpions and spiders and set up the camp bed and mosquito net and collapsible table and canvas chair. He would prepare the Tilley lamp and a hurricane lamp for himself, and set about preparing the evening meal. A good Houseboy was a treasure, but we soon learnt that it took many years of trial and error and training before one was likely to be blest with such a one.

Once on the road north we started to enjoy ourselves. The sky was clear blue for the first time since we reached Africa, for Lagos was humid and dull all the time, and we were fascinated with the local colour, people and bird songs, all so new to us. As we progressed North, bumping across the mighty River Niger at Jebba over the railway bridge, previously having obtained a Pass Paper but with our hearts in our mouths lest we be over-run by a train none-the-less, the jungle gave way to mile after mile of flat and dusty savannah. From here on there was little variation in the scene except for occasional townships, seldom larger than a village, and the only traffic an occasional lorry or Mammy Wagon filled to overflowing with passengers, groundnuts or cotton bales. Occasionally we noticed large pyramids that turned out to be stored ground-nuts (peanuts).

The monotony was again broken at the Kaduna River, where the car was poled across on a pontoon made from drums roped together. Again my heart was in my mouth, but we had no choice but to trust the boatmen, pay the fee, and pray that we, the car, Old Uncle Tom Cobley and all, would not be tipped into the flowing river and certain doom. We arrived safely on the northern bank to be hassled by a voluble and berobed old Hausa who begged for a lift to Bida, our destination for that night, so we squeezed him onto the bench seat next to me, and opened the windows wider, trying to ignore the fine red dust which coated us, our luggage and the stores piled high behind us.

Car ferry, Kaduna River, 1952

Bida turned out to be most interesting and different to anything we had seen so far, being a totally Mohammedan, Hausa town. The Catering Rest House was clean but had no electricity, which was our first taste of the conditions we should expect from now on and we were still finding the heat at night made it very hard to sleep.

Our fourth day on the road was a 270 mile drive to Zaria. There seemed no direct route from Bida to Kaduna, our destination, in 1952, so we had to go a long way round. Our petrol tank held 15 gallons, and we had not yet acquired a jerry can, so we were anxiously watching the empty sign for the last miles. Petrol was obtained from the PWD yard or the divisional office at each overnight stop, which sometimes meant searching out the fellow who had the key to the drums, and an unwanted delay sitting in the hot car.

Lunch on the road each day was a pack of sandwiches and a piece of fruit supplied by the Rest House, with a thermos of cold drink, but we were usually too hot and dry to be hungry, and had not yet acquired a taste for bread flavoured with palm oil or ground-nut oil. We always looked forward to the company of other travelling government officers each evening, from whom we learnt a great deal of local lore. This was just as well because we had been formally told virtually nothing, and we were utterly clueless on matters of servants (how many, what duties, what to pay, how to select etc) and things of a bush-housekeeping nature in general. The biggest problem was that we didn't know WHAT we didn't know, which made it hard to know where to start.

If I seem to keep mentioning Government Officers, D.O.'s, A.D.O's, M.O.'s, and so on when referring to expatriates, it is because the British Government did not permit any white settlers, unlike East Africa, and the only missionaries in the Northern Region were associated with large hospitals run by the Seventh Day Adventists, Sudan Interior Mission and Sudan United Mission. These were in one or two large centres, such as Kano, and because it was a Moslem region, no Christian proselytising was allowed. The Colonial Service provided the local administration, medical, engineering and well-digging personnel, and senior police. Otherwise there was little or no interference with the emirs and District Heads and the region enjoyed considerable peace and prosperity.

We really liked colourful and picturesque Zaria, and appreciated a cooler night's sleep for once. The next day we reached Kaduna, the capital of the Northern Region, where we were glad to have a break from the juddering road, wash the layers of red dust off the car, our hair and clothes, and write some letters. Robin now spruced himself up and reported to the medical headquarters, hoping that someone could be found who had at least heard of us and could inform us of our destination. Here he was at last successful. They had indeed been expecting us and we were to go on to Azare.... AZARE!!!! (pronounced Az'-aree). Flashback to Jim on the voyage out.

It appeared the African M.O. in Azare was being invalided out, and Robin was to relieve there for two months, then three weeks relieving at Bauchi (a provincial HQ north of Jos), followed probably by Rural M.O. at Gombe, further east. Unfortunately Gombe could provide no house, which meant a life of touring around bush rest houses servicing patients in native dispensaries in the most primitive conditions. Robin was given an assurance that at least he would not be left stranded in Azare, which was reserved for African M.O.'s, so not to worry!

Robin was very quiet when he returned from the interview and told me the news, and my heart dropped as we looked at each other and the full significance sank in. We would have no settled home for the baby's arrival and first year of life, and my own health and well being before the birth could also be threatened. The reason for discouraging wives from accompanying officers on their first tour was becoming apparent, and I wondered, not for the first time since leaving England, whether not reporting my pregnancy was such a great idea after all.

I was still troubled by nausea and vomiting most days, which surely should have stopped by now, and was rendering me thin and listless. It was not until our third tour, in 1955, when we changed to Daraprim for malarial prophylaxis, that my constant morning nausea stopped and I realised that it was actually a side effect of Paludrine, and not neurosis, seasickness or pregnancy after all! The only times I felt really well in all those years was when on leave in England and not taking Paludrine, but at the time we put the improvement down to other factors, such as cooler climate and good food. On the sunny side, at least I never developed full-blown malaria.

A piece of good fortune was discovering that a fellow guest at the Kaduna rest house, an Assistant D.O., was an old Merchant Taylor's boy, Robin's old school. He was recovering from some tropical disease and looked most unwell, but very kindly advised us how to go about obtaining house boys. He got his own steward to line up a couple, and helped me interview them, whilst Robin was out. We had expected to take on local servants at our destination, wherever that turned out to be, but were now advised that there would be no house-trained boys (or should I say trained house-boys) available outside of the main towns of Kaduna, Zaria or Jos, and the sooner we started building up our establishment, the better.

And so it was that Sule (pronounced Soo'lee) joined the family, for better, for worse, and was our first house-boy. He was dark, squat and short, with tribal markings on his face and a big smile, which rather diverted me from establishing what language skills he had, English comprehension in particular. We were soon to discover that they were abysmal, limited mainly to "Me sorry, Mudder," and his cooking not much better. His references, typically, said nothing to condemn, but nothing to recommend either, and as he was the only candidate prepared to combine the two roles of cook and steward we piled him into the back of the car, balanced on top of the stores and luggage, with his mat and few belongings, and set off for

Houseboys, Monday & Sule, Azare 1952

Jos on the plateau. We hoped he would later help us select a Small Boy to assist him.

The 172 mile drive was as usual rough, hot and dusty, but the countryside as we came onto the plateau was fascinating and different to anything we had seen before. It reminded us of a moon landscape, with barren and rugged volcanic hills. The local people were referred to as pagans, not being Muslims. The women were well-built, and naked apart from a bunch of green leaves hanging demurely from the waist, front and back. They seemed to do the hard work, carrying heavy bundles of firewood on their heads and a baby on the back, and some had henna coloured legs below the knee that looked like long socks. I thought them singularly unfeminine at the time with their shaven heads. The men wore a simple long white garment and never seemed to be carrying anything heavier than a staff as they walked in front of their laden women.

The road wound up to 4,000 feet and we reached Jos in mid afternoon only to find that the telegram forewarning of our arrival had not arrived, and there was no room at the Hill Station where we had been advised to stay. We were advised to try the Army Leave Camp, and spent two comfortable enough nights there in a round, white-washed mud and thatched hut with clean army beds and the luxury of needing a blanket. Bathing was an adventure, and involved driving or hiking to the bath house some distance away, where one queued up until a bath orderly had run one's bath and withdrawn. Ablutions were not prolonged when the restless queue outside the door was weighing on one's mind.

We discovered Jim and Mary were staying a few huts down the line and had been posted to Gombe. We were able to tell them that we were bound for Azare and might follow them to Gombe in a few months. An A.D.O. at least had the assurance of an allotted house there, unlike the doctor. Like me, Mary was suffering from nausea and losing rather than gaining weight, and she was longing to stop travelling and settle down in her own place. Her baby was due soon after mine, in early July, whilst "Michaelizabeth" was expected at the end of June.

We spent two nights and a busy day in Jos, buying stores and trying everywhere to obtain kerosene, almost non-existent because of a rail strike which meant a shortage of all imported goods which had to be railed up from Lagos. We found a can at the 11th hour, and set off early on the morning of 1st Feb. for Potiskum, a long 232 miles north, with Sule in the back. We had been advised of our duty to pay our respects to the Resident District Officer in Bauchi as we passed through, which we did, since Robin was to be working in his province.

Azare had no Catering Rest House, and as our loads were somewhere between Lagos and who-knows-where (I could accurately say Timbuctu) we had been advised by some official who looked at a map but had obviously never been there, to wait at Potiskum, which had the closest Catering Rest House, and commute the sixty five miles to Azare from there until our loads caught up with us.

As we drove further north we saw a muzzled hyena being led along the road, some camels in line astern, men in big beehive straw hats walking along endless red sandy roads to nowhere, ahead of their burdened, dark blue-robed women, or riding perched over their donkey's rump, their legs dangling almost to the ground. We saw humped Zebu cattle with long up-pointing horns ranging lazily through dusty scrub, watched by small scantily clad boys with big sticks, often standing on one leg, and occasional little groups of thatched huts with people waving as we passed and naked children playing in the dust. Otherwise the countryside was monotonous. The drumming of the car over the corrugations was nearly drowned out by the high-pitched rhythm of cicadas and it was hard to keep our eyes open in the glare, heat and suffocating dust.

We stopped for a lunch break to eat our sandwiches and I turned round to speak to Sule, uncomplainingly perched on the luggage behind us, and gasped. Poor Sule was covered from head to toes in soft, red, laterite dust, which had turned him into a look-alike of Father Christmas, except that his hair and eyebrows were red too. It was hard not to laugh, and there was absolutely nothing that we could do about it except try to dust him down a bit. We were not much better ourselves, and that car, which had van-type doors opening into the back, always did suck in a great deal of dust in addition to that entering via the windows. Needless to say it had no fan to make it more comfortable and we had to drive with the windows open because of the heat.

We reached Potiskum in the early evening and approached the Catering Rest House, trusting that there would be a room available. It was empty except for a touring magistrate from Jos, with whom we chatted after supper and whom Robin would meet again when giving evidence in murder trials. This was far and away the worst catering rest house we were ever to encounter; dirty, fly-blown, with desultory service and unpalatable food. It was run by the African steward with no supervision, and depressed us even more as we faced the prospect of having to spend days, or even weeks, there until our loads caught us up and we could move to Azare.

After a bath and change of clothes we called on the District Officer and explained our position, only to be told that the whole plan was impractical since the direct, dry season road between Potiskum and Azare was virtually a goat track, and "I wouldn't send my worst enemy on it." He was also pessimistic about the chances of our loads arriving within a reasonable time-frame, and he advised us to return to Bauchi, wait until our loads came through on the rail and divert them by lorry to Azare. There seemed nothing for it but to check out of the Rest House the next morning and visit Azare by the long route, about 95 miles, before back-tracking to Bauchi to wait. One thing we had found was that there was usually only one navigable road between destinations, so little need for maps.

We arrived in Azare around midday, and were very relieved to find it quite a picturesque little sub-Saharan town, looking as though it had remained unchanged since biblical times. We surprised the middle-aged D.O., Waller Wood, in his office, and he summed up the situation pretty well and took us home to have a wash, cool drinks and lunch with his charming wife, Jean. We unloaded all the luggage and stores we had been carting around since Lagos, and at about three p.m. reloaded Sule, this time with the comfort of a proper seat, filled up with petrol and set off on the road back to Bauchi, where we arrived long after dark utterly exhausted, hoping against hope that the busy catering rest house would have a room and a meal for us. Thank God, it did.

The next week did much to restore our spirits as we met Jim and Mary again and got to know some hospitable Bauchi residents. The kerosene hunt was resumed, with minimal success, and uniforms made for Sule (khaki drill loose tunic and trousers for work, white with red cummerbund for serving at table). I had been having nose-bleeds since Kaduna, and had such a bad one here that Robin had to pack it, and one night we were awakened with a bang as a kit car crashed into the next door chalet. Otherwise the worst drama was when Robin gave me a driving lesson around the airfield and I inadvertently very slightly scratched the side of the new car against a bush, which elicited as much emotion in certain quarters as if I'd deliberately got a sledge hammer to it! Of course, it was not yet three weeks old and quite our most precious possession; in fact we still could hardly believe it was really ours.

On 7th Feb. the chief steward, informed us that King George VI had died at Sandringham the day before, "Me sorry, Sir; King 'e die", and Sule brought a potential Small Boy around for our approval. Monday Mommon was about 20, stocky and very black, with elaborate tribal markings on his face. He spoke little or no English either, and it was becoming apparent that the quicker I got hold of a basic phrase book in Hausa, the better for all of us.

The Azare D.O. and his wife, Waller and Jean, passed through en route to Jos and returned a few days later with no news of our loads, but inviting us to stay with them until they arrived.

Accordingly we loaded in the two house-boys and hit the road again to Azare, which we were beginning to look to with some affection since it had provided us with such kind friends who seemed bent on looking after us. I was really ready for some of that!

Chapter Nineteen

Azare

Certain memories of Azare are very vivid still. My diary reminds me of our first meal in what was to be our home for the next eighteen months. It was still occupied by the African M.O. and his extended family, who were to leave the next day on sick leave, and we were invited to lunch. We were staying with the D.O. Waller and Jean, who were kindness personified and it was very interesting for us to observe their smooth running household. They had been in Nigeria many years, in fact this was their last tour, and had a loyal and experienced Steward and Cook. They told us that Robin was the first non-African M.O. to be appointed to Azare, The appointment of an English doctor proved very popular all round as at that time there were no trained Hausa doctors, so the incumbents had always been from the southern tribes.

Our arrival coincided with the visit of the Medical Inspector General from Lagos, Dr Manuwa plus entourage, who we had at last caught up with as he toured around the North. With Robin tagging along, he visited the Hospital, prison, meat market, school and leper colony and was then expected to lunch at the Medical Officer's home, after which his party would head back to Bauchi and Robin would officially take over from the M.O.

We were discovering that time has a very approximate quality in Africa, and it was very late in the afternoon before we sat down to lunch, minus the official party who had decided to take to the road before dark. The intense heat for me, unclimatised and pregnant, was totally exhausting and I was feeling nauseated by the long wait. Unsure of correct African etiquette, and not wishing to offend, we both ate as little of the, by now unpalatable, meal as we could get away with, waving away the flies from each forkful in its journey from plate to mouth.

This first impression of our new home was exceedingly depressing, and Waller told us that the M.O.'s allotted house had previously been a cool mud and thatched place, similar to their own, with a certain charm and an established garden and much closer to the hospital and town. When this new bungalow was being built, ostensibly for an Assistant District Officer, the incumbent M.O. stood on his rank and claimed it for himself (much to the A.D.O.'s relief) thus ensuring the discomfort of the families of all the M.O.'s who were to follow him. They had to live out their lives, 24 hours a day, in this small, isolated Public Works Department cement block bungalow, with a shiny tin roof, probably designed for a coastal climate, and certainly totally unsuited to the sub-Saharan climate in which it now found itself. It was two miles out of town, on the Potiskum "goat track", but luckily for me not far from the D.O's compound.

As we walked towards it we were fascinated to see dozens of brightly coloured lizards, 12 or more inches in length, with blue bodies and bright orange heads, doing press-ups on the walls and scuttling around the sandy compound. Although not screened for insects, the house had heavy expanded metal on the windows to discourage burglars, and a wide ribbon of copper ran from the crown of the roof down into the ground to conduct lightning. We later found that it would twang noticeably in the violent electrical storms at the end of the dry season.

The rooms in the bungalow connected in one straight line, having wide, low windows front and back that offered no protection from the glare. Off the bedroom was the Bayan Gida ("back of the house") with thunder box, bucket of sand and a small shovel. The can was emptied once a day, approached from outside through a small trap door behind the seat, by the B.G. man, who disappeared into the bush carrying the heavy can, with accumulation of the day, on his head, and returned with it empty. We had to ask him to knock before removing the can, and stand back till he received an 'all clear', after more than once finding ourselves suspended over space at a very awkward moment. His heavy breathing and chatty greeting while he waited, nonetheless, had a somewhat inhibiting effect on anyone seated.

Next was a dark bathroom housing just a tap-less bath, a large drum of cold water with tin dipper, and a door out into the compound through which hot water was brought in a kerosene tin. The dirty bath water drained into a small cement tank in the ground, out of which it was baled by the garden boy and used on the garden, so that not a precious drop need be wasted.

Also off the bedroom was a dressing room, without a door, with a tiny wash-basin in the corner, again without taps. This area later became the nursery, with a mosquito net suspended from ceiling to floor over the cot, so that I could sit inside to attend to the baby. Later the end wall was knocked out and a tin-roofed, fly-screened sleep-out added, where we slept on camp beds when the heat indoors was intolerable. The down side of this addition was that the nursery (and to a lesser extent, the bedroom) was permanently opened to the elements.

The main bedroom opened into the long living room, as did the front door, and at the opposite end was the dining table, with a kerosene fridge by the back door. Another door led to the scullery, storeroom and kitchen, where the house-boys held sway. Their own living quarters were on the edge of the compound, some distance from the house. The floors throughout the house were cement, treated with red wax, which made them shiny and gave much work to the house-boys who tied dusters to their feet and skated to obtain a polished surface.

The bungalow was perched in the middle of two or more acres of desert, cleared of any vestige of grass or tree, glaringly hot and bare and quite unfenced, and on that first day it was such a relief to return to the clean D.O.'s house for a relaxed meal and pleasant evening outside under the stars, and plan what could be done to make the place habitable. We were getting anxious about locating our loads, without which we could not move in, and were really excited when all the boxes turned up after a couple more days.

The house was very dirty and as soon as the family had left we set Sule and Monday to scrubbing and scraping, aided by a gang of prisoners from the gaol arranged by Waller. On closer inspection it all looked extremely dowdy, with paint peeling and needing fresh distemper, and a soot-blackened, greasy and smelly kitchen. With Jean's help I wrote out an order for groceries from Kingsway Stores, Lagos, trying to look ahead to our needs two to three months down the track, when the stores we'd brought with us would all be finished. Mail went out once a week, on a lorry that had brought incoming mail the day before. There being neither telephones nor radio as a means of communication, all cables, telegrams, parcels and letters travelled the same way, and Wednesday night was always devoted to dealing with the week's correspondence.

So we moved in and set to unpacking china, glass, kitchen gear, bed linen, etc. and making the place into a home. Sounds of chaos drifted through from the kitchen area, with Sule and Monday still very poorly organised, and our first dinner was eventually produced at about 9.00 pm. By this time I was too tired to do more than peck at the very unappetising meal, which did not auger well for our future well-being, especially since Sule reported chasing a rat family out of the kitchen, which accounted for the earlier noises.

Having no curtains, we had to rise early each day before a gang arrived from the gaol to work on putting thatch over the shiny tin roof to help keep it cooler. When that was eventually finished they built a brick patio outside the front door, where we could sit out at night without getting muddy in the wet season, or sand-blown in the dry. This was all organised by Waller, and we benefited greatly by his concern for our comfort (or survival?). Each morning little ceremonies were enacted around the place as I was formally greeted on one knee by the Head

Warder, the B.G. man (Serakin Bayan Gida), the garden boy, the donkey man bringing wood, and anyone else passing by, all conducted, of course, in Hausa. Their greetings are very formal, with questions and answers suited to the occasion, (even for a bridegroom) and I made a point of learning up my part from the phrase book as soon as I could, rather hoping I'd meet a bridegroom to show off to one day.

The bungalow gradually became organised and cleaner, looking quite homely with our own belongings about the place. Robin was kept very busy at the hospital with a large outpatients line-up every morning, and he also had to inspect the prison, school, slaughter slab and look after the leper village outside the town. I defrosted the fridge and trimmed the wick and then couldn't get it going again. Luckily Jean came over and diagnosed what was wrong, and also showed me how to deal with the ceramic water filter candles which must be regularly brushed clean of the residue which soon coated them, using a tooth brush, and then boiled up to sterilise them.

Every drop of drinking water from the well must first be well-boiled, then put to drip through the clean and boiled filter (which took forever) and then bottled in empty gin bottles and refrigerated. For the steward to allow the drinking water to run out was to create a crisis, as providing more was such a lengthy procedure, and we began to appreciate the importance of the nightly gin and lime to provide the necessary bottles, let alone refreshment.

It had soon become apparent that we needed a Garden Boy mostly to carry water from the well, and to scoop up bath water to pour around the trees we were planting to soften the view and provide some shade. Having no piped water, electricity or gas or even phones, everything took a lot longer, which needed to be taken into consideration when planning! The well was very deep, about 60 feet, with water pulled up in a goat skin bag then poured into a kerosene tin for carrying up to the house. Here it was tipped into a 44 gallon drum outside the kitchen door. Periodically the locally-made grass rope would fray and the goatskin would get lost in the well, which entailed our whole establishment dropping tools to become involved in the rescue, mainly as supervisors. The most efficient retrieval occurred after we had acquired a garden rake, which was lowered down on the much-mended rope and managed to snag the goat skin without everyone losing half a day's work! Water for our meagre baths was heated in a kerosene tin with a wooden carrying bar nailed across its top, and carried to the bath by the Steward, to be cooled by a drum of cold water next to it. Life in West Africa would have been greatly improved by a bush shower and by a pedal radio... what a lot a few Australians could have taught us!

Azare house, 1952 - cookhouse on right, sleepout on left

Since I had a Cook, a House Boy and a Garden Boy, for our small establishment, it might be asked what I found to do all day. The answer at that time was "not much" apart from overseeing the Boys, though I did get through a lot of sewing with my faithful Singer, and wrote letters home. Every morning I would meet with Sule, the cook, plan the day's menu, unlock the store and dole out the ingredients as was the custom. Flour by the cup, sugar and yeast for bread; rice, tinned peas, a tin of fruit on special occasions or a packet of jelly, a spoonful of custard powder, a cup of milk powder, tea, coffee and biscuits enough for the day, Vim, soap, Kerosene and so on.

Sometimes there were some potatoes or other fresh vegetables courtesy of someone returning from Jos, and these also had to be kept under lock and key to prevent them disappearing. A rather soft, locally made "Key" soap was bought by the case and doled out by the bar for laundry and kitchen use. Fresh food was haggled for in the market by Sule, and donkeys loaded with firewood came to the door. Hausa traders would also turn up occasionally, with leather and 'silver' wares, carpets and camel hair blankets, but their visits to Azare were very rare. Having little need for cash in the house my trading with them was usually by means of 'changey-changey', bartering unwanted clothing and other goods for leather bags and pouffs and even carpets.

The store room was kept locked at all times. Replenishment came from two sources, neither reliable. Orders could be sent to the Kingsway Stores in Lagos, which had the advantage of coastal prices, and subsidised rail to Jos and thence by the weekly mail lorry to Azare. One allowed the very minimum of six weeks before delivery and faced the possibility of some items being out of stock. Since this could be as vital as yeast or toilet paper (and once was), one opened the box with trepidation as well as excitement. When Christmas 1952 arrived, our order was already long overdue, and we were reduced to celebrating on bush rice and the ubiquitous skinny little chickens, tearing up scarce reading matter for use in the B.G. The Kingsway catalogue was not always easily understandable, and we ended up with a huge tin of dozens of packets of Nice Biscuits. They lasted out the eighteen-month tour and it was about 20 years before we chose to eat a Nice biscuit again.

The other source of supply, particularly for chemist items, was to grab anyone who was not only going to, but also expecting to return from, Jos, and thrust your shopping list and money into their dutiful, if not very willing hands. If these lists were in any way complicated it could entail them in hours of searching and time-wasting, but it was nevertheless a duty that one was not expected to shirk, such opportunities being relatively few and far between, and needs often urgent.

Azare had one or two canteens, as stores were called, but they were basic and not well equipped for Europeans' needs, and I only patronised them for calico (very cheap and called baft), drill for the house-boy's uniforms, checked cotton for curtains, and things like hurricane lamp wicks. The local markets were colourful and much more fun, though I seldom found anything I really needed. Sule bought very small live chickens and ducks and kept them tethered by the kitchen door until dispatched and cooked. It was remarkable how often he would announce "Chicken done go for bush. Me sorry, Mudder," and one could expect tempting aromas from the Boy's quarters without being able to do anything except fume.

Eggs were plentiful and bought by the calabash full, but were very small and had to be tested in water. If they floated they were bad, and many of them did. The rest were scrambled or used in cooking. Beef, from the nomadic Fulani's herds of Zebo cattle, was slaughtered ritually facing Mecca and cut up into unrecognisable chunks. Stewing was the only safe method of cooking, and even so it was crunchy, as if sand or worse was in it, and it probably was. Rice, onions, tiny watery tomatoes and a wild spinach were the other local foods available most of the year, augmented with river fish (if one was lucky enough to be 'dashed' some on tour, slopping around live in a kerosene tin), guinea fowl if Robin shot one, (a real treat) and in the rainy season sweet corn, which we sometimes made a meal of just by itself to give us a respite from Sule's atrocious cooking.

All fresh items were bought home from the market by Sule on his bike, having been entrusted with the money he anticipated needing. Powdered milk was used normally, but when nomadic Fulani herds were in the area Sule would arrange to leave a couple of empty beer bottles and money under a bush, a folded blade of grass serving as stopper, and we would have fresh milk. This was first sieved then boiled until it was reduced to half, and the creamy skin retained in a jar in the fridge. When the jar was half full I would beat it until it formed butter, which was a breakfast treat to stop the marmalade soaking into the toast.

Very occasionally we would have little bananas, limes, papaws, guavas or green but ripe oranges, but fruit was hard to come by unless a traveller brought some back from Jos or Bauchi. Likewise potatoes and fresh vegetables had a very short life in the heat, even if one could obtain them. Sometimes we would be given a lettuce as a great treat, but Dick had warned us never to eat uncooked vegetables or fruit that could not be peeled, and risk round-worms or amoebic dysentery, so we never dared eat them even after routine soaking in potassium permanganate.

Sule produced our food from an unscreened kitchen equipped with a wood-burning stove, table, meat safe and tap-less sink. Unlike the older, mud houses where the cook-house was separated from the main house by a covered way, this kitchen was part of the house, which added to the general heat under the roof. The wood arrived by donkey in two large bundles about 30 inches long. A piece was not shortened before being fed into the fire box, so most of it stuck out into the room and was gradually pushed in as it burnt. This also added to the above-century temperature as, of course, the fire-box door was jammed open and red hot embers frequently fell out onto the cement floor. The kerosene tin of hot water sat permanently on the stove top for washing purposes.

It was no wonder that a European woman found it hard to survive without African servants, and the usual establishment was four, being Cook, Steward, Small Boy (who could be 8 years or 80) and Garden Boy. At first we compromised by having the Cook and Small Boy share the Steward's work between them, but it was never satisfactory and I used to get very frustrated with their lack of hygiene and laziness, as I thought. The truth was that they had probably come from a tribal village situation, and had somehow acquired references but very little training and they must have disliked me heartily with my impatience and constant harping. House-boys always preferred to work in a lone male establishment, where they could be left in peace all day as long as they produced the meals and clean laundry vaguely on time. By the end of the year, after many dismal failures, we did actually achieve an establishment that worked in harmony, and my nerves improved slightly.

Laundry was done by Monday using local soap and cold water, and ironed with a marvellous contraption like a Mississippi steam boat, fuelled by charcoal. I had great respect for this skill, which I never successfully mastered. Because of the climate and dust we seemed to get through a lot of clothes, and always had a bath and changed into formal clothes before dinner in the evening. This was partly as protection against malaria mosquitoes, but it also served to retain our self-respect and identity, I suppose. The steward changed into a white uniform with a red cummerbund and dressing up added a little glamour to the evening. Robin and I both wore mosquito boots, which were soft canvas-topped boots, with a draw-string just under the knee. I wore long cotton skirts (which I had made out of unrationed remnants of curtain material) and long-sleeved blouses, and Robin exchanged his shorts and long socks for long trousers. Any exposed skin was then plastered with DIMP and we sat outside by the light of a hissing Tilley lamp, which sat in a bowl of water to catch the kamikaze insects as they fell, nursing long drinks and watching for shooting stars.

The only other Europeans were one or sometimes two Assistant D.O.s, who seemed to come and go every few months, occasionally with families, and we often invited them over, or had dinner with them, sometimes playing Canasta. Evening was the best time of day, especially when we dined with Waller and Jean, and could enjoy music on their wind-up gramophone. Waller and Jean were followed by Mike and Rosemary Hollis and then by other D.O.'s during our tour, and we still keep in touch with Rosemary after nearly fifty years, though Mike was to die tragically after their return to England some years later.

Rosemary had arrived in Nigeria the month before us, and had the advantage, or possibly disadvantage in some ways, of being the new bride of an experienced District Officer, whose established household, though well-tuned to his ways, resented the intrusion of a woman. Rosemary later wrote a most entertaining book, 'A Scorpion for Tea', about her experiences in Northern Nigeria in the 50's, which included some months with us in Azare and again the next tour in Kaduna. She is an accomplished artist, and this gave her an interest during the isolated and lonely days.

Although I made most of my clothes myself, I did possess a particularly 'good' Horrocks cotton dress, which was rather dramatically patterned in royal blue and white, and was my favourite. Unfortunately, Rosemary had similar taste and had also brought the identical garment out from England. So here we were, the only two white woman for hundreds of miles around, with identical haircuts (self inflicted) and uniform dress. This was the second time it had happened to me in the year! Since my dress disintegrated before Rosie's, I later cut off the bodice and wore the bottom half as a skirt. Incidentally, I had to cut Robin's hair as well as my own, and would take about half an hour producing thirty-nine steps, whilst he groaned and complained under my scissors. After a rather long apprenticeship I eventually gained speed and expertise and he has never been to a barber since.

Apart from the Wood's gramophone, the only other music in our lives, the short-wave radio being a dead loss, even for news, came from our own efforts on recorders, which we had ordered from England with an instruction book and suitable music. When the insects became too annoying outside, we would get onto our bed under the big double mosquito net, and play duets. When Mike replaced Waller, at the end of September, we found to our great delight that he played the flute, and sometimes would join us (though not in the bed), making a very uneven trio as we were never really very good, but made up for it with a lot of laughs!

Every Wednesday in the dry season, which was nine months of the year, Robin would visit three or four village dispensaries, accompanied by the Azare ambulance to transport serious cases needing hospitalisation back in Azare. The local dispensary attendant would have his patients lined up waiting to be seen, and after dealing with them Robin would drive a further thirty or forty miles to the next dispensary, and so on in a big arc until he returned to Azare after dark. Once or twice a month it was necessary to camp in a bush rest house in the villages farthest away, and this way each of the thirteen dispensaries had a visit from the doctor once a month. The whole area Robin covered, in Katagum Province, was said to be the size of Wales.

Ambulance repairs, Azare 1953

A couple of weeks after our arrival, Robin thought it would be interesting for me to accompany him on the Wednesday trip. With us in the car was Mallam Adamu, a turbanned and robed Hausa who was the Out Patients Attendant and Interpreter and Robin's right hand man. The roads between villages were often just sandy donkey tracks, rarely used by any wheeled vehicle, and soft blown sand at times made it impossible to tell whether the road ahead had any firm base, or was deep, dry sand into which the wheels would sink and spin. There were frequent unmapped detours which forced us to choose what looked like the most promising fork, and predictably, around 1 p.m. with the burning sun around its zenith, we took the wrong one and came to a boiling halt, wheels spinning, motor revving as the tyres burrowed into the powdery sand.

Because Robin was needed in the driver's seat, it left Mallam Adamu and me to do the donkey work, and we eventually got the car moving again after a great deal of digging and pushing, me hatless in the desert heat. Hardly surprisingly, the next day saw me unable to leave my bed, vomiting and ill, and deciding that my role would not in future include pushing cars out of sand dunes in the midday tropical sun.

Late that afternoon I staggered out to the kitchen for a drink and found the house-boys gone and everything in a shocking mess. Filter candles for drinking water lay half submerged in a grimy can, cooking pans in a bucket of filthy greasy water outside the door, flies in the open meat safe, ironing still not done after 4 days and so on. I was very angry to see how unreliable the Boys had proved when I was not present, and hauled back Sule from his quarters across the compound and got him cracking. I was relieved to see that both Boys went into efficiency mode after my rocket and scrubbed out the kitchen and scullery. Since our lives are literally in the hands of those who prepare our food and drink we could but hope that the improvement would last. Meanwhile Robin and I were both learning Hausa as fast as we could so as to avoid misunderstandings.

27th February was a very hot Ash Wednesday with a shade temperature still at 98 F at sundown. We were surrounded by bush fires which reached us in the evening, having got closer all day, worrying us that the strong wind might set the new roof thatch on fire from flying embers, but Robin and Monday managed to beat out the burning grass as it neared the house. Thick Harmattan, the dust laden wind that comes across the desert, brought cooler nights which was a relief, but the air was so dry that the camel hair rug on the bed showered sparks as I threw it back in the dark.

I weighed myself at the hospital; 8 stone 2 lbs in cotton dress and sandals, which was 4lbs less than in November, though I was now 5 months pregnant. The heat and Sule's cooking were not conducive to weight gain. Nonetheless I busied myself making maternity clothes in anticipation of a bulge showing up eventually. The skirts had a cut-out circle in the front to go round, but not over the bulge. These were quite the latest Butterick and Vogue maternity fashion and worn under short smocks that concealed the cut-away bit. Robin drove me down to the United Africa Company canteen where I found some blue and white check gingham for bedroom curtains but I ended up hanging them in the dining room as they looked so much nicer than I'd expected. We then decided to put them all through the house as they gave a cool blue light, which helped to keep out glare, and there was little else to choose from anyway. I was thus quite happily occupied with sewing and experimented with making cool drinks from tamarind pods and fresh limes with sugar, to beat the heat.

The days continued to get hotter and the nights almost as bad, and I took to sleeping on a towel to save a sweat soaked sheet and pillow. Jean advised me to close the doors and windows and draw the curtains before the house had time to heat up each morning, to keep out the high wind, which was as hot as a furnace. As my pregnancy advanced I would get through the days alternately sitting, lying or walking around. It was too hot to sit in the leather P.W.D. chairs, so I put up a canvas camping chair in the sitting room and tried to occupy the long hours indoors, wishing there was a local library or a radio that could make contact with the outside world. When Robin returned we would take a gentle stroll around outside before sunset and study our tree seedlings for any sign of growth.

Sule started acting very oddly, complaining about the heat and being thoroughly inefficient, and I began to despair of his ever being satisfactory. One terrifically hot day, when I had spent the morning at Jean's, I came back for lunch to find Sule in a cloud and nothing prepared, and I found myself continually having to roar him up over something or other, such as pouring unboiled water into the filter. This did nothing for my own equilibrium at a time when I was trying to think beautiful thoughts and be placid, and was not producing a happy atmosphere in the home. I wondered if he were taking some sort of drug.

We were experiencing a variety of West African wildlife in the house, as the seasons changed. One evening I nearly put my hand on a scorpion resting on a stone propping the door open and then we were invaded by great big red ants in the bedroom; these we thought we had vanquished with kerosene only to have them return at night in their millions. We had quite a time filling up their holes with kerosene and D.D.T. before we dared turn in. White ants were a constant feature, trekking up inside walls in their corridors of earth overnight, to be knocked down but not out each morning. Occasionally a bat would fly through the open door and around the bedroom, and in the wet season, toads congregated around the lighted wick under the kerosene fridge. A very real hazard was the presence of snakes, which found it easy to enter and settle around the thunder box in the B.G. and also seemed to like the cool environment of the bathroom floor.

Malaria mosquitoes were always on the lookout for a feed and cantharides beetles produced a nasty chemical burn if one slapped at one that had settled on the skin, but probably the things we disliked most were the stink bugs. They swarmed over walls like a heavy curtain, inside and out, nested in the roof by day, and could only be removed by literally sweeping them into tins of kerosene and setting them alight. They got into everything, and the stench was nauseating since it was impossible to avoid crushing them and releasing the smell.

On the pleasanter side, we managed to rear a few baby Baroas; a common deer found in the sub-Sahara region, whose mothers had been killed by hunters. The first one brought to us soon died, but we put sugar in the formula we gave the next ones, feeding them from a ketchup bottle with a rubber teat, as I had learnt to do with the lambs on the farm in Somerset, and we reared them until old enough to return to the bush. We let them roam around untethered, and they would run in rings and high jumps around us when we took our evening strolls, showing no fear of us, but not allowing black skins to approach. Our household also gained two grey kittens from friends in Bauchi, which gave us a great deal of pleasure and amusement, and when Waller and Jean went on tour, as they did frequently, we would look after their big dog, Paddy, who became an ex-officio member of our family.

Chapter Twenty

Michael Alistair, Jos

The pattern of our life was soon to change unexpectedly and rather dramatically. Our baby, preliminarily called "Michaelizabeth", was due on 25th June, and we were so grateful for having been permanently appointed to Azare (at our own request) rather than the Sleeping Sickness team and Gombe as threatened, that we had hardly considered the position I was going to be in with no trained midwife nearer than Bauchi, 140 miles away, let alone a suitable hospital should there be any problems. There might not even be another European wife on the station by then.

The situation was saved by Robin's superior from Jos who was visiting us on tour, with his wife. Pat and Ada Binns were concerned at our situation and kindly invited me to stay with them in Jos for the last month of my pregnancy. It was decided that Robin would drive me there in the first week in June as he had to give evidence in a murder trial then, and he would return to fetch me back a few weeks after the birth when luckily there was another trial scheduled.

As it happened, nature took over and changed our plans precipitously on 31st May, which was a Saturday. We had been driven to sack Sule, the cook, the day before, and were being loaned a cook until Robin could hire another one in Jos. This day started with Monday forgetting to wake us with the usual morning cup of tea, so we overslept after another sticky and mostly sleepless night. Robin left in a rush for the hospital at 8.30 am, an hour late, and was not expected back until at least 10 a.m. for breakfast.

Around 9 a.m. I started to have contractions fairly regularly every three minutes, which soon became impossible to fob off as false labour, and I became more and more convinced that this was 'it'. I got busy packing suitcases for a protracted stay for me (it turned out to be six weeks) and Robin's Palm Beach suit for his court appearance, also getting the baby's few things together. Robin wandered in at 10.30am to be greeted with the urgent change of plans which, I considered, he took far too nonchalantly... perhaps he was in a state of shock. He suggested I have a good breakfast, which we both did, and he drove off afterwards to inform the D.O. and get shopping lists from him and the two ADO's, which took him until after midday. Meanwhile, Jean came across to help me with shutting up the house and briefing a bemused Monday on what was expected of him in my absence, and she was generally a calming influence.

After Robin returned to collect me we had two more ports of call, the PWD yard, to get petrol (hand-pumped from a drum), and then the hospital, to explain the situation to the Head Nurse, and persuade an orderly into pumping up our tyres. It seemed to be taking ages, and I was having serious doubts about getting all the way in time. It was just on 12.30pm when we left Azare on the six hour drive to the nearest European Hospital, 220 miles away in Jos, on a lonely, rough and corrugated laterite road, and as we started to roll out, I said, "But what if we don't make it in time? What about painkillers? We've nothing to cut the cord..." (In books they always needed boiling water, but I was not about to be fussy...). Robin reached out of the car and lifted some scissors from the bewildered nurse's pocket; " Mind if I borrow these?" And so we started on our way... but string to tie the cord... painkillers.... I had to put such concerns out of my mind; we were committed and now must just get on with it.

Robin put his foot down without stopping until we arrived in Bauchi and spent 20 minutes at Sister Peggy Blaize's, the government midwife. Here we ate a tin of pear puree, which was all the food we'd brought from our depleted larder, and had a drink. Peggy told us that our M.V.Apapa friend, Mary, had given birth to a premature baby girl, Caroline, the day before, in Bauchi. She was still under Peggy's care and would join me at the hospital in Jos tomorrow. How strange that our paths were still running so parallel!

Robin, Michael and me with our Standard Vanguard car, Azare 1952

Robin examined me and decided it should be safe to continue the eighty miles to Jos, but speedily, and it wasn't long before the pains started getting intense. The countryside was looking green and very different as we drove up Panshanu Pass, the rains having already started here, which diverted me a little, and the last few miles were speeded up by a bitumen road before we arrived in Jos around dark.

We now had to find the Plateau Hospital. After two false attempts, when we drove first into the Golf Club and then the Residency, I was by now reaching the point of no return, and urged my embarrassed driver to turn and put his foot down as the Resident himself appeared from the house to greet us, with a drink in his hand, and we realised that this was not the hospital either. Mercifully the hospital did turn up next and I was rushed straight into the labour room with no formalities. It was 7 p.m.; Dr Campion was doing his evening round, still in polo clothes, and examined me.

"Won't be long now. If you need me I'll be at the club, Sister." It was not customary for doctors to deliver normal births where there was a midwife.

After three more hours of hard labour, with the baby's head just visible, no progress had been made at all, and the baby's heart was failing, so Dr Campion was recalled (now in evening dress) and performed a forceps delivery under Pentathol. Michael was born at 10:35 pm. I was very disappointed at thus missing the birth and became very garrulous. I had espoused the Grantley Dick Read teachings on natural childbirth and had made up my mind I'd manage without an anaesthetic, or twilight sleep as it was called, which up to that point I had done.

I remember coming round and asking if the baby was O.K.

"Yes, my dear, its a little boy."

"Where is he? Is he all right?"

There was no sound and no sign of a baby; I was suspicious.

"We are just keeping him quiet; he needs to rest now."

"Where is he? I want to see him. Oh please, I MUST see him.... I won't believe you till I see him. "

And so I carried on until the sister produced a bassinet from behind a screen, with a tightly swaddled and battered looking little Michael. But he was breathing and alive and I was mollified. He weighed 5 lbs 3 oz. The excitement of the day and the Pentothal had made me very hyped up and I seem to remember gabbling non-stop to the sister about the day's events and finding sleep impossible.

But what of the new father? As was the custom in those days, Robin handed me in at the hospital with some relief that we'd made it in time, to put it mildly, and went off to find Dr and Mrs Binn's house. They, of course, were not yet expecting us and eventually Robin tracked them down to discover that they had moved house that very day, and were about to dine with friends, their loads still unpacked in the hall. Robin was fixed up with a meal of sorts by the Cook, and stayed by the phone, which eventually rang at around 10.45 p.m. with the glad tidings, before he turned in exhausted. Robin was just 24 then (I was 23) and it was many years later, after he had delivered many hundreds of babies, that he fully considered the risks that we'd taken that day, in the over-confidence of youth, and shuddered.

Two days later, June 2nd was our first wedding anniversary, and I was at the weepy stage, exhaustion having caught up along with feeding difficulties, lack of sleep and the prospect of Robin having to return to Azare without me. He came in early to the hospital with a lovely otter skin handbag for me, but then was so busy attending to the court business and shopping for the station all day, that I hardly had him to myself for a moment. The same the next day when he was tied up interviewing cooks. He eventually picked an Ibo called David, and set off with him back to Azare, the car laden almost to the ground, early on 4th.

I knew it would be some time before he could get news back to me of his safe arrival, and of course he had no means of receiving news about me and Michael until the following Wednesday's mail run at the earliest. A letter from him finally got through to me at its second attempt, on 15th June, having initially been returned to him after non-delivery at the Jos end!

He returned to Jos, on 5th July, to give evidence in another murder trial. He was not feeling well but determined to take Michael and me back home to Azare as soon as possible. We started on the long drive back on the 10th and I will quote my diary: -

"Robin's temperature down and he insisted on driving back to Azare as planned. Left with car piled high and the baby in carrycot perched on luggage behind the front seat. Stopped at friends in Bauchi to eat sandwiches and change baby etc for about 45 mins, then pressed on. Ran into terrible storm. Lightning all on and round us and the rain in such torrents that we couldn't see the edge of car's bonnet and had to stop every few yards. One time the engine stopped and it took about 20 minutes (and R. under the bonnet with baby's cotton wool) to coax it to start again.... so remote and I was scared lest we be stranded.

Michael very good and I fed him as we drove. Arrived at Azare just on dark to find house all shut up and musty. No sign of boys. Very depressing. Awful dust storm straight away and Robin had to go straight out and operate on Mike C.'s foot (touring PWD engineer). Still no rains here, very late apparently. Had trouble getting lamps to light. Feel very strange to be back in my own house. Robin has distempered the baby's room blue, and it looks very nice."

That was one of many sand storms we experienced that preceded the rains. Because the dry atmosphere, over months, had shrunk the timber door and window frames, the sand would blow in and infiltrate everything, even getting between the pages of our books, into drawers, cupboards, food and bedding.

Now a new chapter started for us all, and we remained there in Azare until Michael was about 11 months old. We started out with the minimum of equipment for him, just nappies, tiny singlets sent by Aunt Tryph and the vinyl carrycot with a hood we had brought out with us, making do as best we could. I now had a role which was centred around his survival, assisted only by a book on infant feeding mailed out by sister-in-law, Joan and later by a subscription to Nursery World by my other sister-in-law, Jean. I had never had anything to do with babies and believed firmly in breast-feeding, but when after three months Michael had seldom stopped crying and was failing to thrive we decided he needed to go on the bottle, at least as a supplement.

We sent to Jos for some tins of Cow and Gate Tropical formula, but when it arrived a couple of weeks later it was already three months out of date, so we sent in for more, stipulating FRESH tins. The use-by date of the next lot was the same so we had no choice but to start using it until we could latch onto a new shipment. But somehow we had unleashed a tidal wave of concern among our friends and acquaintances in Bauchi and Jos. These now outdid each other in their enthusiasm to keep Michael's nourishment flowing in, each taking such personal responsibility that I began to dread the sound of a motor approaching the house, knowing that a beaming engineer or touring officer of one sort or another had gone miles out of his way in order to thrust a box full of baby formula tins into my wilting arms. I would regale him with our bottomless supply of Nice biscuits and a cold drink, whilst expressing my thanks and reimbursing him, not daring to examine the tins until he had gone... and they were all more and more out of date.

One day I had just farewelled the bearer of more large tins, and was wondering how we were ever going to be able to turn off the flow, when a man rode up on horseback and removed a bulky parcel from his pannier. Oh NO... it was another two tins. I whisked the others off the table onto the floor behind the settee and went forward to greet him as the steward wearily appeared with more Nice biscuits and squash.

Eventually we must have reduced Jos's supply of Cow and Gate to the point where a cargo of fresh tins started to flow our way, and the message that we were saturated also filtered down the line. I don't think the stale milk powder did the baby any damage, and no doubt saved him from malnutrition, and certainly made us feel much less isolated through the kindness we were shown.

When Michael was eleven months the hottest season was on us again, and it was deemed sensible to dispatch us home to England to build me up for the next baby, due in September, although Robin still had 2 months to go before he could take home leave. Before we could leave the country, Michael had to have a yellow fever inoculation, which meant travelling to Jos and then waiting ten days or more for it to 'take' before being allowed to fly him out. We had a very interesting holiday on the Jos plateau, inexpensively accommodated in the veterinary research centre at Vom, and took the opportunity to have Michael christened by the Anglican missionary in Jos. Michael was more at ease with dark skins than white, and very wary of strangers, and he yelled and wriggled so strongly when held over the font that we all feared he would be ditched. However, the elderly priest gripped him tightly, returning him to me sobbing and deeply affronted.

Since we were to fly home from Kano, Robin drove us there from Jos via the lonely dry season road, which was absolutely terrible in places, crossing dried up river beds, occasional hidden gutters and traps of soft sand. We arrived in one piece, after rather too adventurous a trip for my liking, and spent the night at the Airport Hotel before taking the evening flight to

London next day. I felt desperately sad at having to leave Robin to make his lonely way back to Azare, knowing we would not be together for another two or three months. And it was his twenty fifth birthday!

Kano airport, with Michael, 1953

The four-engine Argonaut flew by night over the Sahara desert to avoid turbulence, the exhausts outside my porthole glowing disconcertingly red in the dark, often with flames shooting out. No-one else seemed concerned, so I settled down with Michael on my lap and tried to sleep. In the early hours of the morning, at Tripoli, we were all turned out of the plane during refuelling, then again in Rome, and I was assisted with Michael's carrycot by a very pleasant couple, who sat me down with a cup of coffee and asked me casually where I was going on arrival in London.

I told them, "To my parents-in-law, in Raynes Park",
They persisted..."Oh! Where in Raynes Park?"
"A cul de sac, Coombe Gardens..."

"Really! What number?"

"Twenty nine," I said, rather surprised at their interest.

"Goodness me! How amazing... that was our house and we sold it before we came out to Nigeria with the police force."

It made me wonder how many other such coincidences we never discover, but are going on all around us just the same.

On arrival in London I was amazed at how out of touch I was, and how fast and noisy everything seemed. Crossing the road was a terrifying experience and I would hesitate on the kerb for ages. I also had to get used to shopping and ration books again. I had told Robin (jokingly I thought) that this time I was going to spend the last six weeks of the pregnancy "on the steps of a maternity hospital" in case this baby arrived early as Michael had done, and amazingly, that is exactly how it worked out... but that's Peter's story.

Chapter Twenty One

Peter Andrew, Kano

1953 was altogether a remarkable year. In May Mt Everest was climbed for the first time by Edmund Hilary and Sherpa Tensing. The news came through just before the coronation of Queen Elizabeth II on 2nd June, with its display of pageantry, colour and public excitement that had not been seen for decades. This day, spent glued to the radio, was also the day of our second wedding anniversary, but Robin was still in Azare, and I was staying with my parents in their little thatched cottage near Stogursey in Somerset. England still had food ration books, but otherwise I felt a new enthusiasm and energy returning in the people.

Two days earlier we had celebrated Michael's first birthday and now I was awaiting the birth of our second child in September. At last I met Tony's wife, Jean, who joined us for a week or two, also expecting a baby later in the year. They had been married while we were in Azare, and I had been longing to meet my new sister-in-law as we had plenty of catching up to do.

A serendipitous set of circumstances now developed as Robin's brother Tony, Joan and toddler Christopher moved into the house of a friend, temporarily overseas, and offered us their flat in New Cavendish Street, just behind the Middlesex Hospital, for three months. Nothing could have suited us better as the baby was due at the end of September and I felt my half-joking remark to Robin had truly been prophetic. Michael and I moved in shortly before Robin returned in July, after he'd spent a few days in Malta en route, and the flat was small and cosy and very convenient for us. Robin managed to get locum work at the Middlesex, and Joan lent me Christopher's pram, which was a great help. I was really enjoying being an English mother and housewife and pushing the pram around the park; so much better than dolls!

Because Michael had arrived so early, I was half expecting the next baby to do the same, and hoped "it" might share my birthday on August 30th. But this day came and went, and the next one too. There were still three weeks to go, so we settled down again to wait. On the first day of Autumn, Tuesday September 1st, Lizzett and her mother came to visit and have supper with us, and we had purposely made it early as they were going on to the theatre. I had been so looking forward to seeing them, and showing off our little son, but around 5 p.m. I started to get strong internal messages that Peter, or was it Diana, was awake and desiring to join the party. I managed to bath Michael and get him to bed and farewell our friends without giving them any hint of what was afoot. I suppose it was a mixture of modesty and pride that kept my mouth shut, anyhow we threw a tooth brush and some nighties into a bag, closed the door on the sleeping big brother, just 15 months old, and Robin walked with me around the corner to the hospital at 8.pm. The baby, who turned out to be Peter, was born around 10 p.m., weighing 6 lbs 11oz, and my bed was wheeled to a phone so that I could ring Robin myself. He then rang Lizzett's father, who conveyed the news to the surprised theatre-goers on their return.

Mothers were kept in hospital for 10 days in those days, until breast-feeding was well established, insides settled down, circumcisions done and the mother given a good rest. In the days when housework was harder work and much more time-consuming, this time-out was very welcome. Soon after my discharge Tony and Joan needed their flat back and we soon found that long leave spent trailing around with two babies, imposing ourselves on family members, however loving, was no fun at all, in fact a big strain on us as well as our hosts. Robin decided that we would be better off on our own in warmer Malta.

Accordingly he booked rooms in the Tigne Court Hotel, Sliema, and we flew out of a very foggy Heathrow early in November.

The previous two days we had spent hours weighing all our baggage to try to keep it within the allowance, regretfully discarding one thing after another. Since we had everything with us for the next eighteen months, trying to anticipate the babies' growing needs, we were grossly over the baggage limit. This was made worse by my keenness to include a number of bottles of concentrated orange juice, issued free to British babies, but not available in Nigeria, and also boxes of .22 ammunition for Robin's rifle.

In the end we hit upon the idea of spreading the bottles of orange and the ammunition on the floor of the vinyl carrycot and covering it with bedding, nappies and then the baby. This looked fine, with tiny Peter bundled up in winter shawls and all kept in place under the rain apron. What nearly gave the game away was the expression on the face of an unsuspecting porter at the airport next day, who grabbed a suitcase in one hand and the carrycot handles in the other and nearly fell over when it wouldn't leave the ground!

This was to be one of those unbelievably long days. After a 5am start, we caught a taxi to London Airport in thick fog, only to have some hours delay waiting for it to lift before we eventually took off at 9am. Our Elizabethan Ambassador dropped in at Nice and then Rome. Here we waited around on the ground before transferring to a shabby old Viking, which ambled down the coast of Italy like a local bus, stopping at Naples for a while before eventually landing us in Malta around twelve hours after we had left Heathrow... very, very weary! This very basic aircraft provided little to make a nursing mother's task easier, and modesty dictated that I had to sit on the uncovered and very draughty toilet to feed the baby, the Italian countryside clearly visible beneath me through the stuck-open hole when I arose! Nappies for the two of them were similarly changed on my lap and I soon had a big swag of wet and soiled ones. No disposables in those days.

Michael had behaved stoically during most of the long day, dozing across our laps or watching the propellers whirr, and been fairly easy to keep entertained. Peter slept a fair bit in his carrycot, which occupied all the floor space at our feet, necessitating contortions on our part to find a parking position for our legs. Unfortunately both decided they had had enough when earache indicated we had begun the final descent into Malta. Michael needed changing (again) having developed diarrhoea, and escaped from our grasp to run up and down the customs counter drawing attention away from the carrycot, which suited us fine... we'd been worrying about it all day! The customs officer waved us through peremptorily and we loaded all aboard a taxi for the hotel.

Our arrival had been expected some hours earlier, but the manager indicated that a cold meal had been left for us in the dining room, which was otherwise closed. We decided I would get the babies fed and hopefully settled down to sleep, whilst Robin had his meal, and then I would go down and eat when he returned. All went well. Robin found the meal laid out and got hold of a bottle of wine. On his return he warned me that the Maltese water was too full of minerals to be drinkable, and by the time I had found the dining room and sat down to eat I was enormously thirsty and downed a tumbler of wine unthinkingly. Alas, the exhaustion of the day, coupled with half a bottle of wine on an empty stomach, had a disastrous effect, and after eating I spent the next half hour wandering unsteadily up and down the empty corridors trying to remember where our room was, until Robin became worried and set out in search of me.

We enjoyed our holiday in Malta, particularly so as Tony's ship was in port and we were able to meet for a meal and celebrate the glad tidings of his daughter Caroline Jean's safe arrival on 17th November, but after a couple of weeks it was time to return to Nigeria and get back to work, first catching a plane to Tripoli in Libya. Our connection from Tripoli to Kano would not depart until after midnight so the airline had booked us into a rather grand hotel in the meantime. We made ourselves at home, lunched and fed the baby and did a little tentative exploring outside before looking into the question of Michael's evening meal. The marble halls of the hotel led into a casino, decidedly unsuitable for a sticky toddler, so we ordered room service, intending to give Michael a soft boiled egg and bread and butter, with a drink of milk. The waiter spoke no English and we spoke no Italian, so Robin went into pantomime mode, clucked, turned red in the face, and formed a circle with his thumb and middle finger, indicating that this was to be brought for the child. The waiter departed with a puzzled look, "Si, si."... and returned shortly with a cold, uncooked egg.

Robin tried again, pointing to his watch and counting off four fingers to indicate minutes. Meanwhile I tried to get across that we would also require bread and milk. This attempt was a little more fruitful, in fact much more as a slice of fruit-cake accompanied a now tepid, runny egg and a can of Pepsi Cola. At this stage we admitted defeat, and Michael, who by this time had developed a cough and was not hungry, was offered this rather unorthodox supper.

Our room had a very well appointed bathroom and I unwisely flushed some soiled paper wadding, which I had used for nappy lining during travel, down the ornate Italian W.C. The water rushed into the bowl and rose and rose... and rose. It kept rising... over the top, onto the floor, over to the door... this was clearly developing into an emergency. I had all the towels on the floor, trying to control the flood and divert it from flowing onto the bedroom carpet, Michael shivering in the bath, wide-eyed peering over the side at his panicking parents, yelling directives at each other, running hither and thither and peering down the lavatory uselessly. After a while Robin ran out to the corridor and found a maid, who took a quick look and fetched a footman, who rolled up his sleeves, dug deep and fished out the offending wad of paper with a flourish. Had he done that before, I wondered? If there had been accompanying music it would have been The Sorcerer's Apprentice! The lesson I learnt is that Italian plumbing has very narrow pipes.

With Peter, Kano, 1954

The babies were eventually settled and we managed a few hours of rest on the bed before it was all go-go-go again, cramming into a taxi with all our luggage for the drive out of town to the airport, the heavy carrycot across our laps, and now accompanied by a thunder storm that was gaining momentum by the minute. At the airport the baby started crying, so I left Robin and Michael with our bags in the draughty waiting area and withdrew to the Ladies Room to perch uncomfortably as I changed and fed him. He seemed fretful and I was worried that he had caught Michael's cold and was getting really sick when the electricity failed and we were plunged into total darkness.

First thoughts of sitting it out until light was restored were soon abandoned. I bundled everything together and clutching the baby tightly to me, groped my way out of the pitch darkness and back into the draughty holding area, half a step at a time, uncertain as to who I might encounter and with my heart beating overtime. Flashes of lightning and dull lighting helped me back to where Robin and Michael were anxiously watching out for me, and in due course we climbed aboard the plane for the flight across the Sahara to Kano, bone weary after another long day.

December is in the dry season in northern Nigeria, very hot by day but with crisp, cool nights and the air dust-laden from the Harmattan. We touched down the next morning and checked in at the Airport Hotel, which was a form of large catering rest house. Peter, ten weeks old, now had a chest infection bordering on pneumonia and the intensely dry air was not helping his breathing. Robin went off for some penicillin and we rigged up a kerosene stove with a pan of water constantly on the boil near his cot, to humidify the air a little.

This tour Robin was appointed to Kano hospital and we were relieved to be allotted a brand new bungalow which had running water and electricity, set in a very large, though totally bare and unfenced compound outside the old city. As soon as we could we located our loads and the Standard Vanguard from the government store and moved in, very relieved when Ali, the last of our Azare stewards, turned up and wanted to continue in the job. There was a snag with this house site however, which did not show up until the rains came in July and submerged the whole area. A line of these bungalows had thoughtlessly been built in the dry season on a swamp, and although the water did not enter the houses, the compounds were all awash and filled with leeches and other interesting fauna and we had to paddle out to the car parked eighty or more yards away on the road. Going out at night, Robin would give me his shoes, socks and trousers, then carry me to the car where he would dry off and squirm back into his clothes.

Another snag was that, being on the very edge of the city, and outside the old city walls, we were but a few hundred yards from a village, just out of sight through the bush behind the house, and the traditional right of way came through our garden and past our bedroom window. At weekends it was impossible to sleep because of the drums beating into the early hours, and thieves trying to break into the house were an ever-present challenge. The bungalow was equipped with the usual expanded metal over the windows, but an arm could reach inside through the gap left for the window latch, especially if equipped with a hook, and we learnt to park our belongings well clear. The children had a set of graduated tins, painted with nursery rhymes scenes, which fitted into each other. These made a most efficient burglar alarm when piled onto the handle of a spade, which had been wedged under the pantry door-knob. This was the preferred port of entry for thieves at night, and we quite often heard the tins crashing down onto the cement floor of the pantry followed by fast departing footsteps.

Our most dramatic thief experience was in the early hours one morning. In bright moonlight, Robin noticed a prowler creeping around our neighbour's house, about a hundred yards away. Taking his .22 rifle from beside the bed, Robin crept out and started across the compound to challenge him. The prowler saw him coming and started running away, whereupon Robin fired two shots into the air to hasten his steps, their echoes ricocheting between the houses. Next door, our neighbour, John, had also seen the would-be thief, and was creeping about inside the house ready to pounce if he gained entry... John was a big fellow! He nearly jumped out of his skin when war broke out, and so did I, still asleep until that moment, and very alarmed when I discovered an empty pillow at my side, not knowing who was shooting at who.

Another night, a friend in transit was sleeping in our dining room when he was woken by an arm reaching through the latch hole in the expanded metal grabbing his clothes from a chair. Ken hit out hard and managed to grab his belongings before they disappeared in front of his eyes. He was quite shaken. After that we made sure that nothing loose was placed near an open window within reach of a stick with a hook on it, which was another trick.

Life in Kano proved to be a great deal easier for me than in Azare, and we made some lifelong friends, especially the radiologist and his wife, John and Marie Chartres, our next door neighbours, John and Pat Duerdon, who had a toddler too, and the specialist physician, Eric Beet and his wife Marguerite. During the course of this tour we had many reasons to be grateful to these three couples, without whose help we would have been sunk, as well as forming enduring friendships.

My life once again revolved around the need to find reliable and reasonably hygienic house-boys. Ali did not stay long and was replaced by Sule, Isa, then Ahmadu the Small Boy. My diary for Saturday 6th February says "Isa's half day; Ahmadu has d & v (diarrhoea and vomiting); Musa (cook) says he's going to Chinade for a week to bury his brother. Isa says he must leave us next Saturday. Heigh-ho!"

The cook's position was initially filled by quite a treasure. Musa was elderly and had a gammy leg and we were very fortunate that he was the closest thing we had had to a real cook, producing edible food on the whole, including a fancy line in deserts which always featured raw egg whites whipped with sugar, spread over the top of a pie or cold custard like uncooked meringue. I felt reasonably confident that a dinner party would be edible, served reasonably on time and not unattractive and we were now able to entertain in modest style and enjoy some social life. Much of this was entertaining a continuous stream of acquaintances from our first tour, now passing through Kano to or from home leave, or on local leave.

Three days after Musa's departure to bury his brother, my diary reads, "Our temporary cook is hopeless, and we wonder how we will ever survive till Musa returns." Fate interceded on our behalf when Robin, returning from the hospital a few nights later, came upon our locum cook, lying with a broken leg by the roadside, having been run over while intoxicated. Robin organised his transfer to hospital and subsequent treatment, not getting home until 1am. We then tried a succession of incompetent replacements. After two weeks Musa returned and took over again from the locum, and I breathed a sigh of relief, only to be told that Ahmadu, who had done so well on promotion to steward after Isa's departure, had abandoned his uniform and disappeared. It seems he was "vexed" because I had threatened to start fining him for all the breakages that were occurring, unless he were more careful. The next steward was to be Dan Karami and then Habu, but after many false starts we eventually found a delightful steward called Dogo (pictured),

who was to stay with us for the next three years until we left Nigeria. He was gentle and honest and very sweet with the children.

I managed to buy a two-burner kerosene stove with a little oven and cooked the children's meals myself in the pantry, and after Musa eventually moved on I soon decided to dispense with a cook altogether. This decision was accelerated by a horrible day when the cookhouse chimney caught fire, the stove having been stoked too much and then deserted by the current incompetent. Thank goodness, being a doctor's house we had a phone, and with Peter on my hip and Michael clutching my skirt, I rang the Fire Brigade, issuing instructions in simple language as to how to find the house (the smoke and flames should have helped). The primitive fire tanker was actually kept quite a short distance away along our road, which was flat and bordered the racecourse, so directions were easy and after some time I heard the bell approaching. The house was set back some way from the road, and as I ran out waving, the firemen sailed past and disappeared into the distance, energetically clanging the bell, eyes fixed straight ahead.

In the interim I had done all I could to dampen the fire, and flames were no longer shooting out of the chimney, but there was still plenty of smoke and a blackened cookhouse by the time the firefighters eventually back-tracked and swept into the drive, ready to save the day. They seemed disappointed that the house was not burning down and it was all over bar the clean-

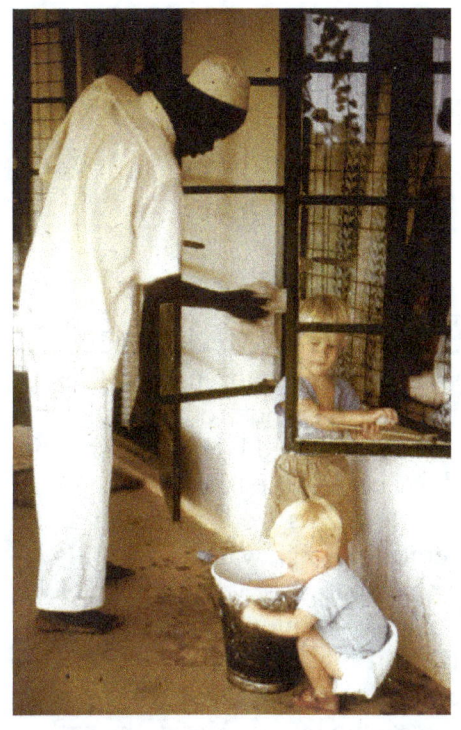

Steward Dogo with Michael & Peter, Kano 1954

ing up, and swarmed over the place with hose at the ready just in case.

As far as I was concerned, regularly cooking out in the cookhouse was out of the question as for one thing the heat became intolerable. When the air temperature was already well over the century at certain times of the year, the sweat would pour down my legs and arms in streams; also, with the burning wood sticking half out of the fire box it was no place for the children. On the other hand, bread could be bought locally, as could cold stores, and I need not be so dependent on the market, which was all so much easier than Azare had been. So I started to do without a cook and never looked back.

Michael and Peter, Kano, 1954

Chapter Twenty Two

Hepatitis A and Kaduna

Some months before this, Michael's second birthday had come round and we had a party with half a dozen small friends, and on September 1st we had a few friends round for Peter's first birthday. As the afternoon progressed I developed a splitting headache, and was glad to farewell the last guest and take a couple of aspirins. The next few days were no better and I started running a high temperature. Robin was not sure if I was incubating Typhoid or Infective Hepatitis or what, until a blood test proved it was Hepatitis 'A'. I was removed to the European Nursing Home and kept there in bed for a month, very sick and very yellow, unable to eat and too weak to lift a finger. Our wonderful friends came to the rescue by day, Marie, the wife of the radiologist, taking Michael, and our neighbour Pat, taking Peter. At night they would be returned home, and Dogo proved what a treasure he was by helping Robin cope. I've forgotten who was doing the cooking at this stage, as my diary is blank for those weeks.

This hepatitis had probably been caught from a friend who had been hospitalised with it a few weeks earlier and I had cared for her little son as they were in transit. Some weeks after my illness, Pat became ill, and turned very yellow and she had obviously contracted it from me. Luckily or unluckily, Pat was not ill enough to be hospitalised, though rest is what is needed, and fortunately her mother-in-law was visiting from England and helped with Pat's own toddler. I was home by then but barely strong enough to cope with getting up in the morning and caring for my own children, without being able to offer assistance, and I felt rather bad about this after all the help she had given me. Luckily Pat recovered, but Hepatitis A does need to be taken seriously and she too remained very jaundiced for months.

Health was always a problem in Nigeria, and Robin had earlier said that if any of us became seriously ill he would send us straight home as soon as we could travel. Nigeria had a reputation of being the 'white man's grave' though anti-malarials, and Smallpox and Yellow Fever vaccinations, had reduced the danger considerably. When faced with my convalescence in practice, Robin was not so keen to ship me back to my parents looking so thin and pale, feeling sensitive that he might be criticised for having taken the babies and me to Nigeria in the first place!

When Peter was still in nappies, he developed a couple of large, hard boils on his buttocks. Robin was very puzzled and on examining them closely thought he detected movement in the crater of one of them. To Peter's intense disapproval he applied pressure on either side and out popped a large Tumbu fly lava. We were horrified, and research came up with the information that on a still day these large flies may lay their eggs on the washing hanging on the line. The attached eggs will hatch out in the warm, moist environment of a towelling nappy and the larvae burrow under the skin of the baby, causing an abscess. Poor little baby! A hot iron was used on all the nappies from then on and we had no more trouble.

Two other problems with the children made us very grateful that we were in Kano, with access to specialist treatment. Michael had a mild squint and we were able to take him to the Sudan Interior Mission Eye Hospital where an American ophthalmologist prescribed atropine drops, which were put into the good eye to dilate the pupil and make the other eye work harder. These would wear off after about ten days, and were followed by ten days of normal use before the drops were inserted again. These were very much more practical for such a small child than spectacles and patches, and his eye straightened out perfectly during the year we were in Kano.

A rather bigger problem was that Peter had been born with mild talipes equino varus, or club-foot, in both feet. From the day after his birth I was taught to mould his feet with my hand when I was nursing him, and this I did automatically, but more was going to be needed, and when he started trying to walk, his little toes would curl in and he would tumble over. Luckily there was an orthopaedic surgeon at the hospital, and he showed us how to hold the foot whilst we applied plaster of Paris up to below the knee. As Peter was growing so fast, we had to renew it every few weeks, and after straightening out the worst foot we started on the other one. Peter accepted all this very patiently and after about six months both feet appeared normal. He grew up to be a fast runner and keen sportsman without any apparent after effects.

At the end of that year Robin was told to transfer to Kaduna, the capital of the Northern Region. This housed the par-

liament of the Northern Region, as well as many government departments. It had shady avenues of trees and some of the original European's houses built in the north around 1902. We were fortunate to be given the oldest of these and we were told it had belonged to Lord Lugard himself. This airy, two-storey, black and white timber house (pictured) was in a large, shady compound, with two entrances connected by a sweeping drive lined with big flowering poincianas. At the back, another drive swept round to the European nursing home and this was lined with frangipani trees. Mango trees cast their heavy shade near the house, under which I would park Peter's pram for his afternoon nap.

When we first moved in, we found a little tabby cat came with the deal. She was very shy and always slept on the roof of our double mosquito net. This was not a Good Idea as she made holes as she scrambled up, which let in the mosquitoes, and it made us feel uncomfortable to know she was suspended, dangling above our heads, until we got used to it and sat up slowly in the dark to avoid collision. There was no reasoning with her. Cats usually went with the house. In Ibadan, later, we inherited a gorgeous ginger fellow called Pumpkin.

Dogo remained my sole helper, and I continued to cook on the paraffin stove, enjoying the freedom from hassles caused by a number of house-boys, when each tends to blame the others for breakages and missing property or food. I was still not feeling well, and ran high fevers, but there seemed nothing much we could do about it. I couldn't face the social life, and would retire to bed as soon as I had settled the children, leaving Robin to attend the official functions and drinks parties we were invited to, and try to make an excuse for me.

Part of Robin's job was to look after the health of the Europeans, and he had the honour of removing the appendix of our friend Rosemary from Azare days. However, his main work was in the Kaduna Public Hospital, where it was his bad luck to walk in at the start of the annual smallpox epidemic. This year, 1955, it was a very bad one, and when it was discovered that patients were catching the disease from the hospital, where it had to be differentiated from a chicken pox epidemic also rife, it was decided to isolate them in a special camp outside the town. Here palm shacks were erected, and the unfortunate patients nursed on mats on the ground, with just a red blanket for cover. Hyenas were a constant menace to be watched out for, as they were quite capable of dragging off recumbent children.

Robin had previously dealt with a smallpox epidemic in Azare, which had coincided with Michael's primary vaccination not taking until about the fifth attempt. Presumably he had immunity from me, but we knew this would soon wear off, and we had not been able to rest easily until he produced a local reaction and we knew he was safe from any infection Robin might bring home. Both babies also had to have yellow fever inoculations at a tender age, and of course we all had to take daily Paludrine, the very bitter anti-malarial. I found that the only fairly sure way to get this little half tablet down them was to add it to a handful of Dolly Mixture, which I gave them in their cots at afternoon sleep time. It seemed better to risk rotten teeth than malaria, but I added drops of fluoride to the drinking water long before it became widely practised and their teeth have remained strong.

Smallpox camp hospital, Kaduna 1955

It was decided that I should return home with the boys in March, three months before Robin's leave was due. I was now under eight stone, and badly needed a change of climate and building up generally, so Robin drove us to Kano and this time waved three of us off on the evening plane back to London. Michael was thirty-four months old and Peter nineteen months, and we were met in London by Tony and Jean and seventeen month old Caroline. They whisked us into a taxi and to a Kensington Hotel, where we eventually managed to stop shivering by piling into bed with all our clothes on.

I learnt what it means when they say "the wind cut like a knife" later that night, when we had fed and bathed the three children and left them sleeping before we went out to find a restaurant. A few yards walk along the street and I became virtually paralysed with the cold and could not take another step. Tony and Jean frog-marched me back inside, bundled me into every vestige of clothing either of us had, and then rushed me out and into the first basement restaurant we passed, where they thawed me out with a long brandy and ginger.

Next day the children and I took the train to Somerset, and my father met us and took us home to their tiny cottage. Mother was not here at this time, having had to be admitted to hospital with another breakdown, and Father valiantly gritted his teeth at this invasion of his peaceful and orderly home and was his usual gracious self. It was not an easy time for any of us but by the time Robin joined us my health had improved dramatically, and we were very happy to be together again as a family.

Since Robin had now finished the stipulated two tours in Nigeria, each of eighteen months, we were free to work anywhere we chose. Robin decided that he would follow a career in surgery, having gained such valuable experience already, and he was successful in gaining an appointment as lecturer in Anatomy in the University of Ibadan, Western Nigeria. This would give him time to study for the Primary exam of the Fellowship of the Royal College of Surgeons, London. It was disappointing that Dick and Pat had left Ibadan and were working in Calcutta, where Dick was a W.H.O professor.

We now had a few months leave to fill in until it was time to drive to Liverpool and once again embark for Lagos in the good ship Apapa, and this time we avoided foisting ourselves on relatives. Robin worked as a locum for a G.P. in Devon which gave the family a pleasant seaside holiday for a couple of weeks, Nigerian friends lent us their house in Oxford, we rented a house in Wiltshire for two weeks and finally spent two difficult weeks with Granny Hebb, who wanted us there, but found it difficult to adjust to having the two lively little boys around. For Robin and me, these long leaves were not restful holidays at all, though it was quite therapeutic for us to be in a temperate climate and my health was always restored dramatically.

I had the feeling that the pattern of my life, being Thursday's child, would never change and was now affecting the next generation too. 'Home' was a movable concept for the boys and was seemingly located wherever I happened to unpack our bags for a few days. Michael was not yet three and a half, and we had already had three 'permanent' addresses in Nigeria, and moved around up to a dozen locations when on long leaves in the U.K. This was no way to provide the children with a secure foundation, and I could see history being repeated, but was helpless to alter the pattern.

We now decided to change our anti-malarial medication to Daraprim, a single tablet of which was taken once a week instead of the daily Paludrine. I had no more problems with morning nausea, seasickness or fits of vomiting....If only we'd done this years ago! We actually enjoyed the two weeks voyage with the children, and it was a relief not to have any domestic duties for a change. This time we were much more relaxed than on our previous voyage out, having more realistic expectations of what lay ahead of us, and I was very positively looking forward to establishing a home of our own again.

Chapter Twenty Three

Ibadan University.

We sailed into Lagos for the second time in September 1955 and were met by an African driver from the University of Ibadan who drove us the 120 or so miles to find our new home. This time it was the wet season; we arrived in the dark with rain deluging down, and it took him some time to identify our allotted bungalow (pictured) on the campus. Our loads and Dogo had hopefully been sent down from Kaduna and would have to be located next day, but in the meantime we had very damp beds, with the usual musty kapok mattresses but no bedding, and the continuous heavy rain and tropical smell made it all rather bleak.

Not wanting the boys to lie on damp mattresses, I spread out our raincoats and cotton dressing gowns. We were all sweating profusely and it was far too hot to need any covering.

Somebody had kindly left a box of basics in the kitchen; a loaf of bread, cereal, milk powder and tea, and we made the best of it and tried to settle down to sleep in this new tropical environment, with frogs and cicadas and the drumming of rain providing constant background noise. Next day everything improved, with a sunny morning sending steam up from the gardens around us, and birds, cicadas and frogs filling the air with their conversation. We gradually met our neighbours, mostly expatriates employed in the university as lecturers or administrators, and very friendly. One family was Dutch, one English like us, two others from New Zealand, and there were four or five school-age children.

Eventually our loads caught up with us, but we were in some difficulty without a house-boy as there was no sign of Dogo. Before leaving Kaduna Robin had told him where and when to meet us and given him the fare. He had seemed keen to carry on with us at the time. We hunted around the likely places that he might be, and began to fear we would have to find another steward. After more than a week... a very difficult week for me, domestically, word filtered through to us that someone was inquiring for Robin at the Hospital, and had been there for days.

Poor Dogo had not grasped that Robin was not in Ibadan to work as a doctor, but was now a lecturer at the University. We were so glad to see him again, and were able to provide him with a marvellous piece of equipment such as he'd never dreamed of. This was an elderly, non-automatic electric washing machine with a little hand-powered mangle attached, discarded by Robin's stepmother when she upgraded, and which we had shipped out with us. We installed this in the bathroom, and Dogo would preside over the washing with a huge grin of pride and enjoyment.

Once again I was able to cope without any additional houseboys, except for a part-time garden boy to wield a langa langa over the grass (the African, very labour-intensive, equivalent of a lawn mower). This bungalow had an electric cooker and running water and had been mosquito-proofed down the bedroom end, so we could dispense with stuffy mosquito nets.

The academic year we spent in Ibadan was particularly enjoyable for me, as there was so much going on, in a cultural sense that made life full and fun. Robin's reason for taking this job was to have opportunity to study for his higher surgical qualification, and to this end he liked to be left in peace at night with his books, leaving me free to have outside interests once the children were settled. There was a very active music group to which I was attracted, and it was decided to put on Gilbert and Sullivan's 'Mikado'. It was an unusual and quite ambitious production and I landed the part of Petti-Sing, one of the 'three little maids'. Robin joined in the actual performances, playing timpani in the orchestra. After that we started rehearsing for Humperdink's 'Hansel and Gretel' and gave a concert of Handel's 'Judas Maccabeus'. The solos were farmed out among those able to sing them, but unfortunately a bout of 'flu' hit just before the performance and the solos had to be hastily re-designated, with me having to practice up two additional ones, in between crouching over a steaming bowl of menthol and eucalyptus inhalation.

Just up our road was 'the club' with a swimming pool where we would take the boys each evening. They soon got the hang of swimming under water, until fished out when we judged their air supply might need replenishing, and Peter was particularly buoyant. Our road was a cul de sac, with virtually no traffic, so very safe for the children living there. We were all university families and the wives swapped recipes and visited each other and we all got on fine.

A big excitement of that year was the visit to Nigeria of Queen Elizabeth and Prince Philip who came to the University and drove around the town. We stood by the roadside as they drove by, and the Duke turned round specially to wave to Michael and Peter in our arms, waving excitedly. There was some local disappointment that the queen did not wear her crown when driving around, but she did wear a tiara for the formal reception at the University.

Dysentery of one form or another was a constant threat, and both children came down with a virulent form shortly before the end of our tour. This confirmed for us that it was time to return to a safer environment and cut our ties once again, so at the end of our year in Ibadan we sold most of our gear, and all flew back to England together.

Much thought and energy was already being applied by the British to prepare the Nigerian civil service to take over the reins of government before Independence in 1960. However, we could not anticipate how devastatingly the peace that we experienced in the 50's would be shattered within a decade. Tribal and religious animosities resulted in the Biafran War of 1967 and have continued sporadically to this present time. Undoubtedly we saw Nigeria at its best, and we are very grateful for our store of remarkable memories from the four and a half years we were privileged to live and serve in that colourful and vibrant country.

Chapter Twenty Four

John Anthony, England

Robin had lined up an appointment as casualty Registrar at Nottingham General Hospital, and so, in September 1956, we found ourselves relocated to the suburb of Aspley, in a semi-detached, dingy, dowdily furnished, two bedrooms plus a box room, rented house, overlooked by passing trains and in a cultural and social desert. This was a rude shock after Ibadan, and I missed the warm climate, blue skies, friendly neighbours, presence of Robin every night, domestic help and interesting cultural and social activities. Here our neighbours on both sides were almost totally invisible as they went out to work all day and had no children. In a full year in Aspley I went into another house only once, and made no friends apart from occasionally meeting some of Robin's colleagues, but since they were also temporary residents, mostly single Indians, there was little socialising. This was undoubtedly the bleakest period of my married life and memories of discomforts and hardships experienced in Nigeria faded as I looked back nostalgically to the pleasant company and cheerful blue skies of our last year there.

Robin worked long hours at the hospital, and had to remain there for two out of three nights as he was on duty one night, on call the next, but we had no phone. We had to keep to a very strict budget so Robin bought a second hand bicycle, with a little motor which could be clicked onto the rear wheel, keeping our small Ford Escort panel van for shopping and weekend exploring when he had time off.

Peter was very interested in Robin Hood, and we had some excursions to Sherwood Forest (rather disappointing) and Nottingham castle, and I made him a set of Robin Hood clothes for Christmas. Robin's boss was the Sheriff of Nottingham at that time, and we were invited to a glittering annual ball for which I made myself a long gown out of beautiful gold damask with a cloak of silver damask, which Tony had brought back from a trip to Damascus. The cloak had a pale blue lining, with a white fur collar, which came from one of Father's rabbits. (He was a great one for breeding rabbits, chickens, geese, ducks and anything he could fit into his current garden as well as the vegetables!) Sadly, although they were the loveliest fabrics I have ever handled, I don't remember ever having occasion to wear either of them again such was the pattern of my life.

Michael & Peter with Grandpa Fletcher, 1957

Strangely, years later I was to discover that my Fletcher ancestors had come from Nottingham, before three generations in the armed services broke the mould. We did know that Robin's grandfather's family (Hebbs) came from Nottingham and his great-aunt still lived there. If only we had been interested in family history when we actually lived there, we might have discovered our common roots decades earlier.

Apart from the days that Robin could get off, the two little boys, now three and four, and unused to the confined life of a damp English winter, were my only companions. As well as learning new skills, such as how to clean the flue (when the coal fire refused to give off anything but smoke) and whiten the doorstep (having noticed after a few weeks that mine was the only grey one in the street) and so on... I was hard put to find enough ways to keep the children amused.

It is not easy controlling small, bored children stuck indoors in some-one else's cramped, poorly furnished home, and I had to insist on the strict rules that had been applied to myself as a child under similar circumstances. One of them was in a rebellious mood one day, and I had to watch as he applied a crayon to the wallpaper at the top of the stairs, and held it firmly there in a wavy line until he had reached his exploding mother at the bottom. That little indelible artwork cost us dearly when we moved out at the end of the year, but how can you get this across to pre-schoolers? I began to appreciate my mother's difficulties a little more.

One day Robin staggered in with an upright wooden box which he placed on the sitting room floor; our first T.V! It was black and white and had only one station, but for us it was wonderful. He had acquired it for ten pounds. Now we could watch the adventures of The Lone Ranger and Tonto, Andy Pandy, Bill and Ben the Flower Pot Men, Sooty and Sweep the glove puppets, Larry the lamb in Toy Town and other wonderful friends.

When Robin's year at Nottingham General was nearly up, he looked around for the next job. He had attained the Primary F.R.C.S. which involved exams in advanced anatomy and so on, and now needed to fulfill certain practical requirements, working under a consultant surgeon in a specified hospital, before attempting the finals. A suitable position came up that also offered a house, and we moved to Blackhill near Consett, on the Northumberland border not far from Newcastle-on-Tyne, and Robin spent the next eighteen months as surgical registrar at Shotley Bridge Hospital.

Our allotted house turned out to be another standard red brick, semi-detached, two and a half bedroom affair, but this time in the middle of a row of council houses. Although it offered the same facilities as the Aspley house, and we approached it with some misgiving, this next period in our family life is looked back on by us both as about the happiest of any we've known. The difference lay mainly in the friendliness of the neighbours and in the fact that we were able to install a phone, so that Robin came home every night.

This house was furnished by the hospital, quite adequately, and had a scullery off the kitchen, where I installed the much-travelled washing machine. In bad weather damp clothes were dried off on rails pulled up to the kitchen ceiling by a pulley, the moist warm air condensing on the ice-cold windows that ran with water. The square iron range in the kitchen, with two hot plates, was heated through the wall by an open coal fire in the sitting room, which had to be stoked all the time if any cooking was to be accomplished, and required much flue-cleaning to stop it clogging up with soot. I seem to remember it heated the bath water too.

Peter, Robin, myself and Michael at Muggleswicks Moors, 1958

The north country winter brought heavy snow, and Michael and Peter had great fun tobogganing down our hill in tandem. We had regular drives over the moors and to the Kielder Forest, and now the boys were old enough to enjoy exploring the countryside with us we had some memorable drives to places like Hadrian's Wall and Blanchlands. We had become more acclimatised to the English winters, but I never got used to my washing freezing into stiff boards on the clothes line, necessitating me retiring indoors every few minutes to thaw out my frozen fingers when hanging up or removing clothes from the line, or having to chip my little dish-mop off the scullery window-sill where it was iced up each morning. When the Nor'easter was blowing a gale the roof creaked and groaned as if it was a sailing ship in a storm, and scared the boys in bed at night in case it blew off.

There were a number of Indian doctors at this hospital with whom Robin became very friendly, and we regularly invited two or three of them to come home for a curry. The routine would start on Saturday with a family excursion to the Newcastle markets, plus Kanti (the chief curry cook), where we would purchase the necessary ingredients. Then back home, to stoke up the fire and get to work cooking up a feast. Robin and Kanti, his junior, would now change roles, Kanti being the chief chef and Robin supplying him with tools and ingredients as they were called for. My role was in the scullery, supplying endless pans (even borrowing them from next door) and washing them up later. Robin learnt how to use a variety of curry spices, and we gave curry parties for years afterwards.

Robin and I decided that a couple more children would complete our family beautifully, preferably two in one hit (say twin girls) and I was delighted when I found I was pregnant. This time I really blossomed and felt wonderful, unlike in my two tropical, Paludrine-nauseated pregnancies.

Michael and Peter were enrolled in the near-by Shotley Bridge Primary School. It was a dour looking, Dickensian place, with 'Board School' and a date from the last century above the door. The bitumen playground was surrounded by tall iron railings, without a blade of grass or tree to soften the exterior, but inside was a first rate Principal, and it was altogether an excellent school, which soon had Michael reading and writing well above his age level, and gave Peter a head start too. If he was home in time Robin would bath the boys and read to them in bed and over this period he read the Jungle Book, Just So Stories, Swiss Family Robinson and Robinson Crusoe, and sometimes he would just make a story up, as his father had done when he was a child. Both boys picked up a Geordie accent which usually disappeared when they were in our company, and was quickly replaced by an Australian one later.

Jill with John, 1959

On September 15, 1958, not twin girls but a third little boy joined the family. Once again I was confined three weeks early, and John Anthony was born in the Richard Murray Hospital, Blackhill. It was much easier for me caring for this baby in a temperate climate and without the travelling and tropical heat that had been Michael and Peter's lot in their early weeks. Michael was now six and a quarter, and Peter just five, and both very good and helpful with the new baby who was cheerful and easy to satisfy from the word go. Once again my sweet mother answered the call from Somerset and helped out for the ten days I was in hospital.

One day, prior to this, a knock on the front door revealed a stout, motherly lady who introduced herself as Mrs Ridge. She explained that her married daughter had moved to another town recently, her first experience away from Blackhill where she had grown up, and a neighbour had knocked on her door and offered to baby-sit any time she and her husband wanted a night out together. This stranger had since become a treasured family friend. Mrs Ridge was so grateful for this woman's kindness to her daughter that she wanted to do the same for us, since we were strangers in her territory. Dear Mrs Ridge, she would never accept any money for baby-sitting, and when we were leaving organised a couple of neighbours to come in with her and clean up the house after us, telling me not to worry about a thing. What a wonderful attitude she had... to pass on to others the blessings you and yours have received and cannot repay in kind.

When we had first moved in at Blackhill, the neighbours, seen only vaguely, treated us with great suspicion, peering through net curtains as we came and went. For two weeks I didn't catch even a glimpse of the woman living next door, whose back door opened right opposite mine along the side passage between our two houses. But one morning she just happened to open her door to attend to the dustbin a few seconds before I emerged on the same errand, and she could not escape. I smiled and introduced myself and asked how to organise coal deliveries or some such question, and she turned out to be another most kind and friendly neighbour who would invite the boys over to watch her TV and would bake a chocolate cake for us every time she baked for her own family. She confided to me that the street had been concerned that a doctor's family suddenly introduced into their community of steel workers, where everyone knew each other and there was little moving around, would be snooty and uppity and not want to mix. She was so relieved to find that I was young and friendly and somewhat lonely, and took me to her heart from then on.

After sixteen months we had to tackle the usual question of where to go next. Robin loved surgery but also hankered for the freedom to operate in all the spheres of medicine that he had experienced in Nigeria. We missed the blue skies and open life-style that we had enjoyed in the tropics, but did not want the enervating heat, dysentery and malaria that accompanied them. Tony had recently returned from two years in Australia, surveying the Barrier Reef on secondment to the Royal Australian Navy, and he strongly recommended that we emigrate to Queensland, which he had loved.

The recently formed National Health Service, by 1958, was not a generous employer. After other expenses, Robin was bringing home about fifteen pounds a week for housekeeping, whereas the steel worker's wives, who were our neighbours, had around forty pounds. They pushed their babies around in big, smart prams with satin sheets, whereas I was happy to find a second hand collapsible Tan-Sad for two pounds, which we later took with us on the ship to Australia. For Robin to attain to the position of consultant surgeon he would have had to face many years of waiting, in a registrar's position, until an incumbent retired or died. Even then there was no certainty that he would be one of the few lucky ones appointed to a specialist position, so remaining in cold, grey England with its chronic housing shortage was not an option that appealed to us then. Robin still had to sit the final exams for his F.R.C.S. but decided it would be better to make the move now, and sit for that in Australia later, when he could first attend a refresher course.

Chapter Twenty Five

We Emigrate to Australia

We applied to Australia House for papers to start the ball rolling, and some months later, after the mandatory interviews and medicals, were accepted as migrants with assisted passage for ten pounds each adult, and allotted births in S.S. Strathnaver, to leave Tilbury in February '59. We were very excited at the prospect, and hungrily sought all the books on Australia we could find, mostly Neville Shute's novels such as "A Town Like Alice", and we set about organising our much travelled belongings into tea chests for transit across to the other side of the world.

With the three children, we caught the early train from a snowy Newcastle down to London on a cold, grey day. There, on the Kings Cross platform to greet us, was my father, who had travelled up from Somerset by train, crossed London, and would later travel straight back, just to spend a few moments seeing us all, meeting the new grandson and saying goodbye. I was immensely touched. I knew he thought he would never see us again, and he always thought he would die before his 'time' as his parents had done. I'm glad I can say he was wrong. He wrote me an encouraging letter telling me how proud he was of me, delivered to our cabin with flowers, before sailing. He was a lovely man and had taken his role as father very seriously. I know I had given him many anxious moments as a know-it-all teenager, but now he could see Robin and I were well and happy and on an even keel and he was very satisfied.

It came as quite a relief to board the P & O liner, Strathnaver, first piling aboard an excessively dirty and dingy train to

Tilbury docks, with the scruffiest lot of fellow migrants imaginable. Unshaven, collarless, with exhausted wives and grubby children most appeared to have travelled all night from Scotland or across Europe, all hoping, like us, for a new and better life in sunny Australia.

Once aboard we were very cheered to discover that we had been allotted adjoining cabins with our own bathroom; Robin and Michael went into one, with Peter and me in the other, plus a cot for Johnny, now five months old. His pram was stored in an alcove outside the door, and he was able to spend much of the day in it out on deck. The boys were happy to have the top bunks, and took to shipboard life with gusto. In the dining saloon Robin and I were placed at the Deputy Purser's table along with two other emigrating doctors and their wives, among others, and found that one couple had spent the last two years in Ibadan Hospital, and were now bound for Tasmania.

The change in our fellow migrants was nothing short of amazing, as they settled in and had a good night's sleep, a shower and change of clothes, and we revised our first impression. Most of them seemed to be from Glasgow or from Finland, both equally difficult to understand, but we soon made some friends, and the boys helped with that. On Gala night there was a fancy dress party. We had been warned about this and I had come prepared with strips of Nigerian cloth for me and his Hausa robe for Robin (presented to him at his farewell party in Azare). I borrowed a pineapple from the galley, plaited a soft pad on my head and walked half the length of the ship in the parade, dressed as a Nigerian, a teddy bear piccaninny on my back, balancing the pineapple on my head. When I reached the judges I managed to drop to one knee and rise again, without touching the pineapple or dropping it, and was awarded the prize for "most original" which raised me greatly in the boy's estimation.

In the Mediterranean we struck a heavy swell off Port Said, which was too steep to allow the pilot to come aboard, so the ship had to wallow. All the crockery in the dining saloon crashed onto the floor and in the lounge the settees and heavy chairs all slid into one corner, occupants still aboard. I was feeding Johnny when it started to get rough, and had Peter with me, but had no idea where Robin or Michael were and just hoped they were together. Peter was in the top bunk, hanging on for dear life, and Johnny back in his cot, when a particularly heavy swell threw me against the door, which was rapidly becoming the floor. I could see the cot starting to slide down towards me, then tipping and spilling the baby, and there was absolutely nothing I could do until the centre of gravity shifted back and I could reach him, alarmed but luckily unharmed.

With John, on the ship to Australia, 1959

Because of the recent Suez crisis we were not allowed to disembark at Port Said, but called in at Colombo where we spent a day mostly ashore. This is where our fathers had met in 1945, to which we owed our own friendship, so it was particularly interesting for us. And so on to Fremantle, with a trip in a train, and a day spent ashore visiting Robin's old Middlesex friend and Best Man, Martin, and his wife in Perth. Our first impression of West Australia, in late summer, was of very dry heat and intense glare from the sandy soil, and the hot wind carried new and exciting smells for us. I had to keep telling myself that this is Australia, the dream is happening and we are really here. On the dock below the ship was a pie-seller selling hot meat pies and for some reason we came to the conclusion that they were made of kangaroo meat and resisted the odours wafting up so temptingly.

Somewhere in the Great Australian Bight disaster struck Michael in the form of measles. The ship's hospital was overflowing with cases, and a temporary measles ward had been opened in the stern above the screws. Here were two or three cots with sick toddlers, and Michael and another child in bunks. By the time we arrived in Melbourne, where Charles and Mal Holmes, cousins of my mother's, met us and took us out for lunch, Michael was covered in a rash and feeling pretty miserable, but mostly sleeping, so we could leave him in the nurse's care for a few hours and take a break ashore. After three days in port we sailed on for Sydney, by which time Michael had taken a turn for the worse and had become delirious and disorientated. He was determined to go ashore and kept getting out of his bunk and heading off to the door, which was a bad idea since we were now at sea again. I left Peter and Johnny to Robin, apart from breaks to feed the baby, and moved into the bunk next to Michael, hardly daring to shut my eyes if I knew he was awake, in case he absconded. The noise of the screws underneath us masked any sound that would otherwise have alerted me to his moving around, so there was nothing for it but to watch him. After two such nights I was dizzy with fatigue, but as the final morning dawned off Sydney Heads I came out on deck at Robin's bidding, leaving Michael at last sleeping tranquilly and in his right mind.

We will always remember our first impressions of Sydney Harbour. It was promising to be a very hot day, cloudless but with a mist softening the view, which was developing into heat haze. With Robin and Peter, and the baby in my arms, I watched the headlands and forested bays slip past as we approached the famous harbour bridge. There were very few tall buildings then, and of course no opera house, and the harbour appeared incredibly beautiful. We were very excited at having reached the end of our long voyage, tinged with apprehension, especially since one big worry completely clouded our enjoyment. We had been told that Michael and the other measles cases would be removed to an isolation hospital and not be allowed to accompany us to Queensland. At first I planned to take a hotel room nearby, with the baby, but was told that no visiting would be allowed and we should proceed north and Michael would be sent to join us when he was no longer infectious. It seemed we had no choice in the matter, and I was feeling sick at heart, especially as he had been too ill for me to prepare him for this.

We sailed under the bridge and came alongside a finger wharf. The big corrugated iron sheds reminded us of pictures of migrants arriving at Long Island, and the ensuing crush of passengers, now sweating in the drab coats and hats they had left England in, brought home to us our new status as we prepared to queue up for disembarkation. At this point a voice over the loudspeaker called our name, to report to the Purser's office, and we received our second blessing of this memorable day. Graham and Margaret Shirley were friends of my brother's and, unknown to us, he had forewarned them of our arrival. Here they were on board to meet us, looking as beautiful as film stars. Having risen at dawn, they planned to take us for a tour of Sydney and a picnic before our train left for Brisbane in the evening.

I explained about Michael and that I wanted to stay with him as long as possible, whereupon these wonderful people said that their two girls had both had measles, it was inconceivable that a six year old could be abandoned in this way on arrival in a strange country, and he must stay with them until he was well enough to travel. They would arrange his transport up to Goondiwindi to rejoin us. What could we do but say a truly heartfelt "Thank you," proceed with our disembarkation and enjoy our first day in Australia to the full. Two weeks later he flew up to us in Queensland all by himself in a DC3. By then brown and well, he had swapped his Geordie accent for a slight australian one. Was this the same little boy?

By 7 p.m. on that long day of our arrival, it was dark and we piled aboard the train to Brisbane at Central Station, filled with fellow migrants also headed for Queensland. Hour after hour the train rattled and swayed through the dark countryside, rarely passing through anything that looked like a large town, and in the morning all passengers were ordered out onto the platform at the small country town of Casino. Here we were seated at trestle tables and served a welcome breakfast of scrambled eggs on toast and tea, waving the flies away from our plates between mouthfuls, before re-embarking for the final hours to Brisbane, arriving at midday.

Robin left me on the station platform, sitting on our luggage with Peter and the baby, whilst he went off to get instructions. He was waylaid by a female reporter who wanted to interview him, but instead he brought her to me and vaguely introduced me to her, but not her to me (he'd not hoisted in her name) so I answered all her questions thinking she was just a friendly well-wisher, and with no idea that she would be writing it all up for the Brisbane Courier Mail... until she produced a camera! Peter, hot and thirsty, hammed it up and was caught pulling an idiot face (also published later, of course, on the front page of the Goondiwindi Argus) and we were later considerably embarrassed by my remarks having been taken out of context and sadly misconstrued. It quoted me as saying we'd spent nearly five years in Nigeria and conditions in Goondiwindi shouldn't worry us. I was referring to the heat, but the locals presumed I was referring to them in a rather derogatory fashion. It took a while before a new friend felt safe enough with me to let me in on this, but by then there was nothing that I could do except hope those offended would come to know me better. Not a very auspicious introduction into our new community.

For now we were all loaded into busses and disgorged at the migrant hostel at Kangaroo Point under the Storey Bridge, and allotted two sleeping cubicles in what appeared to be a huge tin shed. This hostel was not intended to provide long-term quarters, but was purposely very basic in order to encourage migrants to move out and be independent as soon as possible.

We certainly got the message after a sleepless night when we could hear every cough, snore, nightmare, wail, conversation and radio from the hundreds of fellow immigrants under the same ceiling. There were no facilities for babies at all, and I had to bath Johnny in the row of communal wash-basins in the woman's very basic shower block, always wet and smelling from the disinfectant with which it was hosed down every day. Obtaining small amounts of suitable food for him also proved extremely difficult, and the seemingly uncomprehending kitchen hands, probably recent migrants, were less than helpful.

Robin went straight into action getting a car with a previously organised bank loan, registering with the medical board and obtaining a driver's licence, so we hardly saw him. There was nothing I could do to help, so Peter and I pushed the pram for short walks to explore as far as we dared, amusing ourselves as best we could and wondering what Goondiwindi would be like. I was watching him closely to see if he was showing signs of measles, but so far so good and he managed to wait until we had settled into our new home before breaking out in the tell-tale rash. As soon as he could, Robin gave Johnny an injection of gamma globulin to protect him, since he was only six months old.

By the second afternoon, Robin had completed all his business and loaded us aboard our spanking new blue Holden station wagon. We spent that night at a temperance hotel in Toowoomba, such a relief to have a comfortable bed after the previous run of sleepless nights, and next day shopped for some basic furniture, which would follow us to Goondiwindi later. Then we set off on the drive west, with the burning afternoon sun in our eyes, wondering what was ahead of us and what we had committed ourselves to for the next two years, sight unseen.

Chapter Twenty Six

Richard Alan, Goondiwindi

This was the day before Good Friday, and we arrived in Goondiwindi at dusk, after the shops had closed for the long Easter weekend and not even one promised Easter egg was available for Peter from the Greek café. The Medical Superintendent's house was opposite the hospital, across a road as wide as an airstrip, and we were relieved to find that Arthur, the Hospital Secretary, had had some hospital beds made up for us, and a table and four chairs. Otherwise it was an empty house, with no floor coverings or curtains or fridge, and our boxes of belongings would not catch us up until after the Easter holiday.

Arthur introduced himself and said with his slow Queensland drawl "There's half a sheep for you over in the hospital fridge." We laughed at his joke, expecting a generous cut of stewing chops or perhaps a leg, but when I went across to collect it later, I was indeed confronted with half a sheep, cut up, but some of it hard to identify, and I never did discover what to do with all the bits.

In 1959, Australia had a population of about 11 million. 3,000 of them lived in Goondiwindi, which serviced about as many again in the surrounding area. The nearest Queensland town of any size was Warwick, 200 kms away, and it was another 160 Km drive to Brisbane, which at that time had seemed to us just a rather dingy large country town. Goondiwindi had no High School, so children either had to go away to boarding school or have correspondence lessons, which was an important factor that later encouraged us to leave the town when our two years were up.

Robin was the 'free' hospital doctor, but there were also three G.P's, one of whom, Tom Bestic and his wife, Betty, and their four children, became close and lasting friends. Tom and Robin worked together in the operating theatre as a team, one giving anaesthetics and the other operating. Betty looked after me like an older sister, as did another couple, Mabel and Dick Doyle, graziers on a sheep and cattle (and later wheat) property on the New South Wales side of the river, and Mabel's parents, who often invited us out to their property, 'Bangalow'.

Communication turned out to be more of a problem than we had expected, with many turns of phrase being misunderstood. One evening the door-bell rang and I opened it to Arthur. "Good night " he said. I presumed he was just passing on his way home, so I said "Oh! Goodnight Arthur," and shut the door again. Through the frosted glass I was puzzled to see that he was still standing there, so after a minute I opened the door again. "Aren't you going to ask me in?" he drawled. Oh dear! I covered my embarrassment by explaining that for us "Goodnight" was always said on the final parting of the night, not on the first meeting of the evening. By this time he realised we were rather strange, but he never seemed to take offence.

Perhaps my stupidest blue was when I was invited to be guest speaker at the C.W.A. Mother's Day party and told to "Bring a plate." Knowing it was to be held in a hall, I very reasonably asked, "Shall I bring anything else? Knife, fork and spoon... mug?" This was greeted with polite laughter. "No, just a plate." So I took just a plate, but I wasn't trying to be funny! Of course, it was meant to have food on it, but I didn't know that until I walked in and saw the 'plates' of the other women.

I learnt the hard way that my invitation to 'tea' was presumed to refer to the evening meal, and my guests disconcertingly turned up around 6.00pm by which time I presumed they had forgotten, cleared everything away and put the crawler in the bath. On the other hand 'afternoon tea' was served around 3pm, and I was horrified to discover that dress was formal, with stockings worn, even in intense heat, and probably hat and gloves too. The table would be set with scones, slices, cream sponges (and probably Lamingtons) on a lace table cloth, and served with cake forks, napkins and the family silver if there was any. When the grubby children joined their mothers after school, they were relegated to the back yard, where the resident child entertained them with biscuits and cordial. No cream cakes for them!

I was never comfortable in this company, partly due to the heat but also because I always had to control one or two crawling (or bawling) babies, after our family was completed on 18th May 1960 by the arrival, two weeks early, of Richard Alan, known as Rikki. This gave us a polo team, as the locals pointed out, and we decided not to keep trying for those twin daughters after all.

Michael and Peter soon adapted to the Aussie way of life. At the end of the year they both received school prizes, and proved that their English Council School had given them an excellent grounding, with Michael, now seven, a year younger than the average age of his class here. In the meantime we had grown to like the place and particularly the people as the first year melted into the second and the time approached when we would again have to face the question "Where next?" We had some memorable experiences in Goondiwindi and made more life-long friends, and we were to leave with a real love of the Australian outback.

After two years our passports were returned to us and Robin was free to go and find work wherever he wanted. It didn't occur to us to leave Australia. He had long desired to be a Flying Doctor, and even got as far as an interview, but before committing himself, and us, to outback Australia for a long term, he took a holiday and travelled south down the N.S.W. coast to check out an advertisement in the medical journal for an 'Assistant with View to Partnership', placed by a G.P. in a small town called Coffs Harbour.

Robin was enchanted by the beauty of the beaches and hills, a verdant paradise after the flat, dry inland, and was very favourably impressed with Dr Macdonald and his modern surgery. The country practice promised the freedom to do surgery, give anaesthetics, deliver babies and generally use the skills that he had developed over the past eleven years, and it was arranged that we would move to Coffs Harbour in May 1961.

The Hospital Auxiliary gave a wonderful Garden Party on Robin's birthday, the week before we left Goondiwindi. The town band played a selection from Gilbert and Sullivan in his honour, knowing his taste, and two and a half year old Johnny raced home for his toy trumpet and joined them, which we managed to capture on ciné film. There were Marching Girls, a fashion parade, children's pet parade and plenty of fund-raising stalls including 'Guess the weight of the piglet'.

Many kind and appreciative words were spoken about Robin's contribution as Medical Superintendent, and we were presented with some valuable gifts from the Hospital Board, the Auxiliary and other groups, including a fitted doctor's bag, a picnic case, pyrex dishes and a lovely big cut glass vase. We had made many friends in the district who expressed genuine regret at losing Robin from the hospital, and it really was a lovely day and a send-off we will never forget. Granny Fletcher had joined us from England for a few months, and with the seven of us squashed into the Holden, we drove, often on dirt roads, over the Great Dividing Range and down to the coast where a new life awaited us. Could this possibly be the last of our moves?

Chapter Twenty Seven

Coffs Harbour and Journey's End

We were rather surprised to discover that each state has different laws, and that New South Wales had a different health system to Queensland. The small, dark and overcrowded Coffs Harbour District Hospital did not have a government doctor, so the G.P.'s were rostered on call to deal with casualties, and otherwise looked after their own patients after admitting them. We felt that the Queensland system was far superior, and the hospital in Goondiwindi had better facilities. Coffs Harbour then had five other G.P.'s and a population of 7,000. It was still a 24-hour day on call seven days a week job for him, but Robin revelled in it and very soon had built up a loyal following of patients.

In that first month Rikki had his first birthday and then took his first steps. He was a gorgeous baby and my mother had become his loving slave. We soon moved into a brand new bungalow of our own in the centre of town, close to the surgery. It was blue, built of fibro-cement, with a corrugated iron roof, and had three bedrooms and a quarter-acre yard decorated only with grass and builder's rubble. We could hardly believe we had a home of our own at last, and obtained a loan for the four thousand pounds that it cost us, before buying the essential Victa mower.

Mother had to return home to England then, but it soon became certain that our roaming had ended and that Coffs Harbour had everything we had ever wanted, so four years later father sold up and they emigrated and joined us. We all moved into a new home we designed and had built nearby. This had plenty of living space for us and the four boys, and a flat with two bedrooms and living area for my parents. We built the house in the centre of the quarter-acre block and made a walled garden for them in the front, keeping the back garden for our own use. Now we could keep pets and had a series of cats, dogs, rabbits, guinea pigs, ponies and pigeons over the years.

Mother, Rikki and me at Coffs jetty, 1961.

Through Robin's partner Rainy, and his wife Peg, we were introduced to a circle of friends who accepted us and made us welcome. Peg invited me to join her friends at tennis on her own court each Thursday afternoon, and with these families we did many things together and life was full and satisfying. It took some time but I gradually began to feel accepted and that I belonged here. My Pommy accent always stood out however (it still does) and I would often gladly have traded it for something less conspicuous.

We became members of the embryonic Sailing Club and Robin built a small sailing boat for the boys, called Peanut, and then a catamaran for us, (called Echo as it was meant to go there and back as fast as the speed of sound, but it never remotely lived up to its name). For a few years most Sundays would see the same families down at the harbour racing a weird and poorly matched assortment of sailing boats, mostly home-built, having much challenging fun in more senses than one. With the sub-tropical climate and safe harbour, it was an ideal environment for kids and our boys thrived on it.

John and Rikki, 1963

Shortly after arriving, when I was still coming to terms with Australian wildlife, I thought it a good idea to take the four boys to a snake demonstration. An Indian called Ram Chandra toured around with glass cages of live snakes, mostly venomous, teaching the dangers and differences. He wanted to make the point that a bite from a non-poisonous snake will bleed fairly freely, whereas a venomous bite does not bleed. To help us get the message he picked up a small (ish) carpet python and invited a volunteer from the crowd to submit to a bite to prove the point. He assured us that this was a non-venomous snake, it would just feel like pin pricks, the bite would bleed freely and we would therefore always remember the difference. Was he serious? Everything went quiet and there was much studying of the ground. No-one volunteered and the crowd started to thin out a little. He asked again, teasing and cajoling. People were smiling and pushing others forward but no-one was game to meet his eyes.

The tension soon got to me. It sounded logical enough and I thought it a good lesson for my boys to learn so I passed Rick off my hip to Michael, saying

"Hang on to him," and started forward. But I had not reckoned on Peter's reaction, always the imaginative one, he clutched at my skirt, yelling "No, Mummy! No... Don't go... No, No." with the song loudly taken up by Johnny and Rikki and an equally anxious Michael. I stepped back and pacified my panicking tribe but one way or another we did get a lesson we've not forgotten.

In the early years I was kept very busy with a variety of roles. Although Robin and Rainy's surgery was elsewhere, a ring at our front door out of surgery hours could herald considerable drama, with blood, pain or shock needing urgent, dropping-of-everything attention, whilst I waited for Robin to return from the hospital or wherever he was visiting. There was little in the way of government resources. No casualty department or air ambulance, no specialists nearer then Brisbane, not even any social worker closer than Grafton, fifty miles away. Out of surgery hours our phone was always liable to be busy.

Coffs Harbour, 1966.

I very soon identified with the small town community and became a great espouser of causes. In an attempt to organise a network of volunteers to watch out in a neighbourly way for families in distress, a few of us set up the Community Aid Service in 1968, offering help and a small directory of agencies and volunteers from whom advice or help could be sought. It started with a regular advertisement in the local Opinion, giving our telephone number to contact, and it was not long before the telephone pad was sometimes as full of my clients as Robin's, by which time we felt we had proved the point that this service was indeed needed.

A small subsidy was obtained from the Shire Council and our committee permitted to set up an office in the old shire chambers, now empty and recently delegated to Civil Defence. It had a phone and we now staffed it part-time. The Shire Council suggested that in return for their generosity, I undertake training as a Civil Defence Welfare Officer at Mount Macedon, Victoria. I flew down and attended the two-week residential course, which was challenging and enormous fun, and I organised a local Welfare Section on my return. A Field day was held, with our section having to register, feed, clothe and shelter 'the refugees'. We made mud ovens and cooked stews, erected hessian around pit toilets, (leaving some details to the imagination) and had an exhausting but successful day for which I received a very nice letter of appreciation from the Civil defence C.O. who was an ex-army officer from Grafton (where, unlike Coffs Harbour, floods meant they could be doing all this for real).

As a sequel to being appointed Civil Defence Welfare Officer, when the Queen and Prince Phillip and Princess Anne visited Coffs Harbour in April 1970, I was given the job of organising lunch for all the policemen who were shipped in from near and far to control the vast crowds expected. Not having learnt this standard of haute cuisine at Mt Macedon, I gathered a willing band of helpers with C.W.A experience, and we cooked and served a meal in one of the church halls. As it turned out the policemen only totalled 40 and the 'crowds' hardly needed control.

I had to rush off in the middle to attend the reception in the Civic Centre, where much of Coffs' population was lined up in their best finery in long rows behind white lines on the floor. The Queen walked up one row and down the next, speaking now to a person on one side, and then on the other, zig-zagging down the rows. Unfortunately Robin and I were neither a zig nor a zag, though she spoke to each of our neighbours. I was really looking forward to Prince Phillip noticing my Naval crown brooch, prominently displayed on my chest to attract his attention. I could then tell him that my brother was at Dartmouth Naval College with him, and remembers the day the Prince showed the young Princess Elizabeth and Princess Margaret Rose around. Alas, Prince Phillip zigged and zagged just the same route as the Queen, and Princess Anne shot past at high speed, not even zigging, having spent too long being ear-bashed by some-one in the first row. My disappointment was somewhat assuaged later by the sight of the Royal Yacht Brittania raising anchor and sailing out of the harbour with her band playing. The scene took me back to my childhood and I felt tearfully nostalgic.

Incidentally, the Community Aid Service grew and grew over the next thirty years, and after a few name changes has now become the busy Neighbourhood Centre in the centre of a Community Village, though my own involvement ceased over twenty years ago.

Robin had gained his pilot's licence after arriving in Australia, and now he built a two seater wooden plane, a Jodel D11, in our back shed (overflowing into the carport, sitting room and bedroom, naturally). It had the distinction of being the first Jodel D11 to fly in Australia, and he flew it himself on its maiden flight in 1968. We had some memorable adventures as well as flying in a few Air Races. The plane, VH-DRJ (Delta Romeo Juliet) was regretfully sold after about ten years, when finance for education had to take priority, and was later known to be flying in West Australia.

Nearly twenty years later Robin built a fibreglass 'Dragonfly' (later donated to the Wangaratta Air Museum) so his childhood apprenticeship on model aircraft paid off well. All this was spread over thirty years, and of course his real job has always been his medical practice, which was totally consuming for years and still leaves him little free time.

In March 1972 I discovered a small lump in my breast. Michael was working in Papua New Guinea, John was at The Armidale School, eleven-year-old Rikki was at home with his grandparents and we had just settled Peter into John college at the Australian National University in Canberra. Robin and

I had been looking forward to a week's well-earned holiday in Thredbo when I noticed the lump. Now Robin decided we should curtail our holiday and head straight for Sydney. Two days later a leading surgeon had performed a radical mastectomy, removing the right side chest muscles as well as breast, followed a week later by another operation to place a large skin graft over the area, from my thigh.

Robin stayed with our ex-Goondiwindi friends, Tom and Betty Bestic, who by then were living in Sydney. He had to return to work in Coffs Harbour after a few days, but flew back down to Sydney the next weekend in the Jodel. After Tom had waved him off at Mascot Airport for his return home on the Sunday, he reported back that the Jodel looked so tiny amongst the big jets that nothing on earth could have persuaded him, Tom, to fly in her! I was very grateful that Robin didn't have the same qualms.

The following weekend, the Air Traffic Controller at Mascot, having radioed Robin permission to takeoff, came back anxiously on the radio with...

"Delta Romeo Juliet, WHERE ARE YOU?"

"Just in front of the Tower!"

"Oh? ... Ah, I see you ... Roger." I don't know what he had been looking for!

I was always nervous when approaching and landing there. We were usually kept in a holding position circling the Harbour Bridge until our turn came in the queue to land, wondering anxiously if the Controller instructing us had grasped how tiny and vulnerable we were to the preceding jet's turbulent air which could easily flip us over.

In 1987, I developed cancer in the remaining breast, this time undergoing surgery in our local hospital. Although radical this was far less traumatic than the first experience and was followed by five weeks of radiotherapy in Sydney. These two brushes with cancer have given both Robin and me a much greater sympathy for others who are faced with this out of the blue. It certainly does shake one to the foundations. I have been so fortunate in surviving the threat twice, and can honestly say now that I am grateful for the experiences because they have brought home to me how important it is not to take anything for granted. I carry with me a constant reminder to be thankful every day that I am alive and well, and grateful for all the blessings I am surrounded with, particularly for Robin who has been unfailingly loving and supportive through it all, as has my family.

The good side to the second operation was that I could now choose whatever size prosthesis I fancied. I toyed with the idea of being a Dolly Parton, but the impracticality of replacing my entire Size 10 wardrobe soon put paid to that little daydream. I opted for carrying on the same size as normal, and I doubt if many people would guess so much was missing.

My mother and father, Coffs Harbour, 1970.

The years in Coffs Harbour were golden years for my parents. They adapted to the life in the sun as if they'd been here all their lives. My father lived with us in Coffs Harbour for nine years, but the last three or four were marred by Parkinson's Disease, which he handled with his usual strength of character. He had a number of academic interests that he pursued for as long as he was able, and wrote a small book on ancient metrology of which a copy is in the National Library in Canberra. I believe it was a good time for him until his health deteriorated. He was always very grateful to Robin for making them so welcome, and he now need have no anxiety about Mother's future, knowing we would care for her if he died first.

The end came from pneumonia, on 1st March 1974, when he was 77. Mother and I were sitting with him in hospital and I was holding his hand when his pulse stopped. He had expressed the wish that he have no funeral but that his ashes be scattered out to sea off Coffs Harbour, and in due course, Robin and I flew over the waves and farewelled him there.

My sweet and gentle mother was so happy to be safe in the heart of the family, and never interfered or demanded anything. The four boys loved her, especially Rikki, who saw the most of her. She outlived Father by two years, but died of cancer in 1976, eleven years after they joined us. Although confined to her bed with secondaries in the spine for the last year, it was a privilege for me to care for her after all she had done for me over the years, and she never, ever uttered a word of complaint. Her psychiatric disorder had been controlled by Robin with a new daily medication, which meant that it never overwhelmed her in Australia. She had asked that her ashes remain near the family, so they are in our garden, shaded by a Lemon Scented Gum and Bangalow Palms.

I am so grateful for having been granted such parents. They gave me a fine example of courage in the adversities of life, good humour, high personal standards of honesty and integrity, great unselfishness and concern for others, commitment to duty, loyalty and self-control.

To tell the story of our years in Coffs Harbour would need another book to itself. It was a great place to bring up boys in those early days, safe and friendly and uncomplicated, until it exploded with development and eventually has become a city with nearly 60,000 inhabitants (in 2000 AD). Since the six of us had been born in four different continents, in 1968, with Michael turning 16, we had decided to take Australian citizenship and all go on together. There would be no turning back.

After my parents had died and all the boys had left home to pursue their various careers, we bought a five-acre banana plantation in a quiet valley close to town, and built a small house out of western red cedar, where we live still. We have named the place 'Apuldram'. Here we have regular visits from koalas and swamp wallabies, possums in the chimney, monitor lizards and blue-tongues, many types of snake and spider, both venomous and not, and a resident echidna. Dozens of bird species visit throughout the year, including exotics such as Regent and Satin Bower-birds, Pied Butcher Birds (our favourite songsters), Whip Birds, King Parrots, Cat Birds, Rosellas and Lorikeets. Iridescent Spangled Drongos fly in from Indonesia and large Black Cockatoos flap slowly up the valley reminiscent of prehistoric times, their loud raucous calls heralding rain. Today a brush turkey has been pecking at his reflection in a low window.

Robin and me, 1992

Chapter Twenty Eight

My Other Pilgrimage

To look back objectively at my experiences and try to make sense of them, to see the pattern if there is one, to learn from them and hopefully understand things about events, and about myself and others that were puzzling or hidden at the time, is something that fascinates me now from the vantage point of 70 years.

Over time my attitudes subtly changed. In the early years my social attitudes were formed by outside influences and it took many decades before that imprinted structure was replaced by beliefs and standpoints that I chose for myself. Emigrating to Australia when I was 30 released something in me (or released me from something) bringing a greater freedom to be myself and to accept others without judging by appearances, which had always been a fault of mine. I hope that I have been able to retain the best and let the worst go of all that I had been brought up to accept as important and, as someone put it, 'swallow the meat and spit out the bones'.

Polonius, in Hamlet, gave some excellent advice to his son; "And this above all, to thine own self be true, and it shall follow, as the night the day, thou can'st not then be false to any man...." Returning to the past, and trying to map my erratic journey towards maturity, has helped me to understand myself much better as it follows that to be true to myself I must first know myself. This is really very difficult, especially trying hard to be honest and so admitting to being less than perfect.

All through my life I had been drawn towards finding a meaning to life other than just living it out and then passing on who-knows-where. Not finding "It" in Moral Re-armament or the established church, in the my late forties I started experimenting with Transcendental Meditation and read books on Rudolph Steiner and anthroposophy and other religious philosophies, but never gained the satisfaction of finding what I was really looking for. I became convinced that I was just not a very deep person, but still craved for more meaning to life than I had so far grasped.

For a while then I read New Age books on spiritualism and the occult, lent by an acquaintance on a similar quest, and ended up getting myself thoroughly spooked. I reasoned one night that since the spiritual world must definitely be taken seriously, then there was literally only one person "on the other side" who I could trust completely, and that was Jesus Christ. I rejected what I now judged to be dangerous diversions, threw out the New Age and started to really seek him. I don't know why it had taken me so long to come full circle and if only I had known how close the answer would prove to be I could have been spared years of searching in the wrong places.

It occurred to me that we all face eternity sooner or later and an eternity spent outside the realm of God's grace, a place without love, forgiveness, justice and mercy, is surely the ultimate hell, whether it is a fiery furnace or not. I believe that God respects our free will, and the decision to accept Him, and make a real commitment, or reject Him and go our own independent way, is the responsibility of each individual and the decision is vital. We are not puppets.

Soon after coming to the decision to earnestly seek Christ, in fact one evening in May 1977, when I had unexpectedly decided to accompany a rather surprised Rick to a prayer group he had joined, Jesus did indeed dramatically reveal Himself to me. Later tears started running down my cheeks accompanied by a great feeling of release and peace.

After the meeting I remarked to the couple sitting next to me "It's such a relief to let the tears flow. I've not been able to for years." They asked if there was something in my life I really needed to cry about, and I answered that my mother had recently died, but that it was a merciful release from pain and I'd really mourned her more when she was first terminally ill. They asked if I would like prayer to heal these memories and without any more questions quietly prayed over me that Jesus would heal all the past hurts. He did ... on the spot! I walked home with Rick a changed person, and since that evening have never doubted the claims of the New Testament and the reality that Christ is indeed Immanuel, 'God with us'.

Alas, no encouragement was available on the home front at first, and I felt considerably hampered by the (quite understandable) fears of a certain member of the family, who presumed that this sudden change of personality, to a church-going (any and every church was fair game), bible-reading, prayer-group-seeking religious nut, signified that my mother's weakness was now surfacing in me, and needed to be carefully monitored. I reacted by hiding my new books under the bed, and otherwise trying to appear 'normal' when under surveillance; though in reality I was exploding with a new found joy. Was this what it means to be "born again"?

I sought out Don Kemsley, the vibrant pastor of the local Baptist Church, and was baptised by total immersion in the presence of some Christian friends. I felt new and clean and free. The fact that I had been christened in the Church of England as a baby did not seem to me to be the same thing, as my own will had not been involved, and I had obviously not understood 'repentance'. I felt that God, in Christ, had done everything on His part for me, and now I had at least done something on my part to show my genuine commitment.

I am aware that I am continuing to change since that day in May 1977, and it is entirely through the grace of God. It started with being freed from fear... dramatically. Fear of the dark (yes, still carried since childhood), fear of criticism and what others are thinking about me, fear of rejection, fear of failure (whatever that means), all controlled my life to a large extent. Oh, what a relief it was and is to be progressively freed from them. I felt

I was becoming a new person, or perhaps I was being freed to be my real self. I began to like myself better and appreciate all my blessings instead of always wanting to compare and change things.

An added bonus came in 1980, through prayer, when I experienced what can only be described as miraculous healing of my back, which had troubled me on and off since I damaged it aged 15, harvesting. It was showing arthritic changes on Xray, and increasingly I needed anti-inflammatory tablets to combat the pain and keep me mobile. These and other healings, emotional and physical, have remained with me for over twenty years and nothing could now persuade me to doubt the reality of my emancipator.

So that is the story of this Thursday's Child, who had far to go, from conception in New Zealand to arrival in Australia thirty years later via Canada, England and Nigeria. Here I was at last able to put down roots in surely one of the most beautiful places on earth. Now it is forty years since we emigrated, and Robin and I have watched our four sons and eight grandchildren grow and flourish. This is where the ashes of my parents are scattered so we already have four generations here, one way or another. Australia has been very good to us, and here this Thursday's child, for one, has found what her heart always longed for, so she doesn't need to go any further.

For me this is the most important chapter of my story. All that went before was leading me to this point and that is why I prefer to leave it just here. The final destination of Thursday's Child, who had far to go and took her time about it, is now assured. Jesus bid us address God as 'Father'. Let's put it this way, for many years now I am quite sure that I have been safe in the arms my Father, so what more could a child ever wish for?

Coffs Harbour, Easter 2000

Epilogue

It is nearly twenty years since I finished writing this memoir and it comes with some surprise that next year Robin and I will both turn ninety.

Some major challenges have tested us as a family and as individuals, but we have grown in spite of, and probably because of them. We certainly did not envisage then what the future held for us and I welcome this opportunity to reflect a little on the blessed way my life has flowed since trusting in God to lead me safely through troubled waters.

In 2001 our son, Peter, gave us a wonderful surprise Golden Wedding lunch, managing to bring the whole family, including seven of our eight grand-children from Brisbane and Sydney and also Robin's sister-in-law Joan, who just happened to be visiting from UK and had been at our wedding (see photo next page). The only one missing, sadly, was Peter's eldest, Lisa, who was living and working in London. It was a memorable day that I will always be thankful for.

As a family we were shattered when Peter passed away suddenly after a massive stroke in 2003, on holiday near Cairns, aged 49. He had been working as a successful consultant environmental engineer in Coffs Harbour and as well as Lisa, he left two young sons, Jack and William, from a second marriage. He was very involved with the boys, who were then nine and seven, and his loss to them, and to us all was a tragedy. Lisa flew straight from London when she heard Peter was on life support, and those of us who had managed to get flights to Cairns waited for her before we made the inevitable decision to let him go. At his request, repeated only a week before in discussion with his cousin, Christopher, his organs were donated and brought a new lease of life to five recipients. This was an amazing comfort to us, that some good had resulted from his premature death and our great loss.

50th Wedding Anniversary 2001: L to R - Kathy, Michael, Kylie (M&K), William (P), Robin, Timothy (M&K), me, John holding Jessica, James (J&E), Evelyn, Rick, Peter with Jack, Cameron (M&K), Joan.

In 2004 Robin retired from his part time practice and commenced as a part-time lecturer in the Rural Medical School newly established at Coffs Harbour by the University of NSW, retiring finally in 2012. His spine was giving him a lot of pain and his memory becoming increasingly unreliable.

Until my eightieth year I was still living a fairly active and interesting life, but suddenly I found myself a walking invalid with acute rheumatoid arthritis. My back also had been declining with increasing spinal stenosis and in 2010 I had a laminectomy which gave me a few years freedom from pain. Other health problems eventually caused us to have to sell our lovely home (Apuldram) in the North Boambee Valley and enter into Coffs Haven Aged Care Facility nearby, where we have been since July 2014. Here I pass the time caring for Robin as much as I am able, and have started painting again among other things, to pass the time.

On the positive side, our four eldest grandchildren are now happily married and we are the proud great-grandparents of five boys.

Michael and Kathy continue their lifelong involvement with aviation and church related ministries in Papua New Guinea, but also come back to their cottage, near us in Coramba, when they are not visiting their young families in Sydney. Kylie, Tim and Cameron are all married and living in Sydney and they come up to see us once or twice each year with their five wonderful little boys, the eldest who is now seven.

Peter's daughter Lisa is married and living in Los Angeles, Jack is in Newcastle (NSW) and William lives at home with his mother.

John and Evie live in Brisbane on their lychee farm and John is soon due for retirement as an Air Traffic Controller. James and Jessica are working and at university and doing well. Music plays a large part of their lives.

Rick, who works in IT, lives in Sydney with a long time friend and two Golden Retrievers.

So, from the chance wartime friendship of our two fathers in the Navy, which brought us together, we have grown into a family of over twenty souls, counting in the two generations of daughters and sons-in-law.

We celebrate our 66th wedding anniversary this year and are very content with our life and grateful to God for all our blessings.

Coffs Harbour   April 2017

Apuldram, Coffs Harbour

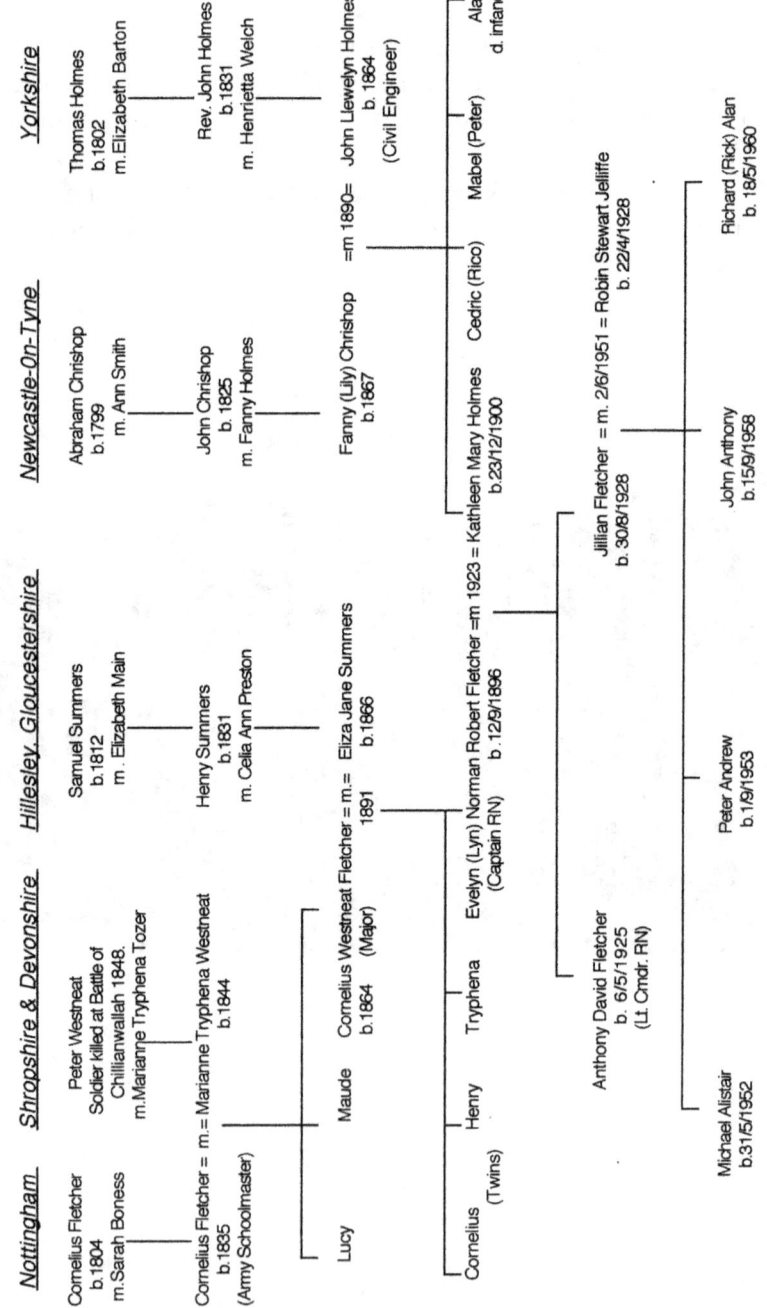

There is a very encouraging little poem going around that has often brought me strength:

What God has Promised

God has not promised skies always blue,
Flower strewn pathways all our lives through.
God has not promised sun without rain,
Joy without sorrow, peace without pain.

But God has promised strength for the day.
Rest for the labourer, light on the way,
Grace for the trial, strength from above,
Unfailing sympathy, undying love.

Annie J Flint (Public domain)

"The Lord is not slack concerning His promises." 2 Peter 3: 9

www.ingramcontent.com/pod-product-compliance
Lightning Source LLC
Chambersburg PA
CBHW071902290426
44110CB00013B/1251